Dedication

This book is dedicated to R. W. McRae, whose vision of assisting Canadian expatriates inspired the authors to create CANADIANS RESIDENT ABROAD.

Canadians Resident Abroad

Second Edition

by

Garry R. Duncan
B.Comm., C.A., C.F.P., R.F.P.
Tax Partner with BDO Dunwoody

Elizabeth J. Peck
B.A. (Hons.), M.Museol.
President, Canadians Resident Abroad, Inc.

CARSWELL
Thomson Professional Publishing

© 1997 Garry R. Duncan and Elizabeth J. Peck

This publication is designed to provide accurate and authoritative information. It is sold with the understanding that the publisher is not engaged in rendering legal, accounting or other professional advice. If legal advice or other expert assistance is required, the services of a competent professional should be sought. The analysis contained herein represents the opinions of the authors and should in no way be construed as being either official or unofficial policy of any governmental body.

Canadian Cataloguing in Publication Data
    Duncan, Garry R.
        Canadians resident abroad

    2nd ed.
    Includes index.
    ISBN 0-459-57488-4

    1. Aliens – Taxation – Law and legislation – Canada.   2. Income tax – Canada – Foreign income.   3. Income tax – Law and legislation. – Canada.   I. Peck, Elizabeth. J.   II. Title.

    KE5864.N6D85 1997   343.7105'26   C97-931445–3
    KF 6441.D85 1997

    Printed in Canada

CARSWELL
Thomson Professional Publishing

One Corporate Plaza   Customer Service:
2075 Kennedy Road   Toronto 1-416-609-8000
Scarborough, Ontario   Elsewhere in Canada/U.S. 1-800-387-5164
M1T 3V4   Fax 1-416-298-5094

Preface

Canadians are on the move. Depressed economic conditions at home combined with an increasingly global outlook have contributed to an exodus of Canadians seeking employment, adventure, a sunny retirement, a lower cost of living and, yes, freedom from Canadian taxes.

If you are a Canadian planning for a future beyond our borders, you will likely investigate many aspects of life overseas — climate, working conditions, cultural differences, compensation and health care to name but a few. You may, however, neglect an essential financial consideration.

Most Canadians going to live abroad wish to become non-residents of Canada for tax purposes. As a non-resident, you would be freed from Canadian income tax obligations (although some Canadian taxes may still apply). You may or may not be taxed in your new country of residence, but even if you are the burden is likely to be less onerous.

If you do not take care in arranging your affairs you may get a nasty surprise when, while toiling, let us say, in a faraway oil field, you find that Revenue Canada still considers you a resident of Canada and liable for Canadian taxation on income you earn anywhere in the world.

How can this be? The answer is based on two disarmingly simple facts:

1) The Canadian income tax system is based on residency, not citizenship.

2) Residents of Canada are liable for income tax on their world income.

This is where things became much less simple. Not only is "residency" not defined anywhere in Canadian law, but becoming non-resident does not depend on adherence to a limited and unchangeable set of criteria. Rather, residency is considered a "question of fact" and the tax authorities reserve the right to examine the particular facts in every individual case before passing judgment.

That is why any Canadian who is now or may want to become a non-resident of Canada needs this book. The contents combine tax law (dreadfully boring) and real life situations (stranger than fiction), all written (we hope) in understandable language. Please write to the authors if something that seems perfectly clear to us leaves you with a terrible headache and badly confused. We shall respond and keep this book from becoming a paperweight. We would also like to hear about any unusual situations you encounter.

CANADIANS RESIDENT ABROAD considers all those factors which conspire to make you a resident or non-resident of Canada for income tax purposes, and provides an overview of current tax law and Revenue Canada's administrative practice.

We look at your life as a non-resident. Even if you have achieved non-resident status, you may still have Canadian tax responsibilities. This will depend on how well you cut your ties and what you left behind — such as investments, business income, employment income, pensions, retirement payments.

If you settle in a country that has concluded a tax treaty with Canada, that document can have a major impact on your life. We review treaties in general and point out some of their more important features. (Those of you who settle in non-treaty countries can skip this chapter.)

We also have information for those Canadians who continue to be residents of Canada while working abroad. Continuing resident status may result from a factual circumstance or simply be deemed to exist. While this is not an ideal tax position, there are a number of provisions which grant tax relief.

Some day you may want to return to Canada. Like departure, coming home requires careful planning to minimize potential tax burdens.

CAVEAT

We have relied on Canadian tax law, Revenue Canada's forms and administrative position at the time of writing. Like most things in life, these change. As well, we have prepared this material so that it is general in nature. This book should not be relied upon to replace specific professional advice.

About the Authors

Garry R. Duncan

Garry Duncan, B. Comm., C.A., and C.F.P., is a tax partner with BDO Dunwoody, Toronto, Canada. His professional experience includes a broad range of tax and financial planning engagements including consulting with Canadians on matters relating to the tax implications of emigration and being a non-resident.

Garry is a Past-president of the Chairman of the Canadian Association of Financial Planners and a frequent speaker on expatriate matters at various seminars.

BDO Dunwoody is a national, entrepreneurially spirited accounting and consulting firm primarily concentrating on the special needs of Canadian independent business. Internationally, the firm has a commanding presence in all the world's important business centres through its membership in BDO Binder.

Elizabeth J. Peck

Elizabeth J. Peck, who received a B.A. (Hons.) from Queen's University and a Master's degree from the University of Toronto, is president of Oakville, Ontario based Canadians Resident Abroad Inc. CRA publishes UPDATE, a quarterly newsletter covering taxation, finance and other topics of interest to Canadians living outside Canada and the United States. With a constantly growing subscriber list, UPDATE is currently distributed free of charge to over 10,000 Canadians worldwide.

CRA invites UPDATE subscribers (and readers of this book) to send to Oakville any questions they may have regarding non-residency or other expatriate concerns. CRA will prepare a written response, at no charge. In taxation matters, CRA relies on the expertise of international tax advisor and co-author, Garry R. Duncan, C.A., Tax Partner, BDO Dunwoody.

CRA also provides access to the services of its associate overseas financial planning firm, Canadian Investment Consultants (888) Inc. CIC representatives travel the globe offering financial planning seminars and related services exclusively to Canadian clients.

Table of Contents

Canadian Resident

GENERAL COMMENTS

The Canadian tax system is based on residency and not citizenship. There are basically two types of residents: factual residents and deemed residents. Revenue Canada's Interpretation Bulletin IT-221R2 (Appendix A: CRA 13) explains Canada's position regarding the determination of an individual's residence status.

- *Factual residence* is a question of fact and is determined by weighing various factors. The principal ones are the location of your permanent home and of your economic, social and family ties.
- *Deemed residence* is determined by statute and most commonly comes into effect when an individual who is normally resident elsewhere remains in Canada for 183 days or more during any calendar year, or when a member of certain defined groups — such as the Canadian Armed Forces — takes a posting outside of Canada.

Residents of Canada (whether factual or deemed) are taxable on their world income. If all or part of their world income comes from foreign sources subject to foreign income taxes, Canada will usually allow a foreign tax credit or a deduction to reduce the incidence of double taxation.

FACTUAL RESIDENCE

If you are a Canadian resident contemplating employment or retirement opportunities abroad and nothing in your circumstances will cause you to be a deemed resident of Canada (see below), then you will need to determine whether you will remain a factual resident of Canada while abroad or whether you will be able to establish non-resident status for tax purposes.

It comes as a surprise to many prospective non-residents that there is no mandatory application process by which an individual requests and is granted non-resident status. Rather, as stated above, Revenue Canada has the right to examine the facts in every individual case in order to determine residency status.

The rule that residency is determined by examination of the facts in each situation is well established in Canadian case law. In *Thomson v. M.N.R.* (1946), a decision of the Supreme Court of Canada which has been used as a precedent as recently as 1990, one of the learned judges stated:

> . . . one is *"ordinarily resident"* in the place where in the settled routine of his life he regularly, normally or customarily lives. One *"sojourns"* at a place where he unusually, casually or intermittently visits or stays. In the former the element of permanence; in the latter that of the temporary predominates. The difference cannot be stated in precise and definite terms, but each case must be determined after all of the relevant factors are taken into consideration, but the foregoing indicates in a general way the essential differences. It is not the length of the visit or stay that determines the question. . . . (emphasis added)[1]

Another judge in the same case (yes, there was more than one judge) expressed the following:

> The graduation of degrees of time, object, intention, continuity and other relevant circumstances, shows, I think, that in common parlance "residing" is not a term of invariable elements, all of which must be satisfied in each instance. It is quite impossible to give it a precise and inclusive definition. It is highly flexible, and its many shades of meaning vary not only in the contexts of different matters, but also in different aspects of the same matter. In one case it is satisfied by certain elements, in another by others, some common, some new.....
> For the purposes of income tax legislation, it must be assumed that every person has at all times a residence. It is not necessary to this that he should have a home or a particular place of abode or even a shelter. He may sleep in the open. It is important only to ascertain the spatial bounds within which he spends his life or to which his ordered or customary living is related. Ordinary residence can best be appreciated by considering its antithesis, occasional or casual or deviatory residence. The latter would seem clearly to be not only temporary in time and exceptional in circumstance, but also accompanied by a sense of transitoriness and of return.[2]

---

[1]   [1946] C.T.C. 51 at 70 (S.C.C.)
[2]   [1946] C.T.C. 51 at 63-64 (S.C.C.)

Establishing Non-Resident Status

If you wish to establish non-resident status for tax purposes, it is your responsibility to ensure that any examination of the facts of your *status quo* would support the contention that you have ceased to be a resident of Canada and have become resident elsewhere.

INTERPRETATION BULLETIN IT-221R2

Revenue Canada's Interpretation Bulletin IT-221R2 (Appendix A: CRA 13) outlines a number of the factors that will be considered in determining whether or not you will remain a resident of Canada for tax purposes while abroad. These include the permanence and purpose of your stay abroad, the residential ties you have retained in Canada, the residential ties you have established elsewhere, and the regularity and length of your visits to Canada.

PERMANENCE AND PURPOSE OF STAY ABROAD

According to Revenue Canada, in order to become a non-resident there must be some permanence to your stay abroad. IT-221R2 indicates that where you are absent from Canada, for whatever reason, for less than two years, you will be presumed to have retained your resident status while abroad unless you can clearly establish that you have severed all residential ties when leaving Canada. If there is evidence that your return to Canada was foreseen at the time of your departure (for example, a contract for employment upon return to Canada), Revenue Canada will presume that you did not sever all your residential ties.

Even if you are leaving Canada for more than two years, Revenue Canada will also insist that you satisfy various other requirements for non-resident status.

IT-221R2 refers to the purpose of your stay but does not elaborate thereon. In absence of any official guidelines, we feel that the purpose of your stay abroad will have a significant influence on your residency status. For example, if you go on a two-year world tour, you will be considered to have retained your Canadian residency. This and other examples are noted below under "Listed Factual Residents".

On the other hand, if you leave Canada to work or retire in another country, sever your Canadian ties and intend to remain outside of Canada for more than two years, you will be considered to be a non-resident unless you are listed as a factual resident. Even then you may not be taxable in Canada if Canada has a tax treaty with the other country. See Chapter 4, "Tax Treaties" for further discussion on this possibility.

RESIDENTIAL TIES WITH CANADA

In order to become non-resident for tax purposes you must sever your residential ties with Canada. Primary residential ties would include your dwelling place and the location of your spouse and dependents. Secondary ties would include your personal property and social ties.

Primary Ties with Canada

DWELLING

If you leave Canada but maintain a dwelling place in Canada that is available for you year-round, Revenue Canada will *not* consider you to have severed your residential ties with Canada. Your Canadian dwelling could remain "available" by virtue of being left vacant, being leased to a non-arm's length party or by being leased at arm's length with the right to terminate the lease on short notice (generally less than three months).

SPOUSE AND DEPENDENTS

If you leave your spouse (spouse includes a common-law partner[3]) and dependents in Canada, Revenue Canada will consider you to remain a resident of Canada during your absence. However, an exception is made where you and your spouse are legally separated and you have permanently severed all other residential ties with Canada.

The primary residential ties of a single person are more difficult to judge. If you were a single person who was supporting someone in a dwelling maintained or occupied by you in Canada and, after your departure, you continue to support that person in the dwelling, Revenue Canada considers you to have retained a significant residential tie and may view you as a resident of Canada.

---

[3]   The term spouse used throughout this book applies to a legally married spouse and a common-law spouse. A common-law spouse is a person of the opposite sex who, at that particular time:
- was living with you in a common-law relationship and is the natural or adoptive parent (legal or otherwise) of your child; or
- was living with you in a common-law relationship and has been living with you for at least 12 continuous months (when you calculate the 12 continuous months, include any period of separation of less than 90 days).

Secondary Residential Ties

Interpretation Bulletin IT-221R2 provides a list of types of personal property and social ties which "generally speaking, an individual who leaves Canada and becomes a non-resident will not retain". These include furniture, clothing, automobiles, bank accounts, credit cards and social ties within Canada. Where you retain these ties in Canada, Revenue Canada will examine the reasons for their retention and determine if they are significant enough to conclude that you have continued to be a resident of Canada while absent. Other obvious ties that may be relevant are provincial hospitalization and medical insurance coverage, a seasonal residence in Canada, professional and other memberships in Canada and family assistance payments.

While the residential ties outlined in IT-221R2 will give you some guidance, the bulletin does not attempt to list all the minor details of day-to-day living that could contribute to a determination of residency. In fact, no such list could be exhaustive as the facts of every individual's life are unique.

Nonetheless, if you wish to find a more comprehensive treatment of the subject, you can turn once again to the courts. A recent case (*Lee v. M.N.R.*, 1990)[4] was noteworthy in that the decision included a list of some of the criteria relevant in determining whether an individual was resident of Canada for Canadian income tax purposes.

In studying the list, you should be aware that no one or any group of up to four of these items will in themselves establish that an individual is resident in Canada. However, a number of additional factors considered together could cause that individual to continue to be a resident of Canada for Canadian income tax purposes.

- memberships with Canadian churches or synagogues, recreational and social clubs, unions and professional organizations;
- registration and maintenance of automobiles, boats and airplanes in Canada;
- holding credit cards issued by Canadian financial institutions and other commercial entities including stores, car rental agencies, etc.;
- local newspaper subscriptions sent to a Canadian address;
- rental of Canadian safe deposit box or post office box;
- subscriptions for life or general insurance including health insurance through a Canadian insurance company;
- mailing address in Canada;
- telephone listing in Canada;

---

[4]   [1990] 1 C.T.C. 2082 (T.C.C.)

- stationery including business cards showing a Canadian address;
- magazine and other periodical subscriptions sent to a Canadian address;
- Canadian bank accounts other than a non-resident bank account;
- active securities accounts with Canadian brokers;
- Canadian driver's license;
- membership in a Canadian pension plan;
- holding directorships of Canadian corporations;
- membership in Canadian partnerships;
- frequent visits to Canada for social or business purposes;
- burial plot in Canada;
- will prepared in Canada;
- legal documentation indicating Canadian residence;
- filing a Canadian income tax return as a Canadian resident;
- ownership of a Canadian vacation property;
- active involvement in business activities in Canada;
- employment in Canada;
- maintenance or storage in Canada of personal belongings including clothing, furniture, family pets, etc.;
- obtaining landed immigrant status or appropriate work permits in Canada...[5]

Establishing Ties In Your New Country

The foregoing deals with residential ties within Canada. Revenue Canada also looks at the ties you establish elsewhere. IT-221R2 indicates that if you go abroad and do not establish a permanent residence elsewhere, there is a presumption that you remain a resident of Canada. In general, the types of residential ties which support the contention that you have established residence elsewhere will parallel those you needed to sever in Canada. However, the fact that you establish a permanent residence abroad does not in and by itself mean that you have become a non-resident of Canada.

Visits to Canada

Fortunately, Revenue Canada concedes that where you leave Canada and become a non-resident, your tax status as a non-resident will generally not be affected by occasional returns to Canada, whether for personal or business

---

[5]   [1990] 1 C.T.C. 2082 at 2085-86 (T.C.C.)

reasons. However, IT-221R2 states that where such visits are regular, these factors together with other residential ties that may exist would be examined to determine whether they are significant enough in total to conclude that you are continuing to be a resident in Canada. Remember, if these occasional visits exceed 183 days in any calendar year, you will be deemed to be a resident of Canada for that year. See "Deemed Residence", below, for more details on this rule.

When Does Non-Residency Begin?

The date you cease to be a resident of Canada and become a non-resident is generally the latest of (1) the day you leave Canada, (2) the date your spouse and/or dependents leave Canada (where applicable) or (3) the date you become a resident of the country to which you are emigrating. An exception is made where you are resident of another country prior to entering Canada and you are leaving to re-establish your residence in that country. In this case, you will generally be considered a non-resident on the date you leave Canada even if, for example, your spouse remains temporarily behind to dispose of your dwelling place in Canada.

Tax Avoidance

Finally, Revenue Canada states that where one of the main purposes of your absence from Canada is to avoid Canadian taxes that would otherwise be payable, they may consider this to be tax avoidance. If this is the case, Revenue Canada would consider you to be a resident of Canada and tax you accordingly.

NR73(E), Determination of Residency Status

Revenue Canada Form NR73(E) (Appendix A: CRA 4) may be used if you plan to leave or have left Canada, either permanently or temporarily and you need to know your residency status for Canadian tax purposes. This situation will arise when you are paid by Canadian employers who want to be assured that you are considered to be a non-resident of Canada. It may also be required by institutions that make pension, annuity, registered retirement savings plan or registered retirement income fund payments.

If you compare the list of queries posed on the NR73(E) with those listed in the court case quoted above (*Lee v. M.N.R.*), you will note a striking similarity. While the NR73(E) may be submitted by anyone wishing assistance in determining residency status, this form is not mandatory unless it is requested to confirm you are a non-resident. As a result, we do not recommend its use unless it is requested.

Listed Factual Residents

Revenue Canada has been good enough to provide a list of certain individuals whom it considers to be factual residents of Canada while living abroad, generally because of ties they retain with Canada while absent. If you fit one of the following categories, Revenue Canada will treat you as a resident, unless you can argue that you are a non-resident.

STUDENTS

When you attend school in another country and you keep your residential ties with Canada, you have to pay tax on your world income. World income can consist of:
- the taxable portion of Canadian and foreign-source scholarships, fellowships, bursaries, and prizes;
- net research grants and similar payments;
- amounts you received from a registered education savings plan; and
- all Canadian and foreign source income you received.

TEACHERS

When you teach outside Canada, and retain your residential ties with Canada, you have to pay Canadian tax on your world income. If your income is being taxed by both Canada and the country in which you are teaching, you may only have to pay tax to one country if Canada has a tax treaty with that country.

When the terms of a tax treaty do not apply, you may be able to claim a credit on your Canadian tax return for the foreign taxes you paid.

MISSIONARIES

As a missionary in another country, you are considered a factual resident of Canada if you:
- are a Canadian citizen or a landed immigrant;
- are in the service of a religious organization that has its national ministry office in Canada; *and*
- are sent out of Canada for five years or less.

If you paid tax to a foreign country, you may be able to claim a foreign tax credit on your Canadian tax return. Alternatively, you may be exempt from

Canadian tax if a tax treaty exists and its provisions deem you to be a resident of the foreign jurisdiction.

VACATIONERS

If you are on vacation outside Canada, you are a factual resident of Canada as long as you keep your Canadian residential ties and your stay outside Canada is not permanent. If you earn income in the country in which you are vacationing, you have to report it on your Canadian tax return and pay tax on it.

COMMUTERS

If you live in Canada and commute to work locations outside Canada, you are a factual resident of Canada, and you have to pay tax on your world income. You may be taxed by both Canada and the country in which you are working. In this case, you may claim the tax you paid to the other country as a credit against your Canadian taxes.

OTHER EMPLOYEES

If you leave Canada to work in another country knowing that you will be out of Canada for less than two years, Revenue Canada will consider you to be a factual resident of Canada. For example, if you have a one-year employment contract and there is evidence that you intend to return to Canada, Revenue Canada will consider you to be a resident of Canada. For instance, this could arise if you failed to completely sever residential ties in Canada or you have some type of commitment for future activities that requires you to be a resident in Canada.

This does not include a situation where you emigrate with the intent of remaining outside Canada for more than two years but return to Canada for reasons beyond your control. The Tax Courts have concluded that unexpected changes to your plans will not jeopardize your non-resident status even where the period outside of Canada has been cut short of the two year-period.

DEEMED RESIDENCE

Canadian tax law contains provisions that deem certain individuals to be residents of Canada. These provisions are summarized in Interpretation

Bulletin IT-221R2. If you fall into one of these categories, you will be subject to Canadian tax on your world income.

Sojourners

Where a resident of another country sojourns (is temporarily present) in Canada for 183 days or more in a calendar year, he or she is deemed to be a resident of Canada for the entire year. While this provision commonly affects foreign visitors, it would apply if you are a Canadian who has established non-resident status and you return often enough to have sojourned in Canada for a total of 183 days or more during a calendar year. The provision will not, however, deem you to be resident of Canada for the full year if you leave Canada to reside elsewhere in the second half of the year. Where you enter Canada with the intention of living here and establish residential ties within Canada, you will generally be considered to have become resident of Canada for tax purposes on the date you enter Canada. Please refer to Chapter 2, "Emigration" and Chapter 5, "Immigration" for details on the taxation of part-time residents.

Other Deemed Residents

The deeming provision will also cause any person who is included in any of the following categories to be a resident of Canada:
- persons who are members of the Canadian Forces at any time during the year;
- persons who are officers or servants of Canada or a province, at any time during the year, who receive representation allowances or who are resident or deemed resident in Canada (members of the Canadian Forces who are not factual residents of Canada and have been serving abroad) immediately prior to their appointment or employment by Canada or a province;
- individuals who perform services, at any time in the year, outside Canada under an International Development Assistance Program of the Canadian International Development Agency (CIDA) described in the regulations of the *Income Tax Act* provided they were resident in Canada at any time in the three-month period prior to the date the services commenced;
- persons who were, at any time in the year, members of the Overseas Canadian Forces school who have filed their returns for the year on the basis that they were resident in Canada throughout the period during which they were such members; and

- the spouse of a person described above, if living with that person during the year and if a resident of Canada in a previous year, and any dependent child of that person who was under 18 years of age at any time during the year or 18 years of age or over throughout the year and dependent by reason of either physical or mental infirmity.

RESIDENCY — QUESTIONS AND ANSWERS

Question – Date of Departure

I left for Saudi Arabia on June 30, 1996. My spouse and children remained in Canada until November 1, 1996. Will I be considered to be a resident of Canada up until June 30, 1996 or November 1, 1996?

Answer

Based on the fact that your spouse and children remained in Canada until November 1, 1996, you will be considered to be a resident of Canada up until November 1, 1996. You must report the income you earned in Saudi Arabia for the period ending November 1, 1996.

Question – Less than two years

I had a three-year contract in Kuwait and severed all my ties when I left Canada. Due to the failure of my foreign employer to renew its contract with the government of Kuwait, my contract was terminated after 18 months. I shall have to return to Canada. Since I have not been out of Canada for more than two years, will I be considered a resident of Canada for the time spent in Kuwait?

Answer

Since you severed all your ties with Canada when you left and your termination was unforeseen, you will not be considered a resident of Canada during the time you spent in Kuwait. This position is supported by Interpretation Bulletin IT-221R2 and a 1984 tax case, *Bergelt v. M.N.R.*[6]

---

[6]   [1984] C.T.C. 2033 (T.C.C.), aff'd [1986] 1 C.T.C. 212 (F.C.T.D.)

Question – Child in Boarding School
I left Canada in June 1996. I severed all ties except I left my child in a boarding school. Will I be considered a resident of Canada?

Answer
The fact that you severed all your ties but left a child in a boarding school will not cause you to be considered a resident of Canada.

We queried Revenue Canada regarding this issue. Revenue Canada responded stating,

> that each determination of residency is done so [sic] on an individual basis and that one factor alone, such as a fee structure at a Canadian boarding school, is not sufficient in itself to make a correct determination. The fee structures at boarding schools vary from school to school, and the type of fee charged would not be a deciding factor when making a determination of residency.
>
> When reviewing a request for a determination of residency, the Department (Revenue Canada) must establish whether or not an individual does in fact have significant residential ties in Canada. When a child is attending a Canadian boarding school additional factors are taken into consideration. For example, would a bank account and credit cards be maintained in Canada, would there be a provincial medical plan for the child, would visits to Canada be frequent and would there be an apartment or home and vehicle available for the parents' use while visiting their child? These and other questions must be answered before residence status can be determined.

Question – Recreational Property
I left Canada on January 31, 1996, sold my principal residence but maintained a recreational property suitable for year-round use and available at any time. Will this jeopardize my non-resident status?

Answer
Revenue Canada would consider the retention of this recreational property as a significant tie and likely rule that you are still a resident of Canada.

Question – Child Living with a Relative

I left Canada in September 1993. I severed all my ties and have been a non-resident ever since. My oldest child has reached an age where there is no school in Saudi Arabia. I propose to send my child, who is 16, back to Canada to live with his grandparents and attend school. Will this jeopardize my non-resident status?

Answer

Based on Revenue Canada's current position on this matter, the fact that your child is living with his grandparents would not cause you to be a resident of Canada.

Question – CIDA

I left Canada to work on a CIDA-sponsored project in a non-treaty country. Will I be considered to be a resident of Canada?

Answer

You will be deemed to be a resident of Canada unless you were a non-resident of Canada during the three months prior to accepting CIDA employment.

Question – Rental of Principal Residence

I left Canada on June 1, 1996. I could not sell my principal residence so I leased it to my brother on a month-to-month lease. Will I be considered a resident of Canada?

Answer

Based on the fact you leased your house to a relative, Revenue Canada would likely rule that you are still a resident of Canada. In order to correct this situation, you should lease your principal residence to an unrelated person and have a long-term lease with a termination clause of at least three months.

Question – 183 Day Rule
I spent half of a day in Toronto while I was a non-resident. Is this considered one day for the purposes of the 183 day rule?

Answer
Revenue Canada states that any portion of a day counts as one entire day for purposes of the 183 day rule.

Question – NR73(E)
I filed Form NR73(E) and received a confirmation from Revenue Canada that, based on the facts provided, I was a non-resident. Several facts have changed since I received Revenue Canada's response. Will this response still be relevant?

Answer
Revenue Canada based their response on the facts given. If these facts have changed, Revenue Canada's original response is invalid and cannot be used to support your non-resident status if it is challenged. You may resubmit the new facts and have them rule again or wait until they challenge your claim and then submit the new information.

Question – Visits to Canada
I ceased to be a resident of Canada on December 20, 1996. I wish to return to Canada for two months in 1997 and every year thereafter for the next three years. Will this jeopardize my non-residency status?

Answer
If you have severed all your ties with Canada and only return for periods of two months each year, your non-resident status should not be jeopardized. However, we recommend that you keep your visits to a minimum in the first year to ensure that you have established non-resident status.

Question – Canadian Employer
I severed all my ties and emigrated from Canada on January 5, 1997. I shall be employed by a wholly-owned foreign corporation of my former Canadian employer. Will I be considered to be a non-resident of Canada?

Answer
Assuming you severed all your ties with Canada and intend to be out of Canada for more than two years, you will be considered a non-resident for Canadian tax purposes.

Question – Sale of House
A friend told me I cannot become a non-resident unless I sell my house in Canada. Is this true?

Answer
The retention of a house is a significant tie in Canada. If you are able to move into it at any time, Revenue Canada will consider you to have remained a resident of Canada. You may rectify this situation by leasing it out to an arm's-length party on a long-term lease with a three-month termination clause.

Question – Payment of Canadian Tax
If I have to have lived outside Canada for two years in order to establish non-resident status, does that mean that I have to continue to pay Canadian taxes for that two-year period?

Answer
If you intend to remain outside Canada for more than two years and have severed all your Canadian ties, you do not have to pay Canadian tax during the first two years.

Question – Retention of Cottage

I want to establish non-resident status but I am very reluctant to give up my family cottage. The cottage is unheated and can only be used in the summer months. Will this jeopardize my non-resident status?

Answer

The retention of a cottage is considered a residential tie with Canada. However, if this is the only tie you retained with Canada and it cannot be used throughout the year, its retention should not cause you to be a resident of Canada.

Question – Rental of House to a Daughter

My 18-year-old daughter will be staying in Canada to attend university. Can I rent our family home to her and some of her friends as long as they sign a proper lease?

Answer

Revenue Canada states that the leasing of a family home to a relative is not sufficient to sever this tie. The fact that her friends are arm's-length may help but a long-term lease with a termination clause of at least three months would be necessary.

Question – Canadian Employer

I am being transferred overseas by my Canadian employer for a length of time which is undetermined but expected to last at least two years. At some time in the future, I will no doubt return to Canada and remain employed by the same firm. Does this arrangement make it difficult for me to establish non-resident status?

Answer

Indicating your intention to return to Canada and the fact that you will be employed by the same Canadian firm will cause Revenue Canada to consider you to continue to be a resident. Even if you can prove that you are a non-resident, you may still be taxable in Canada. See Chapter 3, "Taxation of a Non-resident" — "Persons Deemed to be Employed in Canada".

Question – Leave of Absence
I am planning to take a three-year employment contract in Hong Kong. My current employer has offered me a leave of absence with a guarantee of work when I return to Canada. Will I be able to establish non-resident status?

Answer
If you sever your ties in Canada and establish ties in Hong Kong, Revenue Canada will not consider you to have retained your Canadian residency status due to guaranteed employment upon your return.

Question – World Cruise
I have always wanted to sail around the world. I plan to be away from Canada for at least two years. Will I be able to establish non-resident status for tax purposes?

Answer
Revenue Canada maintains that you must be resident someplace. If you are unable to establish that you are resident elsewhere, Revenue Canada will consider you to have retained Canadian residency.

Question – Canadian Driver's Licence
I would like to retain my Canadian driver's licence while living overseas. Will this jeopardize my non-resident status?

Answer
If you have severed all ties except your Canadian driver's licence, you should be able to achieve the status of a non-resident.

Question – Return to Canada

My wife and I have been non-residents of Canada for 5 years. My wife plans to return to Canada to finish her education. I shall remain in our present home in the Bahamas and continue to work at my present job. I will be supporting my wife while she is going to school. Will the fact that my wife returns to Canada while I remain to live and work in the Bahamas cause me to be a resident of Canada for tax purposes?

Answer

Revenue Canada will consider you to have established ties in Canada upon the return of your spouse. However, all the facts must be reviewed to determine if the return of your wife to complete her education would in and by itself, make you a resident of Canada.

Question – Sojourning

If my husband is in Canada for more than 183 days in a calendar year and is deemed to be a resident of Canada, as his wife, am I also deemed to be a resident of Canada? I never visited Canada during the year.

Answer

The fact that your husband is deemed to be a resident of Canada does not deem you to be a resident as well.

Question – School in Canada

I am a single student from Grand Cayman. I go to a Canadian university for 7 months and return to and work in Grand Cayman for the remaining 5 months. Where am I resident for income tax purposes?

Answer

You will be a resident of Canada and subject to Canadian tax on your world income.

Question – Common-Law

I have been living common-law for the past 3 years in Canada. I plan to go to Nassau, Bahamas to work for 4 years. My common-law partner will remain in Canada to finish school. If I sever all my ties except my common-law spouse, have I ceased to be a resident of Canada?

Answer

A common-law partner is the same as a spouse. As a result, you continue to have a primary tie in Canada and will be considered to continue to be a resident of Canada.

Note:

The foregoing responses are based on situations that did not involve employment in a country that has a treaty with Canada. If a treaty exists and the employment income is taxed in both Canada and the foreign jurisdiction, the treaty should be reviewed to see if it will cause you to be taxed only in the foreign jurisdiction. Please refer to Chapter 4 for more details regarding this matter.

Emigration

When, after faithfully following the guidelines set out in Chapter 1, you leave Canada to become a non-resident for tax purposes, you may still have any one of a number of tax commitments to Canada entailing both current and future filing requirements.

FINAL TAX RETURN

Since you will no doubt leave Canada part way through a calendar year (unless you are incredibly well-organized and leave on December 31), *you will be required to file a "final tax return"*. By completing the area entitled "date of departure" on page 1, you officially inform our tax authorities that you have left Canada. This return must be filed on or before April 30th of the year following your year of departure.

Your final tax return will include your world income up to your date of departure from Canada, along with any capital gains or losses on deemed dispositions of property which may occur on your departure (see below).

For the portion of the year after you cease to be a Canadian resident, you must continue to report certain types of Canadian-sourced income. These may include employment income such as sick leave or vacation pay paid to you by a Canadian employer after you became non-resident, income from any business carried on in Canada, the taxable portion of scholarships, bursaries, research grants and fellowships you received from Canadian sources and gains arising from the disposition of taxable Canadian properties. Certain other types of Canadian-sourced income will be subject to a non-resident withholding tax while others will not be taxable at all.

Question – Final Return on Departure
I left Canada on September 30, 1996. I earned employment income up to September 30, 1996 and received a bonus on or about October 16, 1996. In addition, I continued to operate a business in Canada and realized capital gains from the disposition of real estate in December 1996. Do I include all these incomes in my final return or do I prepare one tax return for the income earned up to the date of departure and a second non-resident tax return for the income earned in Canada after my departure?

Answer
You will prepare one tax return and report the various types of income noted above in that return.

Deemed Dispositions

The government of Canada wishes to ensure that all capital gains which arose during the time when an individual was a resident of Canada are taxed by Canada. For this reason, Canadian tax law requires that individuals realize a deemed disposition of many types of property on departure. The rules regarding deemed dispositions of property upon emigration from Canada are currently undergoing significant changes. While praising Canada's taxpayer migration system as already one of the strictest in the world, Finance Minister Paul Martin has proposed requirements which further broaden the categories of property which must be deemed to be disposed. The new rules apply to all individuals who cease to be resident of Canada after October 1, 1996. While the proposals have been outlined in some detail, the final legislation and forms were not available at the time of updating this edition.

For individuals who left Canada on or before October 1, 1996, the rules were as follows:

You were deemed to have disposed of all capital property at its fair market value when you left Canada with the exception of certain types of property known as Taxable Canadian Property (TCP). TCP assets included assets such as:
- Canadian real estate;
- Capital property used in carrying on a business in Canada;

- Shares of public Canadian companies (where you, together with persons with whom you do not deal at arm's length, own 25% or more of any class of shares);
- Shares of non-resident corporations where more than 50% of the corporation's assets consist of TCP at any time in the 5-year period prior to disposition;
- Interests in trusts resident in Canada or partnerships whose assets are primarily composed of TCP
- RRSPs, RRIFs, IAACs, LIRAs, LIFs, DPSPs and other pension arrangements.

You were not deemed to have disposed of these assets because the entire capital gain on TCP (whether accruing before or after you became non-resident) would be subject to Canadian tax when the property was utlimately sold.

For individuals who leave Canada after October 1, 1996:

All property owned by an emigrant will be deemed to be disposed of and reacquired at its fair market value with the exception of the following assets:
- Canadian real estate;
- Capital property or inventory that is used in a business carried on by the person through a permanent establishment in Canada;
- Stock options and certain pensions and similar rights; and
- RRSPs, RRIFs, IAACs, LIRAs, LIFs, DPSP

These assets will remain excluded from the deemed disposition rules on emigration because Canada maintains the right to tax gains on these assets or income whether or not the individual is a resident of Canada, even under tax treaties with other countries.

The deemed disposition rules will now apply to all other types of TCP (remember that under the previous rules, the deemed disposition rules only applied to property that was not TCP). This means that tax will have to be paid on accrued capital gains on these assets at the time of emigration. In particular, the new rules mean that tax on accrued gains on shares of private Canadian companies must be paid when an individual shareholder leaves Canada. In the past, it was possible to emigrate without having to pay any tax on these shares until they were actually sold and then possibly qualify for treaty protection.

The definition of TCP has been expanded and now includes:
- partnership interests, the value of which arose from holding various assets including TCP which represented more than 50% of the value of all its assets at any time in the preceding 5 years;

- any capital stock which is not listed on a prescribed stock exchange (i.e. over-the-counter or unlisted stock).

Providing Security in Lieu of Tax

Under the new rules, it will be possible to defer paying tax on your accrued gains from TCP if you provide acceptable security to Revenue Canada. The tax can then be paid when the asset is ultimately sold, with no interest charges on any tax that was owing on the date you left Canada. Acceptable security usually means leaving behind funds on deposit or a letter of credit in favour of Revenue Canada. However, Revenue Canada is considering expanding this somewhat and allowing shares of private Canadian companies to be pledged as security when the tax owing is due to the deemed disposition of these shares. Note that because these assets are TCP, the entire gain (attributable to when you were a resident and after you left) on these assets will be subject to tax when they are ultimately sold unless the gain which accrues after you leave Canada is exempt by virtue of a tax treaty.

Valuations — TCP

The new deemed disposition rules will require many Canadians to incur the cost of valuations even though no real sale (i.e. no consideration) occurs. For example, if Canadians own shares of a Canadian private corporation, they must value the shares at the time of departure, report the deemed disposition in their final tax return and either pay the tax or post acceptable security. The new requirement will cause potential emigrants additional cost and aggravation.

Non-TCP

If you own property that is not TCP, such as shares in most Canadian public corporations, shares in foreign corporations, interests in mutual funds or foreign real estate, you will be deemed to have sold this property at fair market value on the date of your departure. Any capital gain or loss arising from this disposition must be included in your final tax return. The tax paid on such a gain is referred to as "departure tax".

Unlike TCP, gains on non-TCP which accrue while you are a non-resident, for example, capital gains on investments in the Canadian stock market or in a Canadian mutual fund, will not be subject to tax in Canada.

ELECTION TO TREAT PROPERTY AS TAXABLE CANADIAN PROPERTY

In order to defer paying tax on assets that are not TCP, you must elect for these assets to be TCP when you leave Canada. You may then provide acceptable security for the tax which is owing. Now whether you pay the tax when you emigrate or you elect to defer the payment of tax until you dispose of the non-TCP, any gain that accrues to you while you are a non-resident is not taxed in Canada.

In the past, an election to have non-TCP treated as TCP was accomplished by filing Form T2061, "Election by an Emigrant to Defer Deemed Disposition of Property and Capital Gains Thereon" (Appendix A: CRA 6). We have been advised that Revenue Canada will require you to complete Form T2161, Election by an Emigrant to Defer the Deemed Disposition of Property and Capital Gains Thereon and send it to Revenue Canada before April 30 of the year following emigration. Form T2161 was not available to be included in the appendix. If you are an emigrant trying to comply with the new rules, you should ensure that you obtain any new forms which may be introduced by Revenue Canada.

Finally, under the old rules, if tax arose on the disposition of non-TCP, by filing Form T2074 and providing acceptable security, you could elect to spread out payment of this amount in up to six equal annual installments. This option will likely remain available under the new rules.

Question – Deemed Disposition
I invested in a Canadian mutual fund. It has a tax cost of $7,000 and is now worth $10,000. Is it deemed to be disposed of when I leave? Should I elect not to have it deemed to be disposed?

Answer
Your investment in the Canadian mutual fund will be deemed to be disposed of when you emigrate. You would allow it to be disposed of if you have capital losses you want to use up. As well, if you expect it to go up in value after you emigrate, you may want to realize the accrued gain now. Due to the new rules, little will be gained if you make this election. While you will be able to defer the incidence of tax until you actually sell the property, you may expose any future increase in value to Canadian tax.

Question – Partnership Interest

I own a partnership interest which will have a negative tax cost when I leave Canada. Will I realize a gain from a deemed disposition of this property?

Answer

Since you have a negative tax cost at the time you emigrate from Canada, you will be required to include the negative amount plus an amount equal to the fair market value in your final return as proceeds. You may wish to take steps to eliminate or reduce the negative tax cost prior to your departure.

Keep in mind, the income you receive from the partnership will likely continue to be taxable even though you are a non-resident. As a result, if you can delay your departure until after the partnership's fiscal period, all or a portion of the negative tax cost may be eliminated by the income.

Question – Life Insurance Policy

I own a life insurance policy. Is it deemed to be disposed of when I leave Canada?

Answer

So far, life insurance policies have been excluded from the deemed disposition rules. They continue to be taxable or non-taxable in the same manner had you remained a resident of Canada. The proposed changes to the deemed disposition of TCP may be expanded to include these. Final legislation was not available at the time of responding to this question to either confirm or deny this possibility.

Question – Business Assets

I own business assets which will not be deemed to be disposed of when I leave Canada. What happens if a year after I leave Canada, I cease to use these assets to carry on a business in Canada?

Answer

Under the new rules, these assets will be deemed to be disposed of and reacquired at their fair market value at that time. Tax must be paid unless you elect to defer payment until the asset is actually sold.

ELECTION TO DISPOSE OF TAXABLE CANADIAN PROPERTY

You may also elect to cause any or all the rest of your taxable Canadian property to be disposed of on your departure. This may be accomplished by filing Form T2061A (Appendix A: CRA 7). You may do this to realize gains, utilize capital losses or create losses to offset capital gains realized on other dispositions. However, you may only elect to cause dispositions that will create losses in order to offset gains realized on deemed dispositions arising on departure.

Elections regarding the treatment of capital property for departure tax purposes would generally be filed as part of your tax return for the year of your departure from Canada. There are provisions to accommodate late filing and also to amend these elections.

Question – Late Filed Election
If I neglect to file the election to have a deemed disposition of taxable Canadian property, is there any penalty for filing a late election?

Answer
If you request to file a late election and your request is granted, you will be liable to a penalty of the lesser of $8,000 and the product obtained when $100 is multiplied by the number of complete months from the day you were required to file the election to the day it was filed. Revenue Canada may waive this penalty under certain circumstances.

EXCEPTION

There is an exception to the deemed disposition rules for short-term residents. If you have been a resident of Canada for less than 60 months in the ten years immediately preceding your emigration, property owned when you last became a resident and property inherited since you established residency will be excluded from the deemed disposition rules. Only property you acquired while resident will be subject to the deemed disposition rules.

A WORD OF CAUTION

Correct filing of deemed dispositions on departure can be a complex matter, depending on the nature of your assets. As well, ascertaining whether or not a property is TCP will be critical to determining if you will be taxed on any gains accruing after you become non-resident of Canada. To further complicate matters, the government has recently expanded the categories of property which are TCP. This means that the same gains which accrue while you are a non-resident of Canada which were not formerly subject to Canadian tax will now be taxable. If you own property which may fall under the deemed disposition rules, we suggest that you seek professional taxation advice.

PRINCIPAL RESIDENCE — CHANGE OF USE

If you owned a home in Canada prior to becoming non-resident and decided to lease it to someone, in taxation terms you will realize a *change of use*. This change of use will cause a deemed disposition of your house (unless you elect *not* to have a change of use — see below).

The property will be deemed to have been sold and reacquired at its fair market value at the time the change of use occurs. As long as the house can be designated as your principal residence for the entire period you owned it, no tax liability will arise from the deemed disposition.

Any gain or loss from a future sale will be calculated on the fair market value of the property used for the deemed disposition. If the future sale price is higher, you will have a capital gain and if it is lower, you will have a capital loss on the land and a terminal loss on the building. Remember a capital loss may only be applied against capital gains while a loss (terminal loss) arising from depreciable property (building) can be applied against both capital gains and other income.

You may elect *not* to have a change of use. This election may be made in the tax return for the year the change of use occurred or later subject to certain penalties. *As a non-resident you cannot designate a property to be your principal residence for those years that you are a non-resident of Canada* (Appendix A: CRA 10).

Change of Use — Deemed Disposition

Should you make this election or not? This decision requires considerable foresight and may be made on a late-filed basis. For example, if you purchased a house in 1980 for $250,000 and it was worth $300,000 in 1994, the year of emigration, and you leased it on an arm's length, long-term lease, you could realize and shelter a gain of $50,000 by having the change of use cause a deemed disposition to occur.

Fair Market Value — Change of Use	$ 300,000
Tax Cost (purchase price)	250,000
Capital Gain	50,000
Less Principal residence exemption*	50,000
Taxable Gain	$ 0.00

Change of Use Election

Let us assume that the property does not go up in value and you sell it in 1996 for $300,000. Since you had a deemed disposition in 1994 from the change of use (leasing), no gain arises on sale in 1996. If you had elected not to have a change of use, you would have paid tax on about $3,000 of the $50,000 gain.

Options	No Election change of use	Election no change of use
Fair market value	$ 300,000	$ 300,000
Tax Cost	300,000	250,000
Gain	–	50,000
Principal Residence		
Exemption (rounded)*	–	47,000
Capital Gain	$ –	$ 3,000

Change of Use Election

However, what if the value of the house goes up to $400,000 in 1996? Then you would have a gain of $100,000 on which you would be required to pay Canadian tax. But if you had elected not to have a change of use, you would have paid tax on only a $9,000 gain rather than $100,000.

Options	No Election change of use	Election no change of use
Fair market value	$ 400,000	$ 400,000
Tax Cost	300,000	250,000
Gain	100,000	150,000

---

* See Chapter 3, "Taxation of a Non-resident" — Question — Sale of a former principal residence for the calculation of the principal residence exemption.

Principal Residence Exemption (rounded)[*]	–	141,000
Capital Gain	$ 100,000	$ 9,000

These results illustrate the tax consequences you can encounter if you elect not to have a change of use in a stable real estate market compared to the tax relief you can enjoy if you elect in a rising market. As noted earlier, it may be prudent to wait and elect at a later date. Remember, you will be subject to a penalty if you file this election late. While Revenue Canada is not obliged to accept the late-filed election even if you pay the penalty, we have not encountered any refusals to date.

If you are still a resident of Canada, either deemed or factual, then this election makes sense because it will extend the number of years (up to four) you may claim it as your principal residence even though it is leased out.

Question – Deemed Disposition, Principal Residence
I am moving to the U.S. I understand that the U.S. tax rules will tax the entire gain since they do not recognize the principal residence exemption.

Answer
The Canada/U.S. rules deem you to have sold your principal residence at its fair market value when you enter the U.S. Only the gain arising after that date will be taxable in the U.S. This appears to indicate that you should elect to have a disposition or if leasing, to permit a change of use to occur. If only life were so simple. Due to the various Canadian implications, you should review all possible results.

Question – Election not to have a Change of Use
I propose to lease my principal residence when I emigrate from Canada. I wish to elect not to have a change of use. How should I do this?

Answer
Revenue Canada does not have an election form. As a result, you write a note in your tax return for the year of departure stating that you elect not to have a change of use occur on your principal residence. You should identify the property you are electing on.

---

[*]   See Chapter 3, "Taxation of a Non-resident" — Question — Sale of a former principal residence for the calculation of the principal residence exemption.

> **Question – Election not to have a Change of Use**
> *If I make an election not to have a change of use and later decide that I should not have done so, can I rescind the election?*
>
> **Answer**
> You may rescind the election at any time. However, the cancellation will not be effective until the year it is made. As a result, the deemed disposition will occur in that subsequent year and Canadian tax may arise.

Deferred Capital Gains

The tax rules permit Canadians to defer the taxation of capital gains if all the proceeds of consideration have not been received. The taxation may be spread over 5 years (10 years for shares of small business corporations, farm property and farm corporations). Unfortunately, this deferral is denied for a taxation year if you cease to be a resident of Canada during that year or in the immediate following year.

Deductions — RRSP

Whether or not you contribute to your RRSP in your year of departure will depend on your previous year's income and your current year's income. The amount of your present year's income that you can shelter from tax (your "deduction limit") is based on 18% of your prior year's earned income minus any pension adjustment. You don't need to calculate this amount because Revenue Canada provides you with the appropriate figures on your assessment notice for the previous year.

Your deduction limit for your emigration year will not be affected by the fact that you were a non-resident for part of the year. However, if you leave Canada early in the year, your taxable income for the year of emigration may not be high enough to utilize your full deduction limit.

What you do will depend on your individual circumstances. If you do not contribute up to your full deduction limit, you have until the end of the calendar year in which you turn the age of 69 to use the deduction limit if you earn taxable income in Canada. You may use your deduction limit to shelter business or employment income you still receive from Canada (on which you pay Canadian tax). If you elect to treat rental income on a net basis (see below) you may also be able to deduct the RRSP contributions from the net rental income.

If you have (accidentally or intentionally) made RRSP contributions which exceed the amount you are able to deduct from any of these types of income in your year of departure, you may request a refund of the over-contribution by filing Form T746(E)–Calculation of Deduction for Refund of Undeducted or Excess RRSP Contributions. As long as this filing is made within certain time limits, you will not be charged non-resident withholding tax, which is usually 25%.

Prior to 1996, the Canadian government actually allowed you to maintain RRSP balances of up to $8,000 in excess of the deduction limit in any year. After 1995, the $8,000 excess allowance is reduced to $2,000. Any amount over the excess allowance is subject to a tax of 1% per month until the excess is removed. Transitional rules were introduced to allow you to reduce excess contributions and avoid this penalty tax.

Even though a number of Canadians have used this scheme, we do not recommend it for non-residents, since a refund of this excess will be subject to a 25% non-resident withholding tax.

And last but not least, what happens if you contribute not only your deduction limit and $2,000, but additional funds? These additional funds will cause you to pay a 1% per month tax until the excess is removed. If the excess arose from a deliberate act on your part, the refund of the excess will be subject to non-resident withholding tax of 25%.

In conclusion, you may contribute to your RRSP in the year of departure or even while you are a non-resident. However, you must analyze the perceived benefits and determine if it really makes sense. It is important to consider the tax laws of your new home and native land. These may not recognize the tax shelter feature of the RRSP and tax the annual income as earned.

RRSP — Home Buyers' Plan

If you took advantage of the RRSP Home Buyers' Plan while you were a resident of Canada, certain tax consequences arise when you emigrate.

If you had withdrawn from your RRSP under the Home Buyers' Plan and became a non-resident before acquiring your Canadian home, your withdrawal will be disqualified and added to your income in the year of withdrawal. You may avoid this disqualification by refunding the withdrawal and cancelling your participation in the plan.

If you have withdrawn the funds and emigrated after acquiring your Canadian home, you must repay the entire withdrawn amount within 90 days of becoming a non-resident. If you have not made repayment within the 90 days, the unpaid balance will be included as income in the tax return you file for the year you departed from Canada.

Deductions — Moving Expenses

Get serious! The only time you will be able to deduct moving expenses occurs when you leave Canada to attend a post-secondary educational institution as a full-time student *and* you receive a Canadian scholarship, bursary, fellowship, or research grant to attend that educational institution.

Capital Gains Deduction

The rules dealing with this area were changed significantly on February 22, 1994. The $100,000 deduction was eliminated for any gains realized after February 22, 1994.

This deduction will have no relevance in 1995 and subsequent years, except for capital properties which are qualified small business corporation shares, qualified farm properties and shares of qualified farm corporations. But like all other so called incentives, these too will likely find their way to the not so great previous government idea recycling area. It is wise to utilize this capital gain exemption sooner than later. This may occur before you leave or on departure because of the deemed dispostion rules. It is important that the shares qualify for this exemption at the time of the disposition. This may require careful planning prior to the disposition to ensure that they do qualify.

Tax Credits

And what about tax credits in the year you emigrate? Well, you get to claim the following non-refundable tax credits to the extent that they apply to the part of the year you were resident in Canada.

- Canada or Quebec Pension Plan Contributions
- Employment Insurance Premiums
- Pension income amount
- Tuition fees
- Education amount
- Medical expenses
- Charitable donations; and
- Gifts to Canada or a province

In other words, if you had any income amount or outlay related to the foregoing while you were a resident, you may claim the resulting credit.

The remaining credits, which are also non-refundable, may be claimed *pro-rata* based on the number of days you are resident in Canada. These include the:

- basic amount
- age amount (now restricted if income too high)
- spousal amount (don't forget spouse includes common-law spouse)
- equivalent to spouse amount
- disability amount transferred from someone other than a spouse
- tuition fees and education amount transferred from a child and
- amounts transferred from your spouse

Under certain circumstances, you may be able to claim these credits for the entire taxation year. For the first set of credits, you need only be reporting Canadian employment or business income for the rest of the year of departure. For the second batch of credits to be used for the entire year, your Canadian return must contain at least 90% of your world income.

Tax Rate

Revenue Canada will require you to pay the federal tax rate and the provincial or territorial tax where you lived just before you left Canada. You may pay different provincial rates if you have a business in several provinces.

OTHER TYPES OF INCOME

As a non-resident you may receive certain types of Canadian source income that will be subject to non-resident withholding tax. The most common examples are interest and dividend income from Canadian bank deposits and investments, pension income and rental income. *Before you leave Canada you should make appropriate arrangements to ensure that the payment of your non-resident withholding tax will be handled smoothly.*

In general, the institution (bank, trust company, mutual fund, pension, RRSP, insurance company) which pays you is responsible for withholding the correct amount of tax, forwarding it to Revenue Canada and sending the balance on to you. It is your responsibility, however, to ensure that all such entities know that you are non-resident and use your non-resident address as the address of record for your account. If you intend to use a Canadian agent, the payer may be given the agent's address but will still need to know your country of residence.

Rental Income

Where rental income is involved, it is the responsibility of your tenants to withhold 25% of their gross rental payments, remit it to our government on your behalf and issue to you a non-resident information slip (NR4B) each year giving details of the rent paid and the tax remitted on your behalf.

If tax has been paid on the gross rent, as a non-resident landlord you have two years after the year the rent was paid to elect to file a Canadian tax return recalculating your tax bill so that you pay tax only on the net rent (the amount which was left over after your expenses).

Alternatively, arrangements can be made in advance to pay non-resident withholding tax on the net rental income. You and your Canadian agent (who usually ends up being a brother or a sister) may file an undertaking (Form NR6 — see Appendix A: CRA 2) before the rental payments commence promising to file a tax return within six months of the end of the year in question reporting the rental income on a net basis. If you have filed an NR6, your agent need only withhold and remit 25% of the net rent. If your rental expenses exceed your rental income you may even end up with a net rental loss and owe no tax. Even in a loss position, however, you must file a tax return reporting your calculations. The NR6 itself is an annual filing and must be submitted prior to January 1st of each rental year.

Sounds good, but there is one catch. *If you read the fine print, the Canadian agent is responsible to remit 25% of the gross rent if the tax return is not filed on time.* This can place an enormous burden on the agent particularly if he or she is unable to file the tax return on time. Please ensure that you give your agent total control over this area. Otherwise, he or she may refuse to be your agent. Recent encounters with Revenue Canada have disclosed that it intends to apply the six-month rule by the book. Agents beware!

Question – NR6
I am a non-resident with a rental property in Canada. Can I take advantage of the benefits arising from filing an NR6 without a Canadian agent?

Answer
Revenue Canada stipulates that the agent must be a Canadian resident.

Question – Tax on Gross Rent

I plan to lease my house when I emigrate from Canada. Who is responsible for withholding and remitting the non-resident tax?

Answer

Technically, the tenant is responsible. However, your tenant will not be too pleased if he has to pay the tax and penalties for not remitting the appropriate tax.

Question – No Tax Withheld

What happens if you are unaware that you should be remitting tax on rent payments? Is there any way to correct this situation?

Answer

We have approached Revenue Canada on several occasions and requested that it consider accepting late-filed tax returns to correct this oversight. We are pleased to report that Revenue Canada usually takes a sympathetic approach to our requests and treats them as voluntary disclosures. When late filed tax returns are accepted, you will pay tax on the net rent and interest and penalties based on the gross rent. Requests may be made to waive the latter if the circumstances warrant.

The voluntary disclosure approach appears to be somewhat costly and may cause you to ponder whether it is really worth the effort. From experience, we feel it is worth the effort. If you do nothing and Revenue Canada assesses, you will pay the 25% tax plus interest and penalties with no opportunity to file on the net basis. Your oversight may be discovered by way of audit or when you sell your property. When you sell your property, the buyer will want confirmation that all taxes have been taken care of which requires you to file Form T2062(E) (Appendix A: CRA 8), and remit 33 1/3% of the gain. The form contains a number of questions, one of which asks if the property has been rented. Need we say more.

Question – Mortgage Interest

I own a house with a mortgage. Effective November 30, 1996, I shall be a non-resident of Canada. I plan to rent my house to an arm's length party on a long-term lease with a three-month termination clause. I have an agent in Canada and will elect to pay tax on my net rental income. Can I deduct the interest expense incurred on my mortgage on my house to determine my net income?

Answer

If the mortgage was obtained when you acquired the house, the interest expense may be deducted to determine your net rental income for purposes of calculating your Canadian tax.

Question – Mortgage Interest

I am a non-resident of Canada and own a rental property there. If I obtain a mortgage on the property, can I deduct the interest expense against my rental income? The money received on the mortgage was used to obtain a five-year term deposit.

Answer

This interest may not be used to reduce your rental income because the interest expense was not incurred to realize rental income. The only time you would be allowed to deduct this interest arises when you use the money obtained from the mortgage to acquire another rental property in Canada and you elect to report the rental income on a net basis.

Question – Net Rent – Capital Cost Allowance

Can I claim capital cost allowance for purposes of determining net rent for withholding tax and remittance purposes?

Answer

No. Capital cost allowance may only be used when you file your tax return for the year in question.

Question – Rental Income, Year of Departure
If I leave in June and earn rental income after that date, do I include the rental income in my departure return or do I file a separate tax return for the rental income?

Answer
First of all, you have a change of use and must decide whether to accept that reality or elect not to have a change of use. Your tenants should remit 25% of the gross rent to the tax authorities, on your behalf. You may file a separate rental return for the rental income earned after you emigrated from Canada.

Question – Filing on a Net Basis
I have had tax withheld and remitted on the gross rent. Can I recover this tax by filing a net basis?

Answer
You have two years from the particular year to file a Canadian tax return, report the rental income on a net basis and recover the previously withheld tax.

Other Income

Finally, there are certain types of income from which non-resident tax is withheld which you may elect (yes, yet another election) to include in your final tax return to receive a refund of non-resident tax withheld. These payments include:

- alimony and maintenance
- certain pension benefits
- death benefits
- certain retiring allowances
- payments under a registered supplementary unemployment plan
- registered retirement savings plan payments
- deferred profit sharing plan payments
- registered retirement income fund payments
- life income funds (LIFs)
- amounts received from a retirement compensation arrangement

This election which is made under s. 217 of the *Income Tax Act* of Canada must be filed within six months of the particular year.

Question – Section 217
I feel that I may benefit by making the election to have s. 217 apply to my pension income. Is there an election form?

Answer
There is no election form. You only need to file a regular Canadian tax return within six months of the year in which you received the pension income, report the income therein and request that s. 217 apply to the income.

Question – Section 217, Year of Departure
I left Canada on June 15, 1995. I received a retiring allowance after I departed which was subject to 25% non-resident withholding tax. Based on my income both from Canada and outside Canada, I feel that I can benefit from a s. 217 election. Do I file a separate tax return for the s. 217 election or do I include the retirement allowance in my regular final return?

Answer
If you elect to use s. 217, the retirement allowance is included in your final Canadian tax return filed for the year of departure.

This particular election is by far the most complex a non-resident must face. Unfortunately, it does not yield significant benefits even when it is applicable. We feel it is really much ado about nothing. We refer you to Chapter 3, "Taxation of a Non-resident", "Other Income" for more information regarding how this election works and when it may be useful.

As noted, these payments are subject to non-resident withholding tax at a rate of 25% unless reduced by a tax treaty. The reduced tax rate may depend on the nature and the size of the payment. For example, lump sum payments from an RRSP will remain subject to the 25% withholding tax except for certain treaties (see Chapter 4 - Tax Treaties). Other payments such as amounts from RRIFs and Life Income Funds (LIFs) will depend on both the amount paid and the treaty. Generally speaking, Revenue Canada treats payments from these as periodic payments except for the portion of the payment in excess of 2 times the minimum amount. The excess is considered a lump sum payment and subject to a 25% tax rate unless a treaty states otherwise.

New Reporting Requirement

The government has introduced a new reporting requirement for individuals who emigrate from Canada. If you leave Canada to reside elsewhere, you must file a new form containing information on all your assets when the total value of these assets exceeds $25,000. You can exclude any asset that you use primarily for personal purposes, such as a car, but only if that asset has a value of less than $10,000. This return will be due with your Canadian tax return for the year in which you leave and must be completed even if there is no deemed disposition of any assets when you leave. This new reporting requirement will affect all individuals who leave Canada after 1995.

These assets could include:
- Automobile
- House
- Cottage
- Airplane
- Bank accounts, GICs, term deposits
- RRSP, RRIF
- Offshore assets
- Antiques
- Jewelry
- Partnership interest

The new reporting rules do not indicate whether mortgages or other indebtedness will be taken into account to determine whether a property should be listed. One can only imagine what Revenue Canada will do with this new information.

PLANNING

We have spent a great deal of paper and ink explaining the finer points of Canadian residency and non-residency. We know that your primary objective is to become a non-resident. With that in mind and a firm conviction that you will achieve non-resident status, you must also plan for your arrival in your new home and not so native land.

It may well be worth your while to talk to a local tax specialist who should be up on the latest ways to legitimately structure your foreign source income so as to minimize both Canadian (if any) and domestic tax. If your new home is a treaty country, you should review both the domestic tax laws and the treaty benefits (if any) or restrictions.

If you can control your departure date, you may either reduce or defer tax. For example, if you leave in December, your income on your final return will include your world income up to the date of departure, plus any gains arising from the deemed disposition of your various properties. The latter will be taxed at the highest marginal tax rate and be payable (unless you are able to defer the payment of tax on taxable Canadian properties) when you file your tax return on or before April 30 (June 15 for individuals who report business income) of the following year. If you are able to delay departure until January of the following year, you may pay less tax and defer the payment of that tax (unless you have to make instalments) for up to 16 months.

New rules relating to business or professional taxation years may have caused you to claim a reserve of untaxed income which will be taxable when you leave Canada and cease carrying on that business or profession in Canada. By delaying your departure until January, you may reduce the tax and defer the payment of tax on that reserve.

If you plan to continue to carry on business through a permanent establishment in Canada after you cease to be a resident, you may be able to continue to claim the reserve permitted by law. This status will require you to continue to file a Canadian return, albeit as a non-resident and report this business income.

You may have claimed other types of reserves during the prior year. In particular, if you sold land inventory and claimed the 3 year reserve, this reserve will not be permitted in the year of departure or the year preceding departure. Once again, careful planning must occur to reduce or defer tax.

Caution must be exercised to ensure that this planning does not cause detrimental tax consequences in your new homeland.

The receipt of certain payments may be more tax effective as a non-resident than a resident. For example, a retiring allowance will be fully taxed unless you are able to roll it to an RRSP. If you cannot roll the entire amount to an RRSP, Canada will only tax it at 25% if you receive it as a non-resident.

Lastly, don't forget the new expanded rules relating to deemed dispositions and reporting assets on hand. The listing should be done prior to departure and presented to your tax preparer to facilitate the preparation of your final tax return in an orderly manner.

Taxation of a Non-resident

As a non-resident of Canada, you remain liable for Canadian tax on most types of income earned in Canada. This may include income from employment in Canada, income from carrying on a business in Canada, gains from the disposition of taxable Canadian property and certain other types of Canadian source income. You may also be liable for Canadian tax on employment income earned outside of Canada (fortunately in very limited circumstances). Income from these sources will be reported on a Canadian tax return similar to the one you completed while a resident. The amount of federal tax payable will be determined according to the same marginal tax rate paid by Canadian residents. Provincial tax may be replaced by an additional federal tax which may be greater or less than provincial rates, depending on the province.

Other types of Canadian income such as interest, dividends, pensions withdrawals from RRSPs and RRIFs will be subject to a uniform level of non-resident withholding tax. This will be deducted and remitted to Revenue Canada by the financial institution which administers your account. The standard rate of non-resident withholding tax is 25%; this may be reduced if you live in a country which has a tax treaty with Canada. In certain situations, you may elect to file a separate return to reduce the overall tax.

This chapter looks at these filing requirements and your responsibility as a non-resident. For more information see Interpretation Bulletin IT-420R3– Income Earned in Canada, which may be obtained from the International Taxation Office.

INCOME TAX — NON-RESIDENT TAX RETURN

Income from Employment

If you earn income from duties performed in Canada, you will be required to include these amounts in your Canadian income. Such income may include employment benefits, living and personal allowances and director's fees, as well as salaries and commissions. This income may be reduced by various expenses such as travelling, to the extent such expenses are reasonable and applicable to the income.

If you perform part of your duties inside Canada and part outside Canada, you are permitted to make a reasonable allocation of the resulting income and pay Canadian tax only on the portion which relates to Canada. For example, if you are a non-resident employed in the transportation of airline passengers partly inside and partly outside Canada, your income allocation may be calculated either on the basis of time worked or kilometres travelled. You may deduct any expense that applies to the employment income on the same basis as the income allocation.

Question – Non-resident Employee

I am currently a non-resident of Canada. However, my employment requires that 15% of my time be spent in Canada while the balance is outside Canada. Since I am a non-resident of Canada, do I have to pay Canadian tax?

Answer

Canadian tax law requires non-residents to pay tax on income from employment performed in Canada. As a result, you would be required to file a Canadian tax return and report that portion of employment income earned in Canada.

If you reside in a country that has a treaty with Canada, you may find that the income is exempt from Canadian tax. This result does not preclude the necessity to file a Canadian tax return. You must still prepare a Canadian tax return, report the Canadian employment income and claim an exemption to the extent that one is available under the treaty.

Income from Business

If you earn income from a business that you carry on in Canada, you are required to include this amount in your income earned in Canada unless the income is exempt by virtue of a tax treaty. Canadian tax laws will deem you to be "carrying on a business in Canada" if:

a) you solicit orders or offer anything for sale in Canada through a dependent agent or servant;

b) you or an agent acting on your behalf produce, grow, create, manufacture, fabricate, improve, pack, preserve or construct, in whole or part, anything in Canada; or

c) you dispose of real property other than capital property.

If you carry on your business both inside and outside Canada, you are permitted to make a reasonable allocation of the income since only income earned in Canada is subject to Canadian tax. Expenses relating to the business will be allocated on the same basis.

If you carry on business in a partnership, you will report your share of the partnership income which relates to Canada.

It is noteworthy that income from business does not include income from property, such as rent, interest or dividends. These amounts are usually subject to non-resident withholding tax unless reduced or eliminated by a treaty. Where these amounts may be attributed to your Canadian business, they may escape the fixed non-resident withholding tax and be included in your business income. Whether this is beneficial will depend on the level of withholding tax which would otherwise have been applicable compared to the rate of Canadian tax applied to your business income. The latter is usually higher.

As noted in Chapter 2, individuals who continue to carry on a business through a permanent establishment in Canada may be able to claim the reserve relating to conversion to calendar year-ends. At the time of writing this section, Revenue Canada had denied this right to non-residents, but, indicated that they would reconsider their application of the law which appears to clearly permit a non-resident to claim the reserve. We do not agree with Revenue Canada's position in this matter and support the ability to claim the reserve to the extent they otherwise qualify.

Question – Non-resident, Consulting Income
I currently provide consulting services to a Canadian client. I do all my work outside of Canada. Do I have to pay Canadian tax on this income?

Answer
Canadian tax law requires you to pay tax on income earned from businesses carried on in Canada. Since you do not carry on this business in Canada, you do not have to pay Canadian tax.

Disposition of Taxable Canadian Property (TCP)

If you gift, transfer or sell TCP as a non-resident, regardless of whether or not the property was deemed to be disposed of on your departure from Canada, you have certain filing requirements and will be required to pay Canadian tax if a capital gain arises. In order to assure the transferee or the purchaser that all Canadian income tax has been paid, you must file Form T2062(E) or T2062A(E) (Appendix A: CRA 8 & 9) and remit 33 1/3% of the gain to Revenue Canada. If you do not comply with these requirements, the transferee or purchaser will be required to remit 33 1/3% of the total purchase price to Revenue Canada. Upon receipt of the required form and remittance, Revenue Canada will issue a clearance certificate which will be given to the transferee or purchaser to assure them that you have complied with these requirements. For more detail on this area refer to Information Circular IC 72-17R4 (Appendix A: CRA 11).

The recent amendments (see Chapter 2) which caused you to have a deemed disposition on departure from Canada of certain types of TCP do not eliminate the requirements listed above with regard to obtaining a clearance certificate. Specific details regarding the necessary procedures were not available at the time of this update. We therefore advise that appropriate inquiries be made at the time of any such sale to ensure that there are no delays for you to obtain your clearance certificate and proceeds from the sale of the property. These new amendments will, no doubt, cause much confusion and result in numerous incorrect filings.

The amendments have also extended the meaning of TCP. As a result, there are now more types of property for which any gain arising after the date of departure will be subject to Canadian tax unless exempt by a treaty. For example, the expanded definition can deem a partnership interest to be a TCP if its assets consisted of more than 50% of TCP in the immediately preceding 5 years (rather than 1 year), shares of any corporation not listed on a prescribed stock exchange (i.e. unlisted shares) and the shares of a non-resident corporation where more than 50% of their value was from taxable Canadian properties in the preceding five years.

If you realized a gain (loss) on the transfer of TCP as a non-resident and remitted the required tax, you must file a Canadian tax return and report the gain (loss). Normally, a refund will arise because various selling costs are not taken into consideration when filing the request for clearance, Form T2062(E). As well, if the taxable portion of the gain is small, your overall Canadian tax rate will be less than 33 1/3% of the gain.

This income tax return is not to be confused with the tax return filed to comply with an undertaking to file a rental return pursuant to Form NR6. This tax return will include the capital gain arising from the sale of your property along with other items of income subject to Canadian tax — e.g. Canadian employment and business income mentioned above. It must be filed on or before April 30 of the following year if tax is owing.

A gain arising from any property other than TCP will not be subject to Canadian tax regardless of whether you paid the tax or elected to defer the payment of tax when you left Canada. These types of property will include shares of public companies, investments in mutual funds and interests in partnerships where less than 50% of their value is attributable to taxable Canadian properties.

Question – Sale of Taxable Canadian Property

I propose to sell my former home. Due to market conditions, I will suffer a loss on this sale. Is it necessary to file Form T2062(E), "Notice by a Non-Resident of Canada Concerning the Disposition or Proposed Disposition of Taxable Canadian Property"?

Answer

Yes. Regardless of whether you realize a capital gain or loss, you must file Form T2062.

Question – Form T2062

I propose to sell a rental property. Do I file Form T2062(E) or Form T2062A(E)?

Answer

If you have both a capital gain or loss and a recapture of depreciation previously claimed, you have to file both T2062(E) and a T2062A(E). The former is for capital property such as land and shares, while the latter is required for property that may be written off such as depreciable property and resource property. If you have to file both, they are filed together. The confusing part of this sale arises when you file your Canadian tax return to report the gain. You file one tax return to report the capital gain and a second tax return under s. 216 to report the net rental income up to the date of sale and the recapture of depreciation.

Question — Sale of Taxable Canadian Property

I filed Form T2062(E) relating to the sale of capital property in Canada. I remitted 33 1/3 % of the gain. Do I have to file a Canadian tax return and do you foresee any benefit for doing so?

Answer

You must file a Canadian tax return and report the gain. This will likely create a refund of tax. Remember, you remitted tax equal to 33 1/3% of the capital gain, which was not reduced by selling costs.

TRANSFER OF TAXABLE CANADIAN PROPERTY

If you transfer a taxable Canadian property to anyone, even your spouse (don't forget this includes a common-law spouse), you will have a disposition at fair market value and Canadian tax may be owing.

As well, if you die (perish the thought) and you leave your taxable Canadian property to your spouse, what would be a tax deferred event for a Canadian resident becomes a taxable event for your estate.

Question – Non-resident Transfer of Property
I plan to gift Canadian real estate to my adult children. The property has a significant unrealized capital gain. Do I have to file Form T2062(E) and will I be subject to Canadian tax?

Answer
Transfers of property by any means will occur at fair market value. As a result you should file Form T2062(E), remit 33 1/3 % of the gain and file a Canadian tax return.

Question – Non-resident, Transfer to Spouse
I plan to gift my spouse a half interest in a Canadian cottage that has a large unrealized capital gain. Do I have to file Form T2062(E) and will I be taxable since it is a transfer to my spouse?

Answer
The tax deferred transfer between spouses only occurs while you are residents of Canada. Since you are a non-resident, the property will be deemed to be sold at its fair market value and a taxable gain will arise. You should file Form T2062(E), remit the required 33 1/3% tax and file a Canadian tax return.

Question – Sale of Taxable Canadian Property
I left Canada on December 30, 1996. I realized and paid tax on a deemed disposition of shares of a private corporation. I plan to sell these shares in 1997 for a value greater than at the date of departure. What filing requirements do I have? Can I claim foreign tax credit treatment against tax in my new homeland?

Answer
You were deemed to have sold and reacquired your property in 1996. As a result, you will be required to file Form T2062(E) and remit 33-1/3 of the gain that arose since the date of departure. You will file a tax return for 1997 and declare that gain.

You should be able to claim the tax paid in 1997 as a foreign tax in your new homeland. However, it is doubtful that you can use the tax paid on departure. This would be the case even if you had elected to defer the payment thereof.

Question – Sale of Taxable Canadian Property

I left Canada on October 3rd (darn!) 1996 and was caught by the new rules. I reported the gain from shares of a private corporation in my departure tax return and elected to defer the payment of the tax. It is now 1997 and I wish to gift these shares to my spouse. Will this action cause me to have to pay the deferred tax in 1997?

Answer

You are permitted to defer the payment of the tax from the deemed disposition until you actually dispose of the shares. A gift to your spouse is considered to be such a disposition. As well, since you are both non-residents, any gain that has accrued since October 3, 1996 will also be taxable. You should file Form T2062(E) before the transfer and remit the required 33-1/3% of the gain and file a tax return for 1997.

Question – Sale of Taxable Canadian Property, Loss

I left Canada in November 1996 and realized a capital gain on the deemed disposition of my shares in a Canadian private corporation. I sold these shares in 1997 at a loss. Can I claim the capital loss against the capital gain in my 1996 tax return?

Answer

Capital losses realized on the disposition of taxable Canadian property may be carried back 3 years and applied to capital gains arising from the disposition (deemed or actual) of taxable Canadian properties. The new rules may restrict the application of these losses.

PRINCIPAL RESIDENCE

Exemption

The most common taxable Canadian property sold by expatriates is the family home. This event may give rise to a capital gain if the date of sale is several years after you cease to be a resident of Canada. As noted in Chapter 2, you cannot designate a property as your principal residence for any full year in which you are not a resident of Canada. Fortunately, you may designate it as a principal residence for those years when you were a resident (including the year of departure). The formula also gives you an extra year. For assistance in the determination of the portion of the gain eligible for the principal residence designation, refer to Interpretation Bulletin IT-120R4 and Form T2091 (Appendix A: CRA 12 & 10).

The formula for calculating the portion of the capital gain arising on the sale of your former residence which will be excluded from your income is as follows:

$$\text{Exempt portion of Capital Gain} = \text{Capital Gain X} \frac{1 + \text{number of taxation years ending after 1971 for which the property was your principal residence } \textit{and during which you were a resident of Canada}}{\text{Number of taxation years ending after 1971 during which you owned the property.}}$$

As a result, if you sell your house after you cease to be a resident of Canada, a portion of the gain that would otherwise have been excluded from income if the house had been sold prior to departure from Canada could give rise to a Canadian tax liability under this formula, even if the value of the property did not increase after you left Canada. Accordingly, in considering the alternatives relating to your principal residence, it is necessary to take into account the increase in the value of the property up to the date of departure, the anticipated change in value while you are out of Canada, and your intentions with respect to the future use of the property.

Question – Sale of Former Principal Residence

We purchased our home in 1985 for $180,000 and became non-resident in 1994. We could not sell our home when we left Canada and leased it out. We elected not to have a change of use at that time. We plan to sell this property in June 1997 for $250,000. What will the tax consequences be?

Answer

You may designate your property as your principal residence for the years 1985 through 1994 (assuming you have not designated any other property). These years (10) plus 1 will form the numerator and the total years you have owned it will be the denominator (13).

Sales Proceeds	$ 250,000
Tax Cost	180,000
Capital Gain	70,000
Deduct: Principal residence exemption	
$\frac{10 + 1}{13}$ X $70,000	59,230
Capital Gain	$ 10,770

You will pay tax on a capital gain of $10,770.

As noted under "Transfer of Taxable Canadian Property", you must obtain a clearance certificate in respect of the disposition by advising Revenue Canada of the transaction (Form T2062(E)) and remitting an amount equal to 33 1/3% of the gain. Failure to obtain the clearance certificate will cause the subsequent owner to be liable to pay an amount equal to 33 1/3% of the purchase price. Revenue Canada's administrative policy is not to require any amount to be remitted in respect of the portion of the gain that will be excluded from income under the formula set out above. In most cases, the purchaser will insist that a clearance certificate be obtained, in light of his or her potential liability.

Change of Use

Should you decide to rent out the house rather than sell it, there are other rules to consider. Such an event will be considered a change of use and our tax rules will cause you to have a deemed disposition. The property is deemed to be disposed of at its fair market value. If this occurs after you leave Canada, the formula may cause you to incur a gain and a tax liability in Canada. You should file Form T2062(E) and a Canadian tax return to report this event. If you return to Canada and move into this property, there will be another change of use and tax may arise from any gain from a deemed disposition.

Both changes of use may be avoided by electing not to have a change of use when you commence renting the house. This election will cause the house to retain its classification as a personal use property. It does not permit you to designate it as a principal residence for these years during which it was rented. If this election is made, you can move back into the property without a deemed disposition.

If no election is made when you commence renting your house, a taxable gain may arise because of the formula. Subsequently, if you cease leasing the property and move into it on your return to Canada, a change of use will occur. You may elect not to realize this change of use and defer any taxable gain until you actually sell the property. If there has been a substantial gain on the property to the date of non-residency, the expected additional increase in value while you are a non-resident will have to be considered. Under the formula, a portion of the gain accruing up to the date of non-residency which would otherwise be exempt from tax may become taxable if the annual rate of increase while you are a non-resident is less than the annual rate of increase during the years that you were resident in Canada and the property was your principal residence. Alternatively, if there has been a relatively small gain on the property up to the date of non-residency and it appears that the value of the property could increase significantly during the period of non-residence, by virtue of the election, a portion of the gain that otherwise may have been taxable will be exempt from tax.

If the sale of the house takes place while you are a non-resident, you should determine whether there are any provisions in a tax treaty between Canada and your country of residence that may help to relieve any foreign tax on the sale.

CAPITAL LOSSES

You may realize capital losses from the sale of taxable Canadian properties. These losses may be offset against capital gains arising from the sale of taxable Canadian property either in the year of the sale, the three preceding years or some future year. Capital losses may only be applied against capital gains. As well, if you realize a capital loss from the sale of an asset you use personally — such as your home — the loss will be deemed to be nil. This is just one more consideration to take into account when you change the use of a property. Remember, an election not to have a change of use may be made. For example, if you elect not to have a change of use when you commence renting out your principal residence, it will remain a personal use asset. If a loss arises on a subsequent sale, the loss will be deemed to be nil. Alternatively, if no election was made, and a subsequent loss is realized, it will be a capital loss, and may be applied against capital gains from taxable Canadian properties.

Other Canadian Source Income

In addition to those mentioned above, a number of less common sources of Canadian income must be included in the computation of your income earned in Canada. These include:
   i)   Negative amounts of Cumulative Canadian Development expenses
   ii)   Recapture of capital cost allowance
   iii) Amounts pertaining to a Canadian resource property
   iv)   The gain on the disposition of an income interest in a trust resident in Canada
   v)   The gain on the disposition of a right pertaining to a partnership
   vi)   Gains arising from the dispositions of certain life insurance policies in Canada

Persons Deemed to be Employed in Canada

Under certain circumstances, you may be required to pay tax to Canada even though you are a non-resident earning income in another country. No, you are not misreading nor have we made a mistake. This situation can and does arise, much to the surprise of some non-residents.

You will be deemed to be employed in Canada if you are a non-resident and are one of the following:

i)   A student in full-time attendance at a university or other educational institution in Canada that provides courses at a post-secondary level in Canada;

ii) A student attending or a teacher teaching at a university, college or other educational institution outside Canada providing courses at a post-secondary school level, if, as either a student or a teacher, you had ceased in any previous year to be resident in Canada in the course of or after moving to attend or teach at that educational institution;

iii) An individual who had ceased in any previous year to be resident in Canada in the course of or after moving to carry on research or any similar work under a grant received to enable you to carry on that research or work;

iv) An individual who had ceased in any previous year to be resident in Canada and who in the current year received remuneration from an office or employment paid directly or indirectly by a resident in Canada; or

v)   A person who received an amount in the current year under a contract, if the amount was or will be deductible by a Canadian taxpayer and can reasonably be regarded as having been received as:

   a) consideration or partial consideration for entering into a contract of services to be performed in Canada (i.e. signing bonus) or for undertaking not to enter into such a contract with another party, or

   b) remuneration from the duties of an office or employment or compensation for services to be performed in Canada.

If you fit into one or more of the above categories, you will be required to include the aggregate of the following amounts in your Canadian income for the year:

1. Remuneration in the year from an office or employment paid directly or indirectly by a person resident in Canada.

    Canadian tax rules allow you to exclude from this income any remuneration attributable to the duties of an office or employment performed by you anywhere outside Canada, provided that it is either:

   a) subject to an income or profits tax imposed by the government of a country other than Canada, or

   b) paid to you in connection with the selling of property, the negotiating of contracts or rendering of services for your employer or a foreign affiliate of your employer or any other person with whom your employer does not deal at arm's length, in the ordinary course of a business carried on by your employer or by the foreign affiliate or that other person.

For purposes of this exclusion, your remuneration is considered to be subject to an income or profits tax if it falls within the taxing jurisdiction of a country other than Canada. You will continue to qualify even if you pay no foreign income or profits tax by virtue of claiming personal allowances and any similar deductions to which a resident of that foreign country would normally be entitled. On the other hand, you will not qualify if you are not taxable in that country because of an exempting provision contained in a treaty between that country and Canada. Similarly, you will not qualify if you are exempted from taxation in that foreign jurisdiction under an agreement between foreign government authorities and you or your employer. Remuneration received by you for certain services will also be excluded. The services must be earned in connection with certain types of work performed in the ordinary course of a business carried on by the employer, its foreign affiliate or a person with whom the employer does not deal at arm's length. The phrase rendering of service would include the performance of work or duties in respect of an office or employment.

2. Canadian source scholarships, fellowships, bursaries and prizes net of allowable expenses.
3. The taxable portion of Canadian source research grants.
4. The taxable portion of registered educational savings plan payments that would have been taxable if you were a resident of Canada.

Reduction of Canadian Tax

The reduction of overall tax in Canada is accomplished by a system of deductions from income and non-refundable tax credits. These are also available to non-residents, in some cases on a restricted basis.

DEDUCTIONS

A number of the deductions permitted in arriving at your net income from Canadian sources are not related to a particular source of income. These include maintenance and alimony payments, RRSP contributions to the extent they are otherwise deductible and Canadian exploration and development exploration expenses. You may also deduct specified portions of benefits arising from employee stock options which have been included in your income, amounts which are exempt from Canadian income because of a tax treaty or other government agreement, income from employment with a prescribed international organization and income from non-governmental organizations. Certain losses may be deductible from your Canadian income.

Maintenance and Alimony Payments

If you are a non-resident who has income which is taxable in Canada and you pay alimony or maintenance, you may deduct these payments from your Canadian income in the same manner you would have done had you been a resident in Canada. Unfortunately, all the same rules apply for these payments to be a deduction. They have to be periodic payments made pursuant to a written agreement.

In the 1996 federal budget, the government proposed major changes to rules determining how child support payments are calculated, the way they are taxed and the ability of custodial parents to collect amounts awarded. These changes were in response to growing pressure on the government to make reforms.

Under the new system, the amount of child support awarded to a custodial parent will be based on the income of the other parent and the number of children. Guidelines will be issued that judges and lawyers will use in setting child support awards. The government hopes that the guidelines will result in fairer and more consistent award payments. In addition, child support paid will no longer be taxable to the custodial parent nor deductible for the payer. This is a major change from existing rules.

The changes are effective for all new court orders or written agreements entered into after May 1, 1997.

Existing agreements will continue under the old rules which means that child support will still be taxable to the custodial parent and deductible to the payer. Both parents can elect, if they desire, to have the new tax rules apply after May 1, 1997 to an existing order or agreement.

These new rules may impact the deductibility of these amounts in the future.

RRSP Contribution

Even though you are a non-resident, you may contribute to an RRSP and deduct the contributions from employment or business income and capital gains which are taxable in Canada. Keep in mind that the amount you can deduct will be governed by the income you earned in Canada in the preceding year. In other words, you will only be allowed to deduct an amount equal to 18% of your earned income, which will include employment and business income (not capital gains) for the preceding year up to a maximum allowed in the current year (1997 to 2003 – $13,500). To the extent you do not have sufficient Canadian income to deduct the RRSP contribution, the excess may be carried forward to a subsequent year.

Earned income for RRSP purposes will be restricted to Canadian employment and business income. Income earned outside of Canada will not qualify as earned income for RRSP purposes unless it is taxed in Canada.

Question – Contribution to an RRSP
I have been a non-resident of Canada for 2 years and have an unused deduction limit of $9,000. Should I contribute to an RRSP?

Answer
You would only contribute to your RRSP if you anticipated earning Canadian income that could be reduced by claiming the RRSP contribution. Current rules permit you to carry forward the deduction limit until you turn 69.

Canadian Exploration and Development Expenses

If you invested in flow-through shares which give you Canadian Exploration Expenses (CEE) and/or Canadian Development Expenses (CDE), you may deduct these from your Canadian income at rates of 100% and 30%, respectively.

Employee Stock Options

You may have exercised employee stock options received from a Canadian employer during the year. Generally speaking, you must include an amount equal to the excess of the fair market value of the share at the time you exercise the option over the option price in your income as a benefit. If you received the option at a time when the option price was equal to the fair market value of the stock, you will be permitted to deduct an amount equal to 25% of the benefit from your income.

If your employer was a Canadian Controlled Private Corporation with which you were dealing at arm's length, the benefit is only taxable when you sell the shares. If you have held the shares for more than two years, a benefit equal to the excess of the fair market value of the shares over the option price (at the time the option is exercised) will be included in your income when you sell the shares, and you may deduct 25% of that benefit from your Canadian income.

Amounts Exempt by Treaty or Agreement

Canada has concluded a number of tax treaties and agreements that contain provisions to exempt certain incomes from taxation in Canada. This subject will be covered in more detail in Chapter 4.

Losses

As a non-resident, you may deduct losses arising from employment, business and capital property if income realized from the same source would normally be included in your taxable income. Obviously, only losses realized in Canada will be eligible.

In order to be deductible, capital losses (which can only be applied against capital gains) must have been realized on the disposition of properties which are taxable Canadian properties or properties you elected to be taxable Canadian properties. Remember, gains from capital properties which are not taxable Canadian properties (e.g. shares of a public corporation) are not taxable when realized by non-residents. As a result, losses arising from Canadian properties which are not taxable Canadian properties are not deductible when computing Canadian taxable income as a non-resident.

TAX CREDITS

The Canadian tax liability of a non-resident may be reduced by certain non-refundable tax credits. These include the charitable donation, disability, tuition fee, Canada Pension, Employment Insurance, medical and personal credits. Some of these may be claimed only if the income reported on your Canadian return represents more than 90% of your world income, a restriction we will refer to as the "90% income test".

Donations

Non-residents can receive a tax credit for donations to Canadian charitable organizations and certain foreign charities recognized by Revenue Canada. The credit will be limited to donations equal to 75% of your net income and any excess may be carried forward for five years.

Gifts to the Canadian and provincial governments have been reduced to 75% of net income while those qualifying as cultural property are still deducted up to the full amount of your net income. Unused balances may be carried forward for up to five years. The charitable donation tax credit is not subject to the "90% income test".

Disability

You may claim the disability tax credit, which is not subject to the "90% income test". However, you must pass that test if you wish to claim the disability tax credit of a dependent.

Tuition

You may claim the tuition fee tax credit for yourself without reference to the "90% income test".

Canada Pension and Employment Insurance

As a non-resident, you may claim Canada Pension Plan and Employment Insurance credits to the extent you made contributions during the year.

Medical

A medical credit may only be claimed by a non-resident if more than 90% of your world income is included in computing your Canadian taxable income.

If you meet the income test, you may claim the excess of medical expenses incurred both inside and outside Canada over the lesser of $1,614 (1997) and 3% of your net Canadian income.

Personal Non-refundable Tax Credits

In order to claim the personal tax credit and unused personal tax credits of your spouse, you must meet the "90% income test".

NON-RESIDENT WITHHOLDING TAX

As a non-resident you will be subject to non-resident withholding tax when certain types of income are paid or credited to you. These incomes include management or administration fees or charges, interest, estate or trust income, certain rents, royalties and similar payments, certain timber royalties, alimony or support payments, patronage dividends, certain pension payments, death benefits, retiring allowances, payments under a registered supplementary unemployment benefit plan, payments out of an RRSP, payments out of a DPSP, payments under an income-averaging annuity contract, annuity payments, payments out of an RRIF or LIF, payments out of a registered education savings plan and certain dividends.

The payer of the income is responsible for withholding and remitting a tax of 25% of the gross amount unless reduced by tax treaty. If the payer does not comply with these requirements, he or she is liable to pay the tax. This responsibility also extends to any agent who receives these amounts on your behalf. Penalties and interest may apply on late payments. Since the payer will not want to pay your tax, he or she will be careful to ensure that the appropriate amount of non-resident tax is withheld and remitted. If unpaid, you remain liable for the tax.

Management or Administration Fees or Charges

If a Canadian pays you management or administration fees, that individual should withhold and remit non-resident tax. No withholding tax is required if you are dealing at arm's length with the Canadian payer and it is your business to provide such services.

However, if your services are performed in Canada, the payer must withhold at least 15% of the fee unless you obtain an exemption from the Canadian tax authorities. This exemption may be granted pursuant to a tax treaty because you do not have a permanent establishment in Canada.

Interest

While interest is subject to non-resident tax, there are a number of exemptions. Several of the more common ones include interest on bonds of or guaranteed by the Government of Canada, a province or municipality; interest payable in a foreign currency; and interest payable by a corporation resident in Canada where you are arm's length, the debt is for at least five years and no more than 25% of the principal amount is required to be repaid in the five-year period.

For most non-residents, the five-year rule has a certain appeal. For example, if you acquired a five-year guaranteed investment certificate, no tax would be withheld on the interest. See Interpretation Bulletin IT-155R3–Exemption from Non-resident Tax on Interest Payable on Certain Bonds, Debentures, Notes, Hypothecs or Similar Obligations for more details.

Question – 5 Year GIC
I purchased a 5 year GIC before I left Canada. Will it qualify for the tax exempt status even though I purchased it a year prior to my departure?

Answer
This GIC will qualify for the tax exemption. The fact you acquired it while you were a resident is irrelevant.

Question – Stock-Indexed GIC
I am a non-resident of Canada and have purchased a 2 year Guaranteed Investment Certificate where interest is calculated by reference to a stock index. If I realize a gain over the next 2 years, how will the income be taxed?

Answer
The gain will be considered interest and subject to a 25% non-resident withholding tax unless reduced by tax treaty.

Estate or Trust Income

An amount paid to you by a Canadian trust will be subject to non-resident withholding tax unless it represents a payment of capital or income classified as a taxable capital gain from a Canadian mutual fund trust.

Question – Taxation of Mutual Funds
I am a non-resident of Canada. I hold several Canadian mutual funds. Please tell me if I pay any Canadian tax on income derived from these mutual funds.

Answer
A Canadian mutual fund may earn income from various sources - interest, dividends and capital gains. Any allocation of interest and dividends will be subject to a Canadian non-resident tax of 25% unless reduced by a tax treaty. Capital gains realized by the mutual fund and allocated to you or a gain realized on the redemption of your interest in the mutual fund is not subject to Canadian tax.

Rent

As mentioned previously, gross rental payments are subject to withholding tax unless you file Form NR6 and undertake to file a tax return by June 30 of the following year. Such an undertaking will permit your agent to withhold tax on the net rental (gross rent less rental expenses). The NR6 must be filed annually and before the year in question (Appendix A: CRA 2).

Timber Royalties

Timber Royalties are similar to rent in that tax is withheld on the gross amount unless you file Form NR6.

Alimony and Support Payments

These are subject to non-resident withholding tax on the gross amount unless they would not otherwise be included in the recipient's income in Canada.

Pensions

Subject to several exceptions, pension payments are usually subject to non-resident withholding tax. For example, withholding tax does not apply to that portion of a pension that can be attributed to services rendered by you in a taxation year during which you were at no time resident in Canada and throughout which you were not employed, or only occasionally employed in Canada. Transfers between registered pension plans or to an RRSP, locked-in RRSP, locked-in retirement accounts (LIRA), RRIF or LIF of which you are an annuitant are not subject to withholding tax.

Old Age Security and Canada Pension Plan payments along with other pension payments will be subject to withholding tax unless otherwise exempt.

Death Benefits

A death benefit is an amount paid by an employer to an employee's estate in recognition of the employee's service in an office or employment. Under Canadian tax law, death benefits up to $10,000 are tax free. As a result, only the excess over $10,000 will be subject to non-resident withholding tax.

Retiring Allowances

Retiring allowances are subject to non-resident withholding tax unless they relate to payment for services rendered in taxation years when you were not resident in Canada. As well, to the extent you can contribute all or a portion of the retiring allowances to an RRSP under which you are the annuitant, non-resident withholding tax will not apply. The amount of the retirement allowance you are able to transfer to your RRSP is restricted. Employment years after 1995 are not counted to determine how much you can transfer to an RRSP.

Registered Supplementary Unemployment Benefit Plan

Payments from Registered Supplementary Unemployment Benefit Plans will be subject to non-resident withholding tax.

Payments — RRSP, RRIF, DPSP, LIF

Payments from an RRSP, RRIF, DPSP or a LIF are subject to non-resident withholding tax unless the amounts are transferred to another plan or annuity of which you are the annuitant. Withholding tax levied on payments to you in a treaty country will vary depending on whether you receive a lump sum payment or a periodic payment. Periodic payment is a defined term and will have the meaning assigned to it by the treaty or the *Income Tax Convention Interpretation Act of Canada*. This area will be discussed more thoroughly in Chapter 4.

Locked-in RRSP or locked-in retirement accounts (LIRA) cannot be drawn out unless they are transferred to a Life Income Fund (LIF). The various provincial statutes regulate how much may be paid out of LIFs and when. Non-resident withholding tax is calculated on the same basis as a RRIF. Any payment equal to or less than 2 times the minimum is considered a periodic payment while a payment in excess of 2 times the minimum is considered a lump sum and subject to 25% unless reduced by treaty.

Question – RRSP Withdrawal
I wish to withdraw amounts from my RRSP on a visit to Canada. I understand that as long as the amount withdrawn does not exceed $5,000, the institution will only withhold 10%.

Answer
If you are a non-resident of Canada, the institution is required to withhold 25% of the payment from your RRSP regardless of how much it may be. You may apply to have a reduction of this tax by filing Form NR5. Alternatively, you may file a tax return within six months of the year in question and receive a refund if substantially all of your world income (more than 90%) is reported thereon.

You should ensure that the institution has your non-resident address so that it may withhold the appropriate non-resident withholding tax.

Registered Education Savings Plans

Contribution to a RESP are not deductible. As a result, the return of these amounts are not taxable. However, any payments which constitute income earned in the RESP will be subject to a 25% non-resident withholding tax unless reduced by a tax treaty or transferred to an RRSP.

TAX RELIEF

The tax laws of both Canada and your new country of residence may offer you relief from tax on various sources of income earned in Canada as a non-resident. These range from reduction in the withholding tax rate to complete exemption and may be contained in Canadian tax law, the foreign jurisdiction tax law and/or the tax treaty between Canada and that country.

Canadian Tax Relief

As you have seen, certain types of income received from sources in Canada may be free of Canadian tax. However, for those which are not, you may benefit from elective provisions which allow you to file a Canadian tax return and file in a specific manner.

Reduction of Tax on Rental Income

As mentioned in Chapter 2, if you have rental property, your tenant must deduct and remit 25% of the gross rent to the Canadian tax authorities. However, you and your Canadian agent may file Form NR6 and undertake to file a Canadian tax return on or before June 30th of the following year and remit only 25% of the net rent (gross rent less related expenses).

If you fail to file an NR6, you have two years after the year in which the rental income was received to file a tax return on a net basis and obtain a refund of tax previously remitted on your behalf.

Section 217 Election

Section 217 of the *Income Tax Act* permits non-residents to pay a reduced rate of Canadian tax on certain sources of Canadian income by allowing them to claim full non-refundable personal tax credits. The sources of income include:

- superannuation or pension benefits
- retiring allowances
- death benefits
- benefits under the *Employment Insurance Act*
- Registered Supplementary Unemployment Plan benefits
- RRSP payments
- RRIF payments
- LIF payments
- DPSP payments
- Alimony and Retirement Compensation Arrangement payments

Only non-residents who include 90% of their world income in their Canadian return will qualify. Experience has shown that it is difficult to benefit from this provision.

If you do qualify to receive a benefit under this provision, you may file Form NR5 – "Application by a Non-resident of Canada for a Reduction in the Amount of Non-resident Tax Required to be Withheld" (Appendix A: CRA 1). If this filing is accepted by the tax authorities, the individual or institution which pays you may reduce the amount of tax normally required to be withheld to that determined on the NR5. You must file a Canadian tax return by June 30th of the following year. Otherwise, the Canadian tax authorities will assess the tax that should have been remitted and advise the payer to commence withholding tax at the statutory rate.

Question – Section 217 Election
I understand that I can elect to reduce my Canadian tax on amounts received from my RRSP. How do I do this and when is it beneficial?

Answer
You may elect under s. 217 to file a Canadian tax return and pay tax as any other Canadian. In order for this election to be beneficial, you must be able to use your non-refundable personal tax credits. The ability to use these tax credits will depend on what portion your RRSP income is of your world income. For example, if your world income and RRSP income included in your Canadian tax return are equal to $6,000, you will not pay any Canadian tax and the non-resident tax will be refunded.

Question – Section 217 Election
I made a s. 217 election and ended up paying more tax than was withheld originally. Can I rescind this election?

Answer
Currently, there is no provision which will allow you to rescind this election.

Question – Section 217, Tax Return
I wish to make a s. 217 election on RRSP income. I currently file a tax return for rental income. Can I include my RRSP income in this rental income return?

Answer
Section 217 requires that you file a separate Canadian tax return. While it does not include rental income, it may include Canadian employment income, business income and capital gains from the sale of taxable Canadian property.

Tax Treaties

Canada has concluded a number of tax treaties with other countries. Various provisions may give you reduced Canadian withholding tax, complete exemption from Canadian tax, the ability to claim tax credits or some combination of these. We shall deal with these in Chapter 4.

Foreign Tax Relief

Your new home country may tax you on income received from Canada. If it does, its laws may contain provisions that will allow you to claim the Canadian tax as a foreign tax credit or deduction. In addition, if the country has a tax treaty with Canada, certain Canadian and possibly foreign taxes will be reduced or even eliminated. As a new resident of any country, you should review its tax filing requirements to ensure that you benefit from all relieving provisions contained in the domestic law and any tax treaty.

Estate Tax

Canada, believe it or not, is one of the few countries that does not levy an estate tax on death. Since this may be relevant in your new homeland, you should seek professional assistance to determine if there is any way to reduce or eliminate the incidence of this tax should you die. Estate tax usually applies to assets located in the jurisdiction or to world assets of persons domiciled in the country. It is important to understand these rules and take the appropriate steps to minimize your exposure.

Offshore Trusts

Now that you are a non-resident of Canada, you should consider setting up an inter-vivos offshore trust or changing your Will to establish an offshore testamentary trust. If you remain outside Canada for more than 18 months, the income earned in these structures will not be taxed by Canada unless income is paid to a Canadian beneficiary. Normally, this income is converted to tax free capital and can be received by a Canadian on a tax-free basis. These structures will be beneficial as long as you remain a non-resident of Canada. If you die and have been out of Canada for 18 months, the capital will never be taxed (under current Canadian law) and can provide Canadian beneficiaries with a lifetime of tax-free money.

If you return to Canada, the trust will be taxed as a Canadian trust. As well, you will be required to comply with the new foreign property reporting rules (Chapter 5 - Immigration).

Due to the cost of maintaining the offshore structure and the additional reporting requirements, it may not prove to be a cost effective investment and should be liquidated. Fortunately, all foreign property will have a tax cost equal to the fair market value of the property on the date when you return to Canada.

We strongly suggest that you seek professional assistance if you propose to establish these structures. While it may cost you some money to establish a trust or amend your Will, in the long run, it may provide your Canadian beneficiaries with a source of tax-free money.

Tax Treaties

OVERVIEW

Canada has entered into a number of bilateral tax agreements. The primary purpose of these treaties is to reduce the incidence of double taxation. For example, if you are living outside Canada, you could be subject to taxation in Canada on Canadian business income and taxed again on that same income in your country of residence. In the absence of a tax treaty, you would have to rely on the tax laws of that country to relieve you from double taxation. If you reside in a country that has a tax treaty with Canada, the possibility of double taxation is reduced by various treaty provisions which either exempt the income from taxation in one of the countries or to permit you to claim a tax credit in your country of residence equal to the tax you paid in Canada.

As noted in Chapter 3, various types of income which originate in Canada are subject to a non-resident withholding tax of 25%. A treaty may either reduce or eliminate this tax. Relief may be provided by reference to a specific lower rate of tax or by allowing only one jurisdiction to tax the income.

Most treaties are based on a model treaty and thus bear a resemblance to one another. However, you should not assume they are exactly the same. You should undertake a careful review of the relevant treaty, together with a thorough examination of the tax laws in your prospective country of residence, before you emigrate. While countries with treaties have tax systems, these systems are not identical to Canada's. Individual countries may tax different sources of income in different ways or may exempt them entirely. Your review should be conducted with a tax specialist familiar with the tax system of your new country. This approach may result in beneficial tax planning prior to entering your new country or a complete reconsideration of where you want to settle. We have found a review of the various booklets prepared by international tax services to be helpful but not as thorough as dealing with a tax specialist living and working in that country. While obtaining the advice of such a tax specialist may cost you a few dollars, it may prove to be money well spent.

Certain words and phrases in a treaty may not be given sufficient description in the treaty to allow you to appreciate their full meaning. If you encounter this problem, you may refer to domestic law for its definition. As well, Canada has an *Income Tax Conventions Interpretation Act of Canada* to facilitate your task. For example, this Act outlines what Canada will consider to be a "periodic pension payment" for purposes of a reduced withholding tax rate.

Question – Periodic RRSP Payments
I plan to withdraw $10,000 each year from my RRSP. Will this be considered a periodic payment eligible for a lower rate of non-resident withholding tax under a treaty?

Answer
Whether this payment is eligible for a lower rate of non-resident withholding will depend on the treaty. In most situations, such a payment will be considered to be a lump sum payment subject to 25% non-resident withholding tax.

If the tax treaty is unclear, you should refer to the *Income Tax Conventions Interpretation Act* which states that a "periodic pension payment" does not include a payment before maturity, or a payment in full or partial commutation of the retirement income, under a registered retirement savings plan.

DUAL RESIDENCE STATUS

The current international employment market could create a situation where you may be considered a resident of both Canada and a foreign country for income tax purposes. If you find yourself in this position, determine whether Canada and the foreign country have concluded a bilateral tax treaty. If a tax treaty exists, refer to Article 4 thereof to ascertain whether any of the so called tie-breaker rules apply.

Tie-Breaker Rules

Where you are a resident of both Canada and a tax treaty country, the tax treaty will usually determine your tax status on the following basis:

1. You shall be deemed to be a resident of the country in which you have a permanent home available to you.
2. If you have a permanent home available in both Canada and the foreign country, you shall be deemed to be a resident of the country with which your personal and economic relations are closer. This is commonly referred to as your centre of vital interests.
3. If the country in which you have your centre of vital interests cannot be determined, or if you have no permanent home available to you in either country, you shall be deemed to be a resident of the country in which you have an habitual abode.
4. If you have an habitual abode in both countries or in neither of them, you shall be deemed to be a resident of the country of which you are a national.

If you are a national of both countries or of neither of them, the competent authorities of Canada and the foreign country will usually settle the question of residency by mutual agreement.

Once you have established your status under the treaty, you can resolve the problem of double taxation by asking the relevant tax authority (Canadian or foreign) to confirm that you are exempt under the tax treaty. If necessary, you may request that the tax authority authorize your employer to cease withholding income tax from your pay cheque in accordance with your status under the treaty. For example, if you are working and residing in Malaysia but considered resident in both Canada and Malaysia, you would contact the Canadian tax authorities to rule on your exempt status. If you were working for a Canadian company, you would request Revenue Canada to authorize your employer not to withhold Canadian employee tax.

The fact that you are considered resident of a foreign jurisdiction for income tax purposes does not relieve you of your filing obligations in Canada. Technically, you must file a Canadian tax return, report your world income therein and claim a deduction thereof on the "additional deduction" line.

If you have been paying tax in Canada and subsequently discover that you were exempt from Canadian tax by reason of a tax treaty, you may write to your district tax office and request an adjustment to reflect your exempt status. For the current year, you may file an income tax return, report your income, claim a deduction on the "additional deduction" line and claim a refund of taxes.

Dual residency can create some interesting results. Even though you pay tax to the foreign jurisdiction, you will still be considered a resident of Canada.

Therefore, you will continue to enjoy many of the tax benefits allowed to Canadian residents. You will be able to designate your house as your principal residence, make tax-free transfers between spouses and maintain preferential tax treatment for Canadian corporations you may still own. And best of all, there will be no deemed disposition of property. Remember, the tie-breaker rule generally only decides where you will pay tax. All other rules will still apply.

A word of caution. The fact that you reside in a country that has a tax treaty with Canada does not always mean you can establish dual residence status. First of all, most treaties require that you be taxable in both Canada and the other country. Depending on the nature of your employment or business, you may find that you are not taxable on that income in the foreign jurisdiction.

Some treaties will not apply to certain individuals. For example, the treaty between Canada and the U.K. may not apply to income not remitted and taxed in the hands of an individual who is resident but not domiciled in the U.K. You should therefore not assume that you have either dual status or even protection under a particular treaty without a thorough review of its provisions.

Question – Treaty, Two-year Period
I have been employed by a foreign company in a country that has a tax treaty with Canada. I pay tax in the foreign country. Will I be subject to tax in Canada if I return before two years has expired?

Answer
You must examine the tax treaty provisions to determine if you will be taxable in Canada. If you are considered to be resident and subject to tax in both countries, you should review Article 4 and the tie-breaker rule to determine where you are taxable.

Question – Treaty, Factual Residence
I have lived and worked in Brazil as a missionary for five years. Revenue Canada feels that I am a factual resident of Canada and makes me file a Canadian tax return. The Brazil tax authorities also consider me to be resident and subject to their tax rules. What can I do?

Answer
You should review the Canada-Brazil tax treaty to determine where you are considered resident for tax purposes. If you are considered to be a resident of Brazil, you may claim an exemption from Canadian tax in your Canadian tax return.

TYPES OF INCOME

Business Income

Canada will tax a non-resident who earns income from carrying on a business in Canada. However, Article 7 of a tax treaty usually provides that as a non-resident you will pay tax in Canada only if you have a permanent establishment in Canada. Article 5 contains the various conditions used to determine whether you have a permanent establishment in Canada. In general terms, there must be a fixed place of business through which the business of an enterprise is wholly or partly carried on. The Article goes on to list a number of situations that will be considered to be permanent establishments:

- a place of management
- a branch
- an office
- a factory
- a workshop
- a mine, an oil or gas well or any other place of extraction of natural resources
- a building or construction site if it lasts more than 12 months
- a dependent agent with the authority to contract on your behalf in Canada

Treaties also contain a list of situations which will not cause you to have a permanent establishment in Canada. We recommend that you review the particular treaty to determine whether or not you have a permanent establishment in Canada. If you have a permanent establishment in Canada, then you will pay tax on that portion of your business income that relates to the Canadian operation in a manner outlined in Chapter 3. Article 7 usually permits your country of residence to tax this income but allows you to claim tax credits or provides some other form of tax relief to eliminate or reduce double taxation.

Rental Income

Article 6 provides for the tax treatment of income from immovable property — real estate, farmland and forests. Under most treaties, with the exception of those with Denmark and Ireland, such income is subject to Canadian non-resident withholding tax of 25% on the gross amount. As noted in Chapter 3, you may reduce the total tax to 25% of the net rental income by engaging a

Canadian agent who jointly agrees with you (on Form NR6) to file a Canadian income tax return within six months after the end of the year in which the income is received.

Article 6 does not preclude your country of residence from taxing this income. However, most treaties provide relief from double taxation through tax credits or exemptions in your country of residence.

Dividends

Article 10 provides that dividends paid to you by a Canadian company will be subject to Canadian non-resident withholding tax. As noted in Chapter 3, the usual non-resident tax is 25% of the gross dividend. This rate is usually reduced by treaty to 15% or 10% depending on which foreign country you live in, how you hold your investment and how much of the Canadian corporation you own. This article usually permits your country of residence to tax the dividend but provides for relief from double taxation.

Interest

Article 11 provides that interest paid to you by a Canadian may be subject to Canadian tax. As noted in Chapter 3, the usual non-resident tax is 25% of the interest. Where there is a treaty, this rate is usually reduced to 15%. This article usually permits your country of residence to tax the interest but provides relief from double taxation.

Royalties

Article 12 provides that royalties paid to you by a Canadian may be subject to Canadian tax. As with most other sources of Canadian income, the usual tax rate of 25% is reduced by treaty to either 15% or 10%. This Article usually permits your country of residence to tax the royalties but provides for relief from double taxation through tax credits or exemptions.

Capital Gains

Article 13 deals with the taxation of capital gains. This article varies from treaty to treaty but usually allows Canada to tax capital gains arising from real property and shares of corporations and interests in partnerships whose value is primarily due from real property. Gains arising from all other property will be left to the foreign country to tax unless the treaty gives Canada the right to tax any gains of a former resident for a period of up to five to ten years after emigration. If this right is specified, it will apply to taxable Canadian property (see Chapter 2). Article 13 usually permits the country of residence to tax the gain as well. As with other sources of income, the treaty will usually provide relief from double taxation in the form of tax credits or exemptions.

Since the taxation of capital gains varies from treaty to treaty, it is important to review the particular treaty to ascertain how it will affect you.

Question – Treaties, Capital Gains

I own a number of investments which consist of shares of public companies. I understand that I can elect to defer the deemed realization of these shares when I emigrate from Canada. I plan to emigrate to the U.S. I understand that gains arising from the sale of these shares will be exempt under the Canada–U.S. tax treaty. Is this correct?

Answer

The election you are referring to will not cause the public shares to be taxable. This fact by itself does not cause the subsequent capital gain to be taxable. Rather, the Canada–U.S. treaty contains a provision which allows Canada to tax you on capital gains arising from the sale of TCP for up to a ten-year period after you emigrate. This election will not cause the Non-TCP to be TCP.

Independent Personal Services (Self-employed)

Article 14 provides for the tax treatment of independent personal services. These include income earned by doctors, engineers, architects, etc. Generally, this will only be taxable in Canada if you have a fixed base regularly available to you in Canada. If you have such a fixed base in Canada, then this type of income is taxable in Canada but only to the extent it is attributable to the fixed base in Canada.

To the extent that it is taxable in Canada, income from independent personal services is taxed as outlined in Chapter 3. Where your country of residence is also permitted to tax this income, the treaty will usually provide relief from double taxation through tax credits or exemptions.

Dependent Personal Services (Employed)

Article 15 provides the rules for the taxation of salaries, wages and similar remuneration. This provision varies from treaty to treaty but taxation in Canada may depend on the amount of money you earned in Canada, how long you remained in Canada to earn the income or who deducted the wage expense. You should review this provision closely to determine how you may be taxed in Canada on such income. The usual type of relief from double taxation will be available.

Pensions

The Article that deals with pension income varies from treaty to treaty. Some treaties permit Canada to levy a non-resident tax thereon but allow you to reduce that tax to 15% or to eliminate it completely depending on your total pension income. This Article will also cover periodic and lump sum payments from your RRSPs and RRIFs. Of all the Articles, this may prove to be the most important one, particularly for those of you who have retired. The usual type of relief from double taxation will be available.

Question — Periodic RRIF Payments
I plan to convert my RRSP to an RRIF and draw out more than the minimum amount each year. I currently live in a treaty country. Will my RRIF payments be subject to the 25% non-resident withholding tax?

Answer
The amount of non-resident withholding tax will depend on the tax treaty and the amount paid out. If the tax treaty is silent on the tax treatment of amounts paid to you from your RRIF, the *Income Tax Conventions Interpretation Act of Canada* (Appendix A: CRA 28) states that a periodic pension payment does not include a payment in excess of twice the amount of the minimum payment you are required to receive each year. If the payment is greater than twice the minimum, the excess over twice the minimum will be subject to the 25% non-resident withholding tax.

Miscellaneous

All treaties contain articles dealing with director's fees, artists, government services, students, estates, trusts and other income. The article dealing with "other income" usually provides that if any item of income is not mentioned in any other article, it will be taxable only in the country of residence.

DOUBLE TAXATION

As noted above, all treaties contain provisions to eliminate or reduce double taxation. These include the ability to use Canadian tax paid on a particular source of income to reduce the tax levied by your country of residence or the complete exemption of that income from tax in that jurisdiction.

SPECIAL PROVISIONS

Most treaties contain a number of other provisions that deal with non-discrimination, mutual agreement procedures, exchange of information and treatment of diplomatic agents and consular officers. If you have to review a treaty, make certain that you obtain the most recent version. As well, once you have examined a particular article in the treaty, determine if any additional provisions have been added at the end. This section is generally referred to as the Protocol. The Protocol may deal with a subject in greater detail than does the Article in the original treaty. And last but not least, look to see if the treaty and/or protocol has been ratified and when the various provisions thereof apply.

It is beyond the scope of this book to provide you with a copy of every treaty. For more information, you may request copies of the following material from the International Taxation Office–Information Circular IC75-6R, "Required Withholding From the Amounts Paid to Non-Resident Persons Performing Services In Canada", Information Circular IC 76-12R4, "Applicable Rate of Part XIII Tax on Amounts Paid or Credited to Persons in Treaty Countries" and Information Circular IC 77-16R4, "Non-resident Income Tax". Information Circular IC75-6R is not current and does not reflect new and or amended treaties. Please refer to our schedule of withholding tax rates for the current status of the relevant tax treaty.

Question – Refund of Non-resident Tax

If Canadian non-resident withholding tax was withheld at 25% when it should have been 15% under the Canada-Australian tax treaty, can I receive a refund of the excess?

Answer

You may file Form NR7 – R(E), "Application For Refund of Non-resident Tax" (Appendix A: CRA 3). This must be done within two years of the year in which you received the payment.

SCHEDULE OF NON-RESIDENT TAX RATES FOR TREATY COUNTRIES
CURRENT AS OF MARCH 31, 1997

COUNTRY	ALIMONY	DIVIDENDS	PERIODIC PENSION PAYMENTS	PERIODIC ANNUITY PAYMENTS	LUMP SUM PENSION ANNUITY	INTEREST	TRUST INCOME	ESTATE/ ROYALTIES	RENT IMMOVABLE
	0	10/15	15	15	25	12.5	25	3/5/10/15	25
ARGENTINE REPUBLIC				15/25	15/25				
AUSTRALIA	25	15	15		25	15	15	10	25
AUSTRIA	0	15	25	25	25	15	15	10	25
BANGLADESH	0	15	15	15/25	25	15	25	10	25
BARBADOS	0	15	15	15/25	25	15	15	10	25
BELGIUM	0	15	25	25	25	15	15	10	25
BRAZIL	25	15/25	25	25	25	15/20	25	15/25	25
CAMEROON	25	15/20	25	25	25	10	0	15/20	25
CHINA	25	10/15	15		25	15	25	10	25
CYPRUS	0	15	15	15/25	25	10	15	10	25
CZECH & SLOVAK FEDERAL REPUBLIC	0	10/15	15	15	25	15	15	15	15
DENMARK	25	15	0	0	0/25	18	25	18	25
DOMINICAN REPUBLIC	0	18	18	18/25	25		18	15	25
EGYPT	25	15/20	25	25	25	15	15	15	25
ESTONIA	0	5/15	15	10	25	10	15	10	25
FINLAND	25	10/15	20	15	25	10	15	10	15
FRANCE	0	10/15	25	25	25	10	15	10	25
GERMANY	0	15	25	25	25	15	25	10	25
GUYANA	0		15		25	15/25	15	10	25
HUNGARY	0	5/10/15	25	10/25	25	10	25	10	25
INDIA	25	15/25	25	25	25	15	15	15	25
INDONESIA	0	15	15	15/25	25	15	25	15	15
IRELAND	15	15	0	0	15	15	15	15	25
ISRAEL	0	15	15	15/25	25	15	15	10	25
ITALY	25	15	15	25	25	15	25	10	25
IVORY COAST	25	15/18	25	15	25	15	15	10	25
JAMAICA	0	15/22.5	25	15/25	25	15	15	10	25
JAPAN	25	10/15	25	25	25	10	25	10	25
KAZAKHSTAN [a]	0	10/15	15	15	25	10	0	10	25
KENYA	25	15/25	15	15/25	25	15	25	15	25

COUNTRY	ALIMONY	DIVIDENDS	PERIODIC PENSION PAYMENTS	PERIODIC ANNUITY PAYMENTS	LUMP SUM PENSION ANNUITY	INTEREST	TRUST INCOME	ESTATE/ ROYALTIES	RENT IMMOVABLE
KOREA	25	15	25	25	25	15	25	15	25
LATVIA	0	5/15	15	10	25	10	15	10	25
LIBERIA [a]	0	15	25	20/25	25	20/15	20	10/15/20	25
LITHUANIA [a]	0	5/10/15	0/25	20	25	15/20	0	10/15/20	25
LUXEMBOURG	0	5/10/15	25	25	25	15	15	10	25
MALAYSIA	25	15	15	15/25	25	15	15	15	25
MALTA	0	15	15	15/25	25	15	15	10	25
MEXICO	0	10/15	15	15	25	15	15	15	25
MOROCCO	25	15	25	25	25	15	25	5/10	25
NETHERLANDS	0	10/15	15	15	25	10	15	10	25
NEW ZEALAND	25	15	15	15/25	15/25	15	15	15	25
NIGERIA [a]	25	12.5/15	25	25	25	12.5	25	12.5	25
NORWAY	0	15	0	0	25	15	15	15	25
PAKISTAN	15	15/20	25	25	25	15	15	15	25
PAPUA NEW GUINEA	25	15/25	15	15/25	25	15/25	25	15/20	25
PHILIPPINES	25	15/25	25	25	25	10	25	10	25
POLAND	0	15	15	15/25	25	15	15	10	25
ROMANIA	25	15	15	25	25	15	15	15	25
RUSSIAN FEDERATION	25					15			
SINGAPORE [a]	15	10/15	25	25	25	10	15	10	25
SOUTH AFRICA [a]		15		25		15	25	15	25
SPAIN	0	5/15	15	15/25	25	10	25	6/10	25
SRI LANKA	0	15	15	15/25	25	15	15	10	25
SWEDEN	0	15	25	25	25	15	15	10	25
SWITZERLAND	0	15	15	15/25	25	15	25	10	25
TANZANIA [a]		15	15	15	0	15		20	
THAILAND	25	20/25	15	25	25	15	15	5/15	25
TRINIDAD & TOBAGO	25	15/20	15	15	0/25	10	25	10	25

COUNTRY	ALIMONY	DIVIDENDS	PERIODIC PENSION PAYMENTS	PERIODIC ANNUITY PAYMENTS	LUMP SUM PENSION ANNUITY	INTEREST	TRUST INCOME	ESTATE/ ROYALTIES	RENT IMMOVABLE
TUNISIA	25	15	25	25	25	15	15	5/20	25
UKRAINE	[a]	5/15	25	25	25	10	15	10	25
UNITED KINGDOM	0	10/15	0	10/25	25	10	15	10	25
UNITED STATES	0	6/15	15	15/25	25	15	15	10	25
USSR	[b] 25	15	25	25	25	15	25	10	25
ZAMBIA	25	15	15	15/25	25	15	15	15	25
ZIMBABWE	0	10/15/20	15	15	25	15	15	10	25

Notes:

1. This schedule has been prepared for general information purposes only. Other treaty provisions may affect specific cases.

a. Signed but not ratified. Until ratification is received, payments to residents of this country are generally subject to a 25% withholding tax.

b. Canada will continue to apply the agreement with the USSR in circumstances involving members of the Commonwealth of Independent States but only on a reciprocal basis. Specific situations involving the Commonwealth of Independent States should be clarified with the International Taxation office.

Immigration

The time may come when you decide to return to Canada. While immigration is a relatively simple event for most Canadian citizens, it should not occur without some planning. Remember, once you commence being a Canadian resident for income tax purposes you will be taxed on your world income.

TIMING

Planning the date when you re-establish Canadian residency will be important. Income earned in a foreign jurisdiction but received after your return to Canada could be taxed in Canada. This may include such items as retirement or termination payments, accrued but unpaid interest and declared but unpaid dividends. You should review all sources of income prior to your arrival to ascertain if the amounts should be received prior to entering Canada.

If you are currently taxed in a foreign jurisdiction and will be taxed when you arrive in Canada, it may be tax effective to arrive in the middle of the taxation year, around June 30. This may permit you to benefit from the various marginal tax rates in both countries. As noted on departure, various tax credits will be prorated for the number of days you are resident in Canada.

DATE OF ARRIVAL

The point of time when you commence residency can be as definite or as uncertain as your date of departure. Its determination will depend on the nature and quality of the ties you establish in Canada compared to those retained in the foreign jurisdiction. As well, if you are coming from a treaty country, the residency article of the treaty may dictate your status.

You will give formal notice of your arrival on the Canadian tax return you file for your year of arrival. Complete the area on page 1 of the personal tax return which requests the date of entry into Canada.

You may need to visit Canada prior to your formal return. Caution must be exercised to ensure that you do not establish ties on any earlier visit that would cause you to be a resident. For example, if you come to Canada and acquire a home, that purchase may be seen as a significant tie which could cause you to be a resident from that point on. It may be prudent to postpone such action or at least delay the closing until the date you plan to actually enter Canada for tax purposes.

Another situation that may be viewed as creating a significant tie would arise if your spouse and children precede you and take up residence in Canada. This event could cause you to be resident in Canada at that time rather than at some future date when you yourself arrive. We suggest that you review the discussion in Chapter 1 regarding the various ties which Revenue Canada considers to determine if you have retained your resident status. The same criteria will be used to establish whether you have reacquired resident status in Canada.

Question – Immigration

I left Canada on June 30, 1995, severed all my ties and intended to remain in Saudi Arabia for three years. My contract was cancelled prematurely, requiring me to return to Canada in August 1996. Will I be considered a non-resident of Canada for the period June 30, 1995 through August 1996?

Answer

If you severed all your ties with Canada and intended to remain in Saudi Arabia for up to three years, the fact that you returned to Canada for the reasons beyond your control should not cause you to be a resident of Canada for the period June 30, 1995 through August 1996.

Question – Immigration, Spouse Returns Early
I have been a non-resident of Canada for five years. I plan to return to Canada in December 1997. My spouse and my children will return in late August 1997. What date will I be considered to be a resident of Canada — August 1997 or December 1997?

Answer
Revenue Canada will consider you to commence being a resident when your spouse and children arrive in Canada to take up residency. You may be able to refute this position if you are coming from a country which has a treaty with Canada.

Question – Immigration, Vacation
I have been a non-resident of Canada for seven years. I plan to return to Canada in October 1997. I will cease my current employment in June 1997 and plan to travel prior to arriving in Canada. When will I be considered to be a resident of Canada?

Answer
As long as you have not established residential ties in Canada prior to your arrival in October 1997, you will not be a resident for Canadian tax purposes until that date.

CAPITAL PROPERTY

You will recall that you were deemed to have disposed of property that is *not* taxable Canadian property at its fair market value when you left Canada. The same rule applies when you arrive back in Canada. All property that is not taxable Canadian property is deemed to be disposed of at its fair market value and reacquired at that value. This rule causes you to realize all gains (or losses) on these properties prior to commencing to be a resident. Such gains will not be subject to Canadian tax. The losses cannot be applied against future capital gains.

Properties subject to this deemed disposition and reacquisition may include shares of public companies, mutual funds, foreign real estate, foreign partnership interests, and foreign business assets.

The deemed disposition rules will not apply to taxable Canadian property. The tax on gains arising from the properties will only be paid when you sell the property, assuming you elected to defer the payment of tax on departure. See Chapter 2 for the deemed disposition rules on departure.

Question – Immigration, Mutual Funds
I own an investment in a mutual fund which has increased in value. I understand that I will be deemed to have disposed of my mutual fund investment when I return to Canada. The fair market value of this investment will be its tax cost for future determination of capital gain on redemption. Will the unrealized gains within the mutual fund also be realized on the date I arrive in Canada?

Answer
The investments within the mutual fund will not be realized when you arrive in Canada. As a result, you may have capital gains allocated to you from unrealized gains which existed within the mutual fund on the day of your arrival in Canada. On subsequent redemption of your units in the mutual fund, you will likely have a capital loss which may be applied against the allocated gains.

TAXABLE CANADIAN PROPERTY

Certain TCPs were not taxable (unless you elected to have them realized) when you left Canada and no deemed realization occurs when you return to Canada. As noted in Chapter 2, TCP which is not deemed to be disposed of includes Canadian real estate and capital property or inventory that is used in a business carried on by a person through a permanent establishment in Canada.

For most Canadian expatriates, the most commonly held taxable Canadian property is the former family home. While this property is not deemed to be disposed of when you return to Canada, the action of ceasing to lease the home and commencing to live in it will constitute a change of use and a deemed realization will occur unless you elected not to have a change of use when you started to lease the house. If the latter action was taken, terminating the lease and commencing to use the house as your home will not have any immediate tax consequences. The tax consequences will arise when you ultimately sell your property. Remember, even though you elected not to have a change of use, you cannot designate the house to be your principal residence for any year throughout which you were a non-resident.

If you did not elect not to have a change of use when you left, you will have a deemed disposition and reacquisition of the property when you cease leasing it and commence using it as your principal residence. If the value of the property is higher at that point, you will realize a capital gain which you must include in your income. This gain would be included in the tax return you file for the year you become a resident of Canada, assuming you commence using the house as your principal residence upon your return.

You may elect to defer the taxation of the gain arising from this change of use until you actually sell the property. This is accomplished by electing with the Minister of National Revenue in writing on or before the earlier of the day that is 90 days after the Minister requests such an election and April 30 following the year in which the property is actually disposed of by you. This election applies only to rental property that becomes your principal residence.

TAX RETURN — YEAR OF IMMIGRATION

The tax return you file for your year of arrival will include not only world income earned after your arrival but employment and business income earned in Canada while you were a non-resident, and gains from both actual dispositions of taxable Canadian properties and deemed dispositions arising from a change in use.

If you have been filing a separate return for rental income, you will still file that return and report the rental income earned up to the date of return. The rental income received after your return will be declared in your regular tax return which includes your world income for the period after your arrival.

Timing

To the extent you can control your arrival in Canada, you may be able to eliminate or reduce your Canadian tax burden on certain income. For example, if you own a property in Canada and you plan to sell it in the year you return to Canada (before or after your return), you will be required to include the gain in your regular tax return for that year. This may cause you to pay more tax than you would have if you were able to sell the property in a year prior to your return. If you are able to do this, only the gain would be reported and a lower tax would be paid because of the application of lower marginal tax rates.

If you receive certain payments for work performed while you were a non-resident after you return to Canada, they may be taxed in Canada. In order to insure this does not happen, you should request payment of the amount prior to your arrival in Canada.

RRSP

Deductions on your first year's tax return may include contributions to an RRSP for yourself or your spouse. Remember, you may not have any deduction limit in the year of arrival unless it arose from the year of departure or from Canadian income earned while you were a non-resident. Incomes which qualify as earned income for RRSP purposes include Canadian employment and business income but not capital gains or any income earned outside of Canada.

You will recall from Chapter 2 that your deductible RRSP contribution is based on the lesser of 18% of your earned income in the previous year or $13,500 adjusted for the pension adjustment. If you examine your most recent assessment notice from Revenue Canada, you should find your current RRSP deduction limit on the deduction limit statement.

Overcontribution

Caution should be exercised when you contribute to your RRSP. Recent amendments reduced the current $8,000 overcontribution allowance to $2,000, effective for 1996 and subsequent years. In order to avoid paying a penalty tax of 1% per month on the excess over the overcontribution allowance, you must remove excess contributions from your account. Transitional rules will make you apply the overcontribution amount on hand at February 26, 1995 to the extent of the deduction limit each year until you are down to $2,000.

Withdrawal

If you have not withdrawn funds from your RRSP prior to returning to Canada, you may want to consider doing so prior to the date of your arrival. This action will permit you to receive amounts at a maximum tax of 25%, which is likely lower than the rate you would pay as a resident of Canada. It is important to remember that any such withdrawal must occur prior to the day you become resident in Canada.

RRIF WITHDRAWAL

You may also wish to consider making your annual minimum withdrawal or perhaps an additional withdrawal from your RRIF before re-establishing Canadian residency. RRIF payments received by a non-resident are subject to a 25% withholding tax. Although the rate may be reduced by treaty, under most treaties, any payment in excess of two times the minimum amount will be subject to the 25% tax. The minimum amount is a defined amount that must be paid out annually.

OFFSHORE INVESTMENTS

As a resident of Canada, you will be subject to tax on your world income. This will include income earned from bank accounts located in various tax havens, offshore trusts and corporations. You no doubt have read about establishing an immigration trust and hope to capitalize on its benefits. While this is a well recognized vehicle to achieve a five-year tax holiday, you may not be able to benefit from it. We have prepared the following outline regarding how immigration trusts work and suggest that you seek professional assistance if you feel that you are eligible to use one.

Immigration Trust

An immigration trust may be created when a non-resident person (settlor) transfers assets to trustees (non-residents). These trustees are responsible for managing the assets in accordance with the trust document for the beneficiaries of the trust.

You may settle an immigration trust if you are moving to Canada. You would establish the trust in a jurisdiction that has no income tax, is politically stable and has the appropriate infrastructure and trust laws.

In order to avoid Canadian tax for up to a five-year period you must ensure that you were not a resident of Canada for more than 60 months at any previous time. This rule eliminates most Canadian expatriates unless you marry a person who has never been a resident of Canada. This situation will permit your new spouse to settle and contribute to a trust of which you are the beneficiary and allow you to benefit from a five-year tax holiday on the income earned by the trust.

This area of taxation, like many others, is extremely complex and requires due care to ensure that you do not run afoul of any one of the many tax avoidance provisions created to make certain that you do not benefit from a tax reduction through the use of an offshore trust. It is important that the trust be properly set up. You should pay particular attention to the following matters:

Residence of the Trust

Under Canadian tax law, the residence of a trust is generally considered to be the place of residence of a majority of the trustees who exercise management and control of the trust. The place of residence of the settlor or the beneficiaries of the trust is generally not relevant as long as they do not exercise any control over the trust. In short, no resident of Canada should have authority to control the trust. Select trustees who reside in tax havens.

Discretionary Trust

You should ensure that the trust document gives the trustees full discretion as to the payment of income and capital of the trust. If the trust is non-discretionary, Canadian tax rules will require the trust income to be taxed in Canada in the hands of any beneficiary who has at least a 10% interest in the trust.

Funding of the Trust

Canada has a number of tax rules, known as attribution rules, that are designed to prevent an individual from loaning or transferring property to a related person in order to split income and save tax. These rules should be considered when establishing an immigration trust.

Payment of Income and Capital of the Trust

No income of the trust should be paid or be payable to the beneficiaries during the five-year period of exemption from Canadian tax. If funds are required by the beneficiaries, the trustees may make a distribution of trust capital and avoid any Canadian tax consequences.

Winding up the Trust

After the five-year tax holiday period has expired, the trust will be deemed to be a person resident in Canada and pay Canadian tax on income earned in Canada and its Foreign Accrual Property Income (FAPI). These tax consequences are extremely complex and beyond the scope of this book. Suffice to say, if you have an immigration trust and the five-year period has expired, you should consider transferring the residence of the trust to Canada and winding it up. The former is accomplished by obtaining the resignation of all non-resident trustees and replacing them with trustees resident in Canada. As a result of the change in the residence of the trustees, the trust would become resident in Canada. Upon becoming a Canadian resident, the trust would be deemed to have acquired all of its property at its current fair market value. The assets of the trust could then be rolled out to the beneficiaries at no tax cost and the current fair market value of the assets would become their cost base for Canadian tax purposes.

Granny Trusts

If your trust is settled by someone who is not planning to come to Canada, it is possible to defer Canadian tax on trust income indefinitely. This is sometimes referred to as a "Granny Trust" since it is usually settled by a non-resident grandparent. You must exercise the same degree of care when you establish this trust as you would with an immigration trust.

Foreign Accrual Property Income (FAPI)

Canada has a number of tax rules that were introduced to ensure that you pay tax on investment income located in foreign jurisdictions. The FAPI rules are one such set of provisions. These are very complex and intended to cause you to pay tax on various types of investment income even though you have not received them. You may not have received the FAPI due to the fact it was earned by an offshore trust or corporation. Regardless of whether you received this income or not, if you meet the conditions (which are far too complex for this book), you will be taxable thereon as a resident of Canada. This area requires specific professional assistance to ensure that you abide by Canadian tax law.

Foreign Asset Reporting Requirements

Commencing in 1996, Revenue Canada will require you to report certain information concerning your foreign holdings. This will include details of transfers to and deposits with foreign corporations, partnerships, trusts or estates. If you made a transfer to a non-resident trust, you will have to provide financial statements and details of transfers to and distributions from the trust on an annual basis. As a result, if you established an immigration trust or any other offshore structure, you will be required to provide details of its existence to Revenue Canada. This will no doubt cause Revenue Canada to scrutinize the structure of the offshore entity and challenge its integrity.

Four new forms have been introduced to accumulate this information.

Foreign Property

Form T1135 must be completed by all Canadian residents where, *at any time in the year*, the total cost of foreign investments exceeds $100,000. This does not include assets held in your RRSP or other pension plans. It also does not include business assets or personal-use property, such as a Florida condominium. However, it does include the following:

- Shares and debt of foreign corporations, even if they are held in a Canadian brokerage account;
- Debt of foreign governments such as US treasury bills;
- Foreign rental properties (this could include a foreign vacation property that you rented for part of the year);
- Interests in foreign partnerships, such as a US limited partnership;
- Low interest loans to non-residents including family members.

If the total cost of this type of property exceeds $100,000 at any time in the year, Form T1135 must be completed. It is due at the same time that your Canadian income tax return is due, which for individuals will be April 30th (June 15th if you are reporting business income).

Partnerships are also included in this reporting requirement. Any partnership, whether foreign or Canadian, will have to report its foreign investment assets to Revenue Canada annually if the total income allocated to Canadian residents exceeds 10% of the total income of the partnership.

Foreign Affiliates

If you, together with persons related to you, own 10% or more of a non-resident corporation, it is considered to be a foreign affiliate. This is true whether you own your shares directly or through another entity such as a Canadian corporation, another non-resident corporation, or a non-resident trust.

Form T1134 must be completed for all shares that you own in foreign affiliates. There is no dollar threshold; all foreign affiliate holdings must be reported to Revenue Canada no matter how small.

Transfer and Loans to Foreign Trusts

Non-resident trusts are set up for many reasons. Many Canadians who operate businesses offshore choose to do so through foreign trusts. Immigrants to Canada frequently take advantage of immigration trusts set up in tax havens, which allow them to escape Canadian tax on the income earned in the trust for a period of up to 5 years. Also, many Canadians who are concerned about protecting their assets have transferred investments to offshore trusts in jurisdictions that have strong asset protection legislation.

In order to accumulate information on these trusts, new Form T1141 requires the reporting of all loans and transfers to foreign trusts that are done on a "non-arm's length basis". Usually, this means the beneficiaries of the trust are related to you, such as family members. However, other loans and transfers are also caught unless a market interest rate is charged on loans or fair market value consideration is taken back on transfers.

Distributions from Foreign Trusts

Are you a beneficiary of a foreign trust? Perhaps a non-resident relative has set up a trust for your benefit. You may have even set up your own offshore trust.

If so and you received a distribution from the trust, or the trust became indebted to you (likely because they issued you a promissory note rather than making a distribution), you have to report this to Revenue Canada on new Form T1142. You are only taxed in Canada if the distribution is out of trust income; however, Revenue Canada still wants to know about it.

Extension of First Filing Deadlines

There will be an extension of the first filing deadlines for all four forms. Forms T1135, T1141 and T1142 will only be due on the later of the actual filing deadline for a taxation year and April 30, 1998. This basically gives many taxpayers (individuals, corporations, trusts and partnerships) a one year filing extension for the first year that the forms are required (for example, without this change, individuals would have been required to file these forms for 1996 by April 30th or June 15th 1997). The first filing deadline for Form T1134 (information return for foreign affiliates held) cannot be earlier than June 30, 1998. Keep in mind that this is only an extension of the first filing deadline - returns will still be required for taxation years which end after 1995 and subsequent years' returns will be required by their normal due dates.

Exception for First-Year Residents of Canada

Individuals will not be required to file any of the foreign property information returns for the year in which they first become resident in Canada. Non-residents returning to resume residence in Canada will be required to file for the year of return.

Dual Resident Status

Individuals who claim to be residents of both Canada and another jurisdiction will be required to comply with these filing requirements even though the tax treaty indicates that they are taxable in the other jurisdiction. As a result, they will not only have to file a Canadian tax return to claim the exemption from tax but will also have to complete any or all of the new foreign property reporting forms.

What If the Returns Aren't Filed?

In order to encourage Canadians to comply with these new reporting requirements, severe penalties have been introduced if the required forms are not filed by their due dates. For all the returns except Form T1142 (Distributions From Foreign Trusts), the late filing penalty is $500 per month up to a maximum of $12,000. If the return is not filed within 24 months of its due date, an additional amount can be levied which increases the penalty to 5% of the total cost of foreign property that should have been reported. The late filing penalty for Form T1142 is $25 per day up to a maximum of $2,500.

Addition of a Due Diligence Test

Taxpayers required to file Form T1141 (Loans or Transfers to a Non-Resident Trust), Form T1135 (Information Return in Respect of Foreign Property) and Form T1134 (Information Return for Foreign Affiliates), will be excepted from the penalties for omissions in the return if they can prove that they exercised due diligence in attempting to obtain the required information. Note that to qualify for the due diligence exception, a taxpayer must give reasonable disclosure in the information return of the unavailability of the required information and must have made diligent attempts to get the information. In addition, if the information subsequently becomes available to the taxpayer, it must be filed with Revenue Canada within 90 days. Note that the due diligence exception does not apply to Form T1142 (distributions from a non-resident trust).

6

Miscellaneous Tax Relief, Residents of Canada

If you are a resident of Canada for tax purposes and earn income from a foreign source, it will be included in your Canadian income tax return and taxed accordingly. Generally, tax relief will be in the form of credits or a deduction of tax paid on such income in the foreign jurisdiction. As noted in Chapter 4, specific provisions of a treaty may reduce or eliminate double taxation through exemptions or tax credits.

There are, however, a number of types of income earned by residents of Canada which receive special tax treatment through tax credits or complete exemption.

OVERSEAS EMPLOYMENT TAX CREDIT (OETC)

If you are leaving Canada to work for at least six months abroad, you may qualify for the OETC. This credit will appeal to you if you will be outside Canada for less than two years or you cannot establish non-resident status because your family remains in Canada. To qualify, you must work on a construction, agricultural, engineering, installation or exploration project. In addition, your employer must be either Canadian or a foreign affiliate of a person resident in Canada.

The calculation of the credit is (typically) overly complicated. But assuming you qualify and you will be working abroad for the required period of time, you may reduce your Canadian tax by a significant amount. For example, if you work abroad throughout a tax year, only 20% of foreign remuneration up to $100,000 will be subject to tax in Canada. But there is one further consideration — minimum tax. For whatever reason, our legislators feel that anyone who is entitled to the OETC should also be subject to minimum tax. This is a tax which, even though you pay some Canadian tax, may cause you to pay more, because you have received a benefit from using the OETC. Fortunately, minimum tax is recoverable over the next seven years. It is like a tax instalment against future tax. In other words, it may be recovered in years while you are working in Canada, earning income not eligible for the OETC.

The OETC has proved to be popular for those Canadians who work offshore for Canadian employers.   In fact, certain Canadians establish corporations to permit them to use the OETC while interacting with what would otherwise be a foreign employer. The ability to do this was curtailed by recent amendments which require the Canadian contractor/employer to have more than 5 full-time employees.

We (the authors) feel that this credit should be extended to anyone who sells, installs or markets Canadian products. As it stands now, the credit is too narrow and extremely discriminatory.

In some situations, your foreign employment income may be subject to tax in the foreign country. Normally, you would be able to reduce Canadian tax by claiming some or all of the foreign tax as a credit. This is not the case if you claim the OETC. Although it is possible to claim a combination of an OETC and a foreign tax credit, you cannot claim both on the same income.

In order to claim the OETC, you must obtain Form T626, "Overseas Employment Tax Credit" from your employer (Appendix A: CRA 5). For more information regarding the OETC, we refer you to Interpretation Bulletin IT-497R3 which outlines Revenue Canada's position (Appendix A: CRA 16).

To assist you in determining if this provision will benefit you, we present a simplified version of the formula of the OETC:

$$\text{OETC} = \frac{\text{Lesser of A and B}}{C} \times D$$

Where

A	=	$80,000 x No. of days you were abroad ÷ 365
B	=	80% of your remuneration while abroad
C	=	Your total income for the year
D	=	Your Canadian tax for the year

Question – OETC, Alternative Minimum Tax
I am eligible to benefit from the OETC. However, I have been told that Alternative Minimum Tax may apply.

Answer
The OETC is considered a tax preference and subject to Alternative Minimum Tax. In the event Alternative Minimum Tax is payable, you may recover it in a future year when your regular tax exceeds the Alternative Minimum Tax. You have seven years to recover this tax.

Question – OETC, Foreign Tax Credits
I am eligible to benefit from the OETC. I pay tax in the country in which I work. Can I claim the foreign tax paid as a credit against Canadian taxes payable after I use the OETC?

Answer
You may use either the OETC or foreign tax credits to reduce your Canadian tax, but not both.

Question – OETC, Canadian Income
I am presently eligible to benefit from the OETC. However, I have an opportunity to earn Canadian income on my regular rotation back to Canada. This income is not from the employer which employs me for the work which is eligible for the OETC. Will this jeopardize my eligibility for the OETC?

Answer
As long as you otherwise qualify for the OETC, the ability to earn additional income from another source while on rotation in Canada should not cause you to lose your eligibility for the OETC.

> **Question – Six Consecutive Months**
> *I entered a contract of employment on January 15, 1997. It ended on June 30, 1997. Does this qualify as six consecutive months?*
>
> **Answer**
> Revenue Canada states that if the starting date for the six consecutive months was January 15, 1997, the minimum qualifying period of more than six consecutive months, would run from January 15, 1997 to July 15, 1997. As a result, you would not qualify for the OETC.

TREATIES

Our tax laws allow you in arriving at taxable income to deduct from income any income that is exempt by virtue of a tax treaty. This provision appears to eliminate any Canadian tax on income exempted by treaty provisions. However, a closer look at the relief discloses that the provision allows you to deduct the exempt income to arrive at taxable income rather than net income. This may not be detrimental unless your net income causes you to lose certain benefits. For example, if your net income is over $25,921, you will lose part or all of your age credit; if your net income is over $53,215, your Old Age Security may be subject to clawback or not paid to you. So, even though you may not be taxed on certain types of foreign income because of a treaty provision, you may still face tax consequences.

EMPLOYMENT INCOME – PRESCRIBED INTERNATIONAL ORGANIZATIONS

If you are either a deemed or factual resident of Canada, you will pay Canadian tax on world income. However, if you earn employment income from an employer referred to by our tax laws as a "prescribed international organization", you may deduct it from your calculation of taxable income. In other words, you include the income from a prescribed international organization to determine your net income, then deduct the same amount from net income to arrive at taxable income.

Revenue Canada prescribes that the United Nations and any specialized agency that is brought into relationship with the United Nations in accordance with Article 63 of the Charter of the United Nations will qualify. Revenue Canada addresses this issue in comments contained in its memorandum titled "Employees of International Organizations: Department Guidelines".

Question – UN Income
I am a factual resident of Canada and work for the U.N.'s Food and Agriculture Organization (FAO). This is my only source of income. Do I have to file a Canadian tax return?

Answer
Based on the fact that you are a resident of Canada, you should file a Canadian tax return and report your world income regardless of whether you will be required to pay Canadian tax on this income. Since this is employment income, it will establish your contribution room for purposes of your RRSP.

INTERNATIONAL NON-GOVERNMENTAL ORGANIZATIONS

As mentioned numerous times throughout this book, if you become a resident of Canada, you will be taxed on your world income. Certain world income may not be subject to Canadian tax either because a treaty exempts it from Canadian tax or it came from a prescribed international organization. A further exception is provided for employment income received from so called prescribed international non-governmental organizations. Unfortunately, this exception will only apply if you meet all of the following conditions:

1.   You are not a Canadian citizen,
2.   You were a non-resident of Canada immediately before commencing your employment in Canada, and
3.   You became a resident of Canada solely for the purpose of employment.

To date, this exception will only apply if you meet the foregoing conditions and you are employed by either the International Air Transport Association or the International Society of Aeronautical Telecommunications.

Revenue Canada's guidelines are contained in its memorandum "Employees of International Organizations: Departmental Guidelines.

FOREIGN TAX CREDITS/DEDUCTIONS

If you earn income from a source outside of Canada, it may be subject to tax in the country from which it originates. Subject to any exception which may be available under a treaty or our own tax law, it will be included in your income and subject to Canadian tax. If this income has already been taxed by a foreign jurisdiction, it would be subject to double taxation if not for certain provisions in the tax treaties and in our own domestic tax laws which allow you to reduce your Canadian tax on such income by tax paid in the other country. This relief may come in the form of a tax credit, a deduction or a combination of a credit and deduction.

Interpretation Bulletin IT-270R2 (Appendix A: CRA 14) discusses the foreign tax credit, which is a deduction from Canadian tax otherwise payable. This foreign tax credit may be claimed in respect of income or profits tax you paid to a foreign country. You must calculate this credit on a country-by-country basis. In general terms it is limited to the lesser of the income and profits tax paid by you to the particular foreign country and the Canadian tax otherwise payable for the year on income from sources within that particular country.

Foreign tax credits come in two forms: business and non-business. While the basic formula to determine your tax relief is similar for each, the results differ. Business foreign tax credits may only be claimed to reduce federal tax while non-business foreign tax credits may reduce both federal and provincial tax. If you incurred more foreign business tax than you are allowed to claim, you may carry the unapplied balance over for up to five years to be applied against tax on foreign business income in those years. There is no carryover for non-business foreign tax. However, to the extent it is not utilized, non-business foreign tax may be deducted as an expense in determining your net income. Please refer to Interpretation Bulletin IT-506–Foreign Income Taxes as a Deduction from Income for a more thorough discussion of this deduction.

7

Safeguarding Your Health

HEALTH INSURANCE

The Ontario Ministry of Health recently placed notices in airports warning, "Don't Leave the Country Without Reading This...Whether you are a business traveller, a student or a vacationer — whether you plan to be out of Canada for half a day or a half a year — you need extra health coverage."

Because of restrictions on the amounts which provincial/territorial health insurance plans will reimburse for medical expenses incurred outside of Canada, Canadians who spend even a short time abroad now require supplementary private health insurance coverage. If you plan to live outside Canada for an extended period, you will need a complete package of private medical and hospital benefits.

LEAVING CANADA

We have already stated that Canadians wishing to establish non-resident status for income tax purposes must cancel their government health insurance because participation in such a plan constitutes a significant residential tie with Canada.

If you leave Canada to reside elsewhere and do not cancel your government health insurance, you will likely find yourself ineligible for coverage in any case. Whether you qualify for provincial/territorial health insurance is determined by whether you are a resident of the jurisdiction in question. However, since residency regulations vary widely across Canada (and, by the way, are totally unrelated to the residency rules for income tax purposes), you should never assume that your coverage is continuing or has lapsed without checking with provincial/territorial authorities. While the consequences with regard to provincial health insurance for a family who pack up all their belongings and head overseas for five years may be fairly predictable, other cases involving, for example, rotational employment or a pattern of seasonal migration in search of warmer weather, may be less clear cut. In some instances (if you are not concerned about the residency implications for tax purposes), you may be able to apply for an extension of provincial/territorial coverage.

PROVINCIAL/TERRITORIAL INSURANCE

If you plan to live outside Canada, it is essential that you investigate the impact on your government health insurance both at the time you leave Canada and upon your return. We are grateful to MetLife for their permission to publish the following summaries of relevant information for each province and territory. Government regulations are, of course, subject to change. In every instance we strongly recommend that you contact your provincial or territorial health insurance authorities at the addresses given to confirm current rules and their effect on your particular situation.

The following information regarding provincial/territorial health insurance regulations is reprinted from *Provincial Hospital and Medical Plans – Canada,* by permission of MetLife, Ottawa.

ALBERTA
1. **Title**
-   Alberta Health Care Insurance Plan

2. **Coverage**
-   all residents and their dependents must register with AHCIP; registration is required by law in Alberta
-   residents coming from other provinces in Canada must register themselves and their dependents within one month after becoming eligible for coverage
-   residents coming from outside Canada must register within one month of the date they become a resident
-   a resident may opt out of the program for a 12 month period starting July 1st following the date such resident signs a declaration to that effect

Eligibility
- all residents regardless of health, age or financial status
- members of the Canadian Armed Forces, RCMP, tourists, transients and visitors, or individuals serving terms in penitentiaries are not eligible for benefits
- an eligible dependent is:
  • a spouse
  • an unmarried dependent child under age 21 (age 25 if in full-time attendance at an accredited educational institute)
  • an unmarried child age 21 or over who is dependent due to mental or physical infirmity

Coverage Begins
- new residents from outside Canada are eligible for benefits on the date of their arrival
- new residents from elsewhere in Canada are eligible for benefits the first day of the third month following the date of arrival

Dependent Coverage Begins
- later of date of insured's coverage or date first dependent is acquired

Coverage Extended
- coverage continues during temporary absences of up to 12 months
- students attending an educational institution outside the province are entitled to benefits if they intend to return to the province

Coverage Terminates
- a resident leaving the province to establish permanent residence elsewhere in Canada may purchase coverage for the period from the date of departure to the last day of the second month thereafter
- a resident leaving the province to establish permanent residence outside Canada may purchase coverage for the three month period following the date of departure

BRITISH COLUMBIA
1. Title
- Medical Services Plan

2. Coverage
- coverage is not compulsory; it is the responsibility of every resident to enroll themselves and their dependents

Eligibility
- all residents regardless of health, age or financial status who are Canadian citizens or lawfully admitted for permanent residence, make a home in British

Columbia and are physically present at least 6 months per year are eligible for benefits.
-    eligible dependents are spouses or children ordinarily resident in British Columbia. A child means a person who is not married and is under the age of 19 or is in full-time attendance at school or university and under the age of 25, and who is wholly or mainly supported by an adult
-    landed immigrants and persons on student or employment authorization are covered on first day of third month after entry in B.C.
-    tourists, transients, visitors, members of the RCMP and Canadian Armed Forces are not eligible

Coverage Begins
-    new residents are eligible to become subscribers the last day of the second month following the month of arrival in the province

Dependent Coverage Begins
-    later of date of insured's coverage or date dependent is acquired providing application for dependent coverage is made within 60 days of acquisition and the appropriate premiums are paid

Coverage Extended
-    full-time students outside the province who remain B.C. residents are covered upon submission of satisfactory proof of attendance at school
-    coverage continues during temporary absences of up to 12 months providing the necessary premiums have been paid

Coverage Terminates
-    residents leaving the province to establish full-time residence elsewhere in Canada are eligible for benefits until the expiration of
     •   a reasonable period for travelling time, not to exceed three months, and
     •   a further period ending at midnight of the last day of the second month following the month in which the travelling period ended
-    residents leaving the province to establish full-time residence outside of Canada are eligible until the last day of the second month following departure; no travelling time is available

MANITOBA
1.   Title
-    The Manitoba Health Services Insurance Plan

2.   Coverage
-    compulsory
-    all residents and their dependents must register with the Manitoba Health Services Commission directly or through a registrar (i.e. employer, municipality or person authorized by the Commission)

Eligibility
- all residents regardless of health, age or financial status who make their home in Manitoba at least six months a calendar year
- dependent means:
  - a spouse
  - a dependent, widowed mother if no spouse
  - dependent child under age 19 (19 or over if mentally or physically incapacitated), or to age 21 if attending full-time school; and also the spouse or child of these dependent children
- members of Canadian Armed Forces, RCMP and inmates of penitentiaries are not eligible

Coverage Begins
- a new resident from elsewhere in Canada is eligible for benefits the first day of the third month following the date of arrival in Manitoba
- a new resident from outside of Canada is eligible for benefits the date of arrival in the province
- new residents are not eligible for care in Personal Care Homes until resident for 24 months

Dependent Coverage Begins
- later of date of insured's coverage or date dependent is acquired

Coverage Extended
- during temporary absences of up to 12 months

Coverage Terminates
- residents leaving the province to establish permanent residence elsewhere in Canada and who obtain an out-of-province certificate are entitled to benefits until the first day of the third month following the month of arrival in the new place of residence
- residents leaving the province to establish a permanent residence outside Canada having obtained an out-of-province certificate are entitled to benefits up to the last day of the second month following the month of departure

NEW BRUNSWICK
1. Title
- Medicare New Brunswick

2. Coverage
- coverage is not compulsory

Eligibility
- all registered residents regardless of age, health or financial status

- members of the Canadian Armed Forces, the RCMP, visitors to the province, students from another province or country, students in Canada on a Students visa, some non-Canadians and penitentiary inmates are not eligible
- dependents are:
  - spouse
  - unmarried, dependent children under age 19

Coverage Begins
- on the first day of the 3rd month after the month of arrival in the province if they establish residence in the province:
  - a new resident to the province
  - regular members of the Canadian Armed Forces, RCMP, and persons serving a term of imprisonment in a penitentiary maintained by the Government of Canada upon discharge in New Brunswick
  - non-Canadian spouses of Canadian residents assuming residence in Canada for the first time, landed immigrants, repatriated Canadians, returning Canadians, returned landed immigrants and Canadian citizens establishing residence in Canada for the first time

Dependent Coverage Begins
- later of date of insured's coverage or date dependent is acquired

Coverage Extended
- during temporary absences, vacations, or terms of education outside the province for up to 12 months

Coverage Terminates
- 1st day of 3rd month following month of arrival at his new residence
- when a resident leaves to establish full-time residence outside of Canada coverage ceases on the date of departure from Canada

NEWFOUNDLAND
1. Title
- Medical Care Plan

2. Coverage
- coverage is compulsory
- residents must register themselves and their dependents

Eligibility
- all residents regardless of age, health or financial status
- tourists, transients, visitors, members of the RCMP and Canadian Armed Forces, members of the armed forces from other countries, students from other countries, applicants for landed immigrant status and others who do not meet residency requirements are not eligible

- eligible dependents are:
  - spouses
  - unmarried dependent children
  - other dependents for income tax purposes

Coverage Begins
- the first day of the third month following the month of arrival from elsewhere in Canada
- date of arrival if from outside of Canada

Dependent Coverage Begins
- later of date of insured's coverage or date dependent is acquired

Coverage Extended
- during temporary absences from the province but not beyond 12 months, except with special extension from the Provincial Plan authorities

Coverage Terminates
- benefits terminate on the date of permanent departure from Canada
- residents moving elsewhere in Canada are eligible for benefits until the last day of the second month following the month of arrival in the other province

NORTHWEST TERRITORIES
1. Title
- Medical Care Plan

2. Coverage
- coverage is not compulsory
- all residents must have a registration certificate
- each resident is registered individually

Eligibility
- all residents regardless of age, health or financial status
- tourists, transients, visitors, students whose permanent residence is outside the Northwest Territories, temporary workers, members of the Canadian Armed Forces, the RCMP (their families and dependents can register if they live in the NWT), and penitentiary inmates are not eligible for coverage
- dependents consist of:
  - a spouse
  - unmarried dependent children
  - other dependents for income tax purposes

Coverage Begins
- all residents are eligible for coverage the first day of the third month after becoming a resident

-   newborns and individuals who have not had the opportunity to acquire coverage elsewhere in Canada are eligible for immediate coverage

Dependent Coverage Begins
-   date of registration

Coverage Extended
-   during temporary absences from the Territories but not beyond 12 months
-   students attending an educational institution outside the Territories are eligible for coverage up to 12 months

Coverage Terminates
-   residents leaving the Territories to establish residence elsewhere in Canada are entitled to benefits during the time of travel and the waiting period in the new province, but not to exceed three months
-   residents leaving the Territories to establish permanent residence outside Canada are not covered beyond the day they leave the Territories

NOVA SCOTIA
1. Title
-   Hospital Insurance Plan
-   Medical Care Insurance Plan

2. Coverage
-   not compulsory for hospital insurance
-   compulsory for all residents for medical insurance

Eligibility
-   all residents regardless of health, age or financial status
-   members of the Canadian Armed Forces, RCMP, tourists, transients or visitors are not eligible for coverage
-   dependents are:
    -   spouse
    -   unmarried dependent children
    -   other dependents for income tax purposes

Coverage Begins
-   individuals moving to the province from elsewhere in Canada are eligible for coverage the first day of the third month following the month in which he becomes a full-time resident
-   a new Canadian citizen is eligible for coverage on the day he becomes a full-time resident

Dependent Coverage Begins
- later of date of insured's coverage or date dependent is acquired

Coverage Extended
- during temporary absences or terms of education outside the province, up to 12 months

Coverage Terminates
- any resident leaving Nova Scotia to establish permanent residence elsewhere in Canada will be eligible to receive coverage for health insured programs, up to the last day of the second month following the month in which they arrived in the new province (e.g. persons leaving on January 20th, their eligibility will cease on March 31st)
- a resident leaving the province to establish full-time residence outside of Canada the coverage ceases on the date of departure

ONTARIO
1. Title
- Ontario Health Coverage

2. Coverage
- not compulsory
- participation is on an individual basis
- there are no premiums

Eligibility
- all permanent residents of Ontario regardless of health, age or financial status are eligible. Permanent residents are Canadian Citizens, landed immigrants and convention refugees.
- NOTE: tourists, transients, and visitors; members of the RCMP and Canadian Armed Forces; and inmates of federal penitentiaries and temporary residents, primarily international students and foreign workers and their families are not eligible and will not be covered (with the following exception).
EXCEPTION: People who come to Ontario for the primary purpose of working temporarily are eligible for OHIP coverage if, before coming to Canada, they are issued an Employment Authorization allowing them to work for a named Ontario employer, at a specific job, for a limited time and for at least six months. This exception does not apply to accompanying family members.

Coverage Begins
- new residents of Ontario will have to wait 3 months before OHIP coverage begins (the first day of the third month)
- the day a permanent resident of Ontario ceases to be:
  - a serving member of the Canadian Armed Forces
  - a serving member of the RCMP
  - an inmate of a federal penitentiary

-      the day a non-resident becomes:
       •   a recipient of social assistance
       •   a ward of the Children's Aid Society

Coverage Extended
-      under certain circumstances, residents may apply to continue Ontario coverage
       while living temporarily outside Ontario
-      Ontarians who spend more than 183 days outside Canada will face a 3 month
       waiting period after their return before OHIP coverage resumes, unless prior
       approval was given for the extended absence

Coverage Ends
-      for Ontarians who establish residence outside Canada: three months following
       departure
-      for Ontarians who establish residence elsewhere in Canada: the last day of the
       second month following departure
-      for Ontarians who remain in Canada but do not establish residence in another
       province or territory: twelve months following departure
-      the day a resident becomes:
       •   a serving member of the Canadian forces
       •   a serving member of the RCMP
       •   an inmate of a federal penitentiary
-      the day that a non-resident's social assistance is terminated *or* the day a non-
       resident is no longer a ward of the Children's Aid Society
-      the end of the month following the month of expiry of a document issued by
       Employment and Immigration Canada

PRINCE EDWARD ISLAND
1.   Title
-      Hospital and Health Services Plan

2.   Coverage
-      coverage is not compulsory
-      residents must register themselves and their dependents to obtain coverage

Eligibility
-      residents must register themselves and their dependents to obtain coverage. A
       resident is defined as anyone who is legally entitled to remain in Canada and
       who makes their home and is present on an annual basis for at least six
       months plus one day in Prince Edward Island. Residents lose their eligibility
       if they are absent from the province longer than six months, unless they obtain
       a waiver of this requirement from the Agency.
-      tourists, transients and visitors are not eligible
-      members of the Canadian Armed Forces, the RCMP, or inmates of
       penitentiaries, foreign students, tourists and transients are not eligible

- dependents are
  - spouses
  - unmarried dependent children
  - other dependents for income tax purposes

Coverage Begins
- new residents are eligible for benefits three months after establishing permanent residence in the province
- immigrants establishing permanent residence in the Province having registered with the Commission within three months of arrival are eligible for benefits from the date of registration

Dependent Coverage Begins
- later of date of insured's coverage or date dependent is acquired

Coverage Extended
- during temporary absences from the province
- residents absent for educational purposes are eligible for benefits for up to 12 months

Coverage Terminates
- a resident of Prince Edward Island leaving the province to establish full-time residence elsewhere in Canada is eligible for benefits during normal travelling time and during the waiting period in the new province but not to exceed three months
- a resident leaving the province to establish full-time residence outside of Canada is eligible for benefits for three months from the date of departure

QUEBEC
1. Title
- The Quebec Hospital Insurance Plan
- The Quebec Health Insurance Plan

2. Coverage
- coverage is compulsory

Eligibility
- all residents regardless of health, age or financial status
- a person who is:
  - a permanent resident
  - a repatriated Canadian
  - a Canadian returning to the country
  - a permanent resident returning to the country
  - a Canadian Citizen or his spouse who takes up residence in Canada for the first time

- a member of the Canadian Armed Forces, or the RCMP who is not a Quebec resident
- a prisoner who was not a Quebec resident upon confinement in Quebec and has indicated intentions of becoming a resident of Quebec, along with each of his dependents, shall be considered a resident of Quebec upon his arrival, discharge or liberation, as the case may be
- a person who legally resides in Canada, who makes his home in Quebec and who lives there at least 183 days per year
- a foreign national who legally resided in Canada and resides in Quebec (must provide proof of permanent resident status from Canadian and Quebec immigration authorities)
- foreign national employed in Quebec for three or more months (must hold a work permit from Canadian Immigration authorities)

- tourists, transients and visitors, students from another province or country (except if student agreements are in effect) are not entitled to insured services
- dependents are:
  - spouses
  - unmarried persons under 18 living permanently with the resident

Coverage Begins
- individuals moving to the province from elsewhere in Canada are covered under the plan as soon as the other province's plan ceases to cover him
- new citizens are entitled to benefits on becoming a full-time Quebec resident

Dependent Coverage Begins
- later of date of insured's coverage or date dependent is acquired

Coverage Extended
- during temporary absences or for education purposes, while retaining Quebec resident status
- to Quebec civil servants in service outside Quebec
- to a person staying outside Quebec, while his family resides or maintains a dwelling therein, looking for temporary work or executing a contract, who returns to Quebec at least once a year (or informs the Quebec Health Insurance Board why he can't)
- a person employed by a non-profit organization which has its head office in Canada and works abroad within a program recognized by the minister of Social Affairs in Quebec

Coverage Terminates
- a Quebec resident leaving the province to establish full-time residence elsewhere in Canada, coverage ends on the first day of the third month following the date of arrival in the other province
- a Quebec resident leaving the province to establish full-time residence outside of Canada ceases to be covered under the plan immediately upon his departure

-   anyone who lives outside Quebec for at least 183 days per year (excluding periods of less than 21 days)

SASKATCHEWAN

1. Title
-   Saskatchewan Medical Care Insurance Plan

2. Coverage
-   compulsory for all residents

Eligibility
-   if you make your home in Saskatchewan and you normally live in the province at least six months a year, regardless of health, age or financial status you are eligible for health care benefits.
-   members of the Canadian Armed Forces and inmates of Federal Penitentiaries are not provided medical and hospital benefits — their dependents must be registered to be eligible for benefits
-   dependents are:
    -   spouse
    -   unmarried dependent children to age 18

Coverage Begins
-   residents must be registered by the first day of the third month following establishment of residence
-   when a married individual arrives in the province and his spouse arrives at a later date, the date of "establishing residence" will be from the date of arrival of the spouse

Dependent Coverage Begins
-   later of date of insured's coverage or dependent is acquired providing dependent is registered

Coverage Extended
-   residents temporarily absent from the province may maintain coverage for up to 12 months
-   students attending an educational institution outside the province are entitled to receive benefits for the entire time they are studying and for up to 60 days travelling time to or from their studies
-   extended coverage is available to students provided the student returns to Saskatchewan at least once a year

Coverage Terminates
-   residents leaving the province to establish full-time residence elsewhere are eligible for benefits up to the first day of the third month following the date the new residence is established

- when a married resident leaves the province and the spouse leaves at a later date, benefits are provided up to the first day of the third month following the date the spouse establishes residence elsewhere

YUKON TERRITORY
1.   Title
- Yukon Hospital Insurance Services
- Yukon Health Care Insurance Plan

2.   Coverage
- not compulsory for hospital
- compulsory for health care
- a resident who fails to register for health care is guilty of an offence
- residents do not have to register for the hospital plan

Eligibility
- all residents regardless of health, age, or financial status
- members of the Canadian Armed Forces or RCMP are not eligible — they may register their dependents only
- dependents mean, in relation to any person:
  - a spouse
  - unmarried child under age 21 who is a dependent for income tax purposes of that person, or, less than age 25 if in full attendance at an accredited institute, college or university
  - unmarried child age 21 or over, who is a dependent of that person for income tax purposes of that person by reason of mental or physical infirmity

Coverage Begins
- after three months of consecutive residence in the Yukon
- immediately for landed immigrants if they establish residence within 3 months of being admitted to Canada

Dependent Coverage Begins
- date of insured's coverage or date dependent is acquired

Coverage Extended
- during temporary absences or extended vacations up to a period of 12 months

Coverage Terminates
- after normal travelling time and a waiting period not exceeding 3 months for residents leaving to establish full-time residence elsewhere in Canada
- three months after date of departure from the Territory to establish full-time residence outside Canada

CONTACTS

We recommend that you contact your provincial/territorial health insurance office with any questions regarding coverage:

Alberta
Alberta Health Care Insurance Plan
P.O. Box 1360
Edmonton, Alberta
T5J 2N3
Canada
Tel: 403-427-1432

British Columbia
Medical Services Plan
P.O. Box 1600
Victoria, British Columbia
V8W 2X9
Canada
Tel: 604-683-7151 (Vancouver)
Tel: 205-386-7171 (Victoria)
Toll Free 1-800-663-7100 (within BC)

Manitoba
Manitoba Health Insured Benefits Branch
Box 925 – 599 Empress Street
Winnipeg, Manitoba
R3C 2T6
Canada
Tel: 204-786-7101
Toll Free: 1-800-392-1207 (within Manitoba)

New Brunswick
New Brunswick Medicare
P.O. Box 2500
Fredericton, New Brunswick
E3B 7J3
Canada
Tel: 506-453-2161

Newfoundland
Medical Care Plan
Public Services Division
Elizabeth Towers
P.O. Box 200, Station A
St. John's, Newfoundland
A1C 5J3
Canada
Tel: 709-758-1588
Fax: 709-758-1576
Toll Free: 1-800-563-1627 (within Newfoundland)

Northwest Territories
Health Service Administration
Department of Health, G.N.W.T.
Inuvialuit Corporate Centre
Bag #9
Inuvik, Northwest Territories
X0E 0T0
Canada
Tel: 403-979-7401

Nova Scotia
Medical Services Insurance
P.O. Box 500
Halifax, Nova Scotia
B3J 2S1
Canada
Tel: 902-468-9700 (Halifax)
Toll Free: 1-800-563-8880 (within Nova Scotia)

Further Hospital Information
Department of Health
P.O. Box 488
Halifax, Nova Scotia
B3J 2R8
Canada
Tel: 902-424-5615

Ontario
Ministry of Health
Central Region
Service Manager
P.O. Box 1700
Station A
Toronto, Ontario
M5W 1G9
Canada
Tel: 416-440-4400

Prince Edward Island
Health & Community
Services Agency
P.O. Box 3000
Montague, P.E.I.
C0A 1R0
Canada
Tel: 902-368-5858 or 838-4064
Fax: 902-832-2050

Québec
Régie de l'assurance-maladie
du Québec
1125, Chemin Saint-Louis
8e étage
Sillery, Québec
G1S 1E7
Canada
Tel: 418-682-5162
Fax: 418-643-7312

Saskatchewan
Saskatchewan Health Insurance Registration
Saskatchewan Health
3475 Alberta Street
Regina, Saskatchewan
S4S 6X6
Canada
Tel: 306-787-3251
Toll Free: 1-800-667-7551 (within Saskatchewan)

Yukon Territory
Health Services Branch (H-2)
P.O. Box 2703
Whitehorse, Yukon
Y1A 2C6
Canada
Tel: 403-667-5233 (Whitehorse)

PRIVATE HEALTH PLANS

Private Health Insurance While Living Abroad

While we are gradually becoming more accustomed to the idea, the average Canadian has little experience in purchasing medical and hospital insurance coverage. If you accept an international posting, your employer may provide health insurance for yourself and your dependents. If no such benefit package is available to you, you may be responsible for choosing and purchasing your own insurance. In some instances, it may also be possible to obtain coverage under a government-sponsored scheme in your new country of residence.

In any case, you would be wise to review your coverage options carefully with a professional insurance advisor familiar with the needs of expatriates. We have compiled a list of some Canadian, British and US insurance companies, all of whom offer medical insurance to expatriates (see below). Although this list is not exhaustive and should not be taken as an endorsement of any particular company, it should help you to get started.

While the authors are not insurance experts, a little research has enabled us to identify some of the concerns you will want to keep in mind when consulting an insurance professional. As is the case with insurance policies generally, expatriate medical coverage will have a maximum coverage limit, either per year or by type of benefit. Policies frequently also have territorial limits, largely because of the high cost of medical expenses incurred in North America. The premium for a policy which covers your family not only in your new country of residence but also on visits home or while travelling in the United States may be as much as double the cost of a similar policy excluding North America. Some policies are designed to accommodate business travel and visits home by allowing North American coverage for a limited number of days in each year.

Insurers may offer a range of benefits depending on whether you choose the economy or luxury version of their coverage. For example, one policy may cover in-patient hospital care only while another may cover out-patient care and even home nursing or visits to a general practitioner. Services may also be subject to a deductible or user fee. Medical care related to a pre-existing condition may or may not be covered. Policies can sometimes be supplemented with coverage for pregnancy and delivery (there may be a waiting period before coverage commences), prescription drugs, dental care (emergency and/or routine), long-term disability and income replacement, accidental death or dismemberment, life insurance and even insurance of personal liability and possessions.

A 24-hour helpline, access to English or French-speaking doctors and air evacuation service may be essential if you will be living or travelling to areas of the world where medical care is inadequate. Provision for a family member to travel with the patient, especially if the patient is a child, may also be a concern. You will want to give some thought to the specific evacuation provisions, bearing in mind that evacuation may simply take you to the nearest source of adequate care, not necessarily to the location of your choice. If your work involves travel to any of the world's "hot spots", you will also want to enquire as to whether war and other similar risks are excluded.

An insurance company's reputation for prompt processing and payment of claims is an important consideration but one which is difficult to assess. You may have to rely on the recommendations of colleagues. However, you should be able to investigate questions such as whether the policy provides for payment directly to the hospital and whether efforts have been made to eliminate any difficulty with currency exchange in the payment process.

The following is a list of some Canadian, British and US insurance companies offering health insurance coverage to Canadian expatriates:

CANADA

Compass International
(A division of Wright Mogg & Associates Ltd.)
100 Regina Street South
Suite 270, P.O. Box 96
Waterloo, Ontario
Canada
N2J 3Z8
Tel: 519-886-1690
Fax: 519-886-8559

John Ingle Insurance
438 University Avenue, Ste. 1200
Toronto, Ontario
M5G 2K8
Canada
Tel: 416-340-0100
Fax: 416-340-2707
Toll Free: 1-800-387-4770 (within Canada and U.S.A.)

The Norfolk Group
Suite 510, 940 – 6th Ave. S.W.
Calgary, Alberta
T2P 3T1
Canada
Tel: 403-232-8545
Fax: 403-265-9425

Telfer International Consultants Inc.
Suite 200-59 rue St. Jacques
Montreal, Quebec
H2Y 1K9
Canada
Tel: 514-284-2002
Fax: 514-284-3203

UNITED KINGDOM

BUPA International
Russell Mews
Brighton, East Sussex
BN1 2N12
England
Tel: 44-1273-323563
Fax: 44-1273-820517

ExpaCare Insurance Services
Dukes Court, Duke Street
Woking, Surrey
GU21 5XB
England

Attn: Mr. David Pryor
Tel: 44-1483-740090
Fax: 44-1483-776620

Goodhealth Worldwide Limited
Mill Bay Lane
Horsham, West Sussex
RH12 1TQ
England
Attn: Mr. Paul Davies
Tel: 44-1403-230000
Fax: 44-1403-268429

International Health Insurance danmark a/s
64A Athol Street
Douglas
Isle of Man, IM1 1JE
British Isles
Tel: 44-1624-677412
Fax: 44-1624-675856

PPP Health Care
20 Upperton Rd.
Eastbourne, East Sussex
BN21 1LH
England
Tel: 44-1323-410505
Fax: 44-1323-731325

UNITED STATES

International Medical Group, Inc.
135 North Pennsylvania
Suite 1700
Indianapolis, Indiana
U.S.A. 46204
Tel: 317-636-4721
Fax: 317-687-9272
E-mail: 75223-2575@compuserve.com

Returning to Canada

Until recently, a Canadian who fell ill while living overseas could return to Canada and count on virtually immediate acceptance into a provincial/territorial health insurance plan. You should be aware, however, that in an effort to ensure that only those individuals genuinely resident in their jurisdiction receive coverage, certain provinces (British Columbia, Ontario and New Brunswick at time of writing) have instituted waiting periods of up to three months for returning Canadians. Ontario and B.C. will require that you further demonstrate your intent to take up permanent residence by spending no more than 30 days outside the province in the first six months after your arrival.

You should investigate whether any waiting period will be covered by the provisions of the policy which insured you and your family while you lived overseas. Three-month extensions are becoming routine for Canadian companies with expatriate clients but will be less familiar to insurers based outside Canada. Never assume you will be covered without checking with your insurance provider. Always discuss how coverage would be handled in unusual circumstances, such as a sudden return to Canada part way through your employment contract or a prolonged round the world vacation at the end of your assignment. If you cannot arrange continuation of your overseas policy to cover a provincial waiting period, some assistance is available from insurance companies who offer insurance for travellers. These companies (see list below) will provide you with the same type of "emergency" coverage you can buy for visitors to Canada. Policies are likely to cover emergency care but not treatment for pre-existing conditions, checkups and the like.

If you are considering "visitor to Canada" medical insurance, take note that most insurers require that coverage begin within a few days of entry into the country. Delay in applying may make you ineligible. Depending on the company, it may be possible to arrange in advance for coverage to commence on your date of arrival. Payment can generally be made by credit card.

The following companies provide short-term emergency medical coverage to returning residents of Canada:

E. T. F. S.
73 Queen Street
Lennoxville, Quebec
J1M 1J3
Canada
Tel: 819-566-4298
Fax: 819-566-4449
Toll Free: 1-800-465-8602 (within Canada)

John Ingle Insurance
438 University Avenue, Ste. 1200
Toronto, Ontario
M5G 2K8
Canada
Tel: 416-340-0100
Fax: 416-340-2707
Toll Free: 1-800-387-4770 (within Canada and U.S.A.)

Liberty Health
Visitors to Canada
3500 Steeles Avenue E.
Markham, Ontario
L3R 0X4
Canada
Tel: 905-946-4050
Fax: 905-946-4849
Toll Free: 1-800-268-3763 (within Canada)

The Norfolk Group
Suite 510, 940 – 6th Ave. S.W.
Calgary, Alberta
T2P 3T1
Canada
Tel: 403-232-8545
Fax: 403-265-9425

Travel Insurance Coordinators
#300 – 2609 Westview Drive
North Vancouver, B.C.
V7N 4M2
Canada
Tel: 604-986-4292
Fax: 604-987-4527

For further information call the Canadian Life and Health Insurance Association (in Canada 1-800-268-8099 or 416-777-2344.)

SAFEGUARDING YOUR HEALTH

There are many resources in Canada to assist the prospective expatriate to maintain good health while abroad. Numerous travellers' clinics, public service organizations and a variety of books provide information on the risks associated with travel to all areas of the world and advice regarding precautionary measures such as immunization, prophylactic drugs and portable medical supplies.

Travellers' Clinics

Commerce Court
Travel Clinic
Commerce Court East
Suite 314
Toronto, Ontario
Canada
M5L 1A1
Tel: 416-361-0564
Fax: 416-361-0637

Mississauga
Travel Clinic
2200 Credit Valley Road
Suite 512
Mississauga, Ontario
Canada
L5M 4N4
Tel: 905-820-9556
Fax: 905-828-4101

The Canadian Society for International Health publishes a list of close to 100 Travellers' Health Centres in Canada. Clinics may offer pre-travel advice, post-travel or both. The full list, included in a pamphlet entitled "Health Information for Canadian Travellers", is available by writing to:

Canadian Society for International Health
170 Laurier Ave W.
Suite 902
Ottawa, Ontario
K1P 5V5
Canada
Tel: 613-230-2654
Fax: 613-230-8401
The list is also available via the Internet at www.csih.org

Information on travellers' clinics is also available from your local Public Health Unit.

Travel Information Line

For easy access to basic information on the region or country to which you will be travelling, call the Travel Information Line, sponsored by the Toronto Hospital, at 416-340-4030. The Information Line is a computerized system of recorded information available from a touch-tone telephone. A series of detailed messages cover topics such as food and water precautions, incidence of disease and immunization recommendations for specific countries worldwide.

IAMAT

The International Association for Medical Assistance to Travellers was established over 30 years ago by a Toronto doctor. The Association's stated aim is "to make competent care available to the traveller around the world (even in very remote places) by doctors who usually speak either English or French and have had medical training in Europe or North America."

While membership in IAMAT is free, donations are appreciated to support the work of the association, which is funded solely through voluntary contributions.

Members receive the IAMAT Directory, which lists physicians in countries worldwide who have agreed to IAMAT's standard fee schedule. IAMAT has reviewed their professional qualifications and determined that all speak English or another language in addition to their native tongue.

IAMAT also publishes detailed information regarding the world risk of malaria, schistosomiasis and Chagas' disease. If you make a substantial donation, you can also request the "24 World Climate Charts" which provide information on climate and the sanitary conditions of water, milk and food for hundreds of locations worldwide. The Association also sells a free-standing bed "mosquito" net.

For further information contact: **IAMAT**
40 Regal Road
Guelph, Ontario
Canada
N1K 1B5
Tel: 519-836-0102
Fax: 519-836-3412

Canadian Medic Alert Foundation

If you have a medical condition such as diabetes, hypertension or asthma, a drug allergy, or an implant such as a pacemaker, a Medic Alert bracelet or necklet could save your life. If you are ill or injured and cannot communicate, the Medic Alert "ident", engraved with your primary medical information, your membership number and the 24 hour Medic Alert Hotline number, will give emergency personnel essential information. A collect call to Medic Alert will enable medical staff to obtain information on your medical history, the medications you take, your allergies and how to reach your physician and other emergency contacts.

For further information contact: **Canadian Medic Alert**
Box 9800
Station Don Mills
Toronto, Ontario
Canada
M3C 2T9
Tel: 416-696-0267
Toll Free: 1-800-668-1507
Fax: 416-696-0156

HEALTHY READING

There are numerous health guides for travellers available. Reference to other sources can be found in the bibliographies of the following books:

Don't Drink the Water
Dr. J.S. Keystone, Editor
Co-published by the Canadian Public Health Association
and the Canadian Society for International Health
Distributed by CPHA
400-1565 Carling Ave.
Ottawa, Ontario
K1Z 8R1
Canada
Tel: 613-725-3769
Fax: 613-725-9826

International Travel Health Guide
Stuart R. Rose, M.D.
Travel Medicine, Inc.
Suite 312 – 351 Pleasant Street
Northhampton, MA
01060, U.S.A.
Tel: 1-800-872-8633
Tel: 413-584-0381
Fax: 413-584-6656

HEALTH SUPPLIES

If you will be travelling to areas where sanitation and medical care may be inadequate, you may wish to check out the following sources for water filters and purifiers, mosquito nets and a wide variety of medical kits ranging from basic first aid needs to sterile syringes, hypodermic needles and other supplies designed to reduce the risk from contaminated medical equipment.

Steri-Aid
P.O. Box 81614
1057 Steeles Ave. W.
North York, Ontario
M2R 3X1
Canada
Tel: 416-650-0900
Toll Free: 1-800-567-8374
Fax: 416-661-1900
(Sterile medical kits only)

Travel Medicine, Inc.
Suite 312 – 351 Pleasant Street
Northampton, MA
01060, U.S.A.
Tel: 413-584-0381
Toll Free: 1-800-872-8633
Fax: 413-584-6656

HEALTHY PETS

If you plan to take family pets to live with you outside Canada, you should, of course, check with the relevant authority on your new country of residence regarding vaccination requirements, import restrictions, quarantine periods and so on.

For information on bringing animals back into Canada, contact:

Agriculture and Agri-Food Canada
Lester B. Pearson International Airport
P.O. Box 11
Toronto AMF, Ontario
L5P 1A2
Canada
Tel: 905-676-2545
Fax: 905-676-3804

CANADIAN CONSULAR ASSISTANCE

Canada's embassies, consulates and other missions abroad provide assistance to Canadians resident or travelling in their areas. A full listing of Canadian missions is contained in the booklet, *Bon Voyage, But...* available from Canadian passport offices and by contacting:

InfoCentre
Department of Foreign Affairs and International Trade
125 Sussex Drive
Ottawa, Ontario
K1A 0G2
Canada
Tel: 613-944-4000
Toll Free: 1-800-267-8376

Canadian missions offer 24-hour assistance. For emergency assistance, you can also call the Department of Foreign Affairs and International Trade in Ottawa at 613-996-8885.

Canadian Driver's Licences

Canadians planning to live overseas frequently ask us whether they must relinquish their provincial/territorial driver's licences. Most are concerned that retention of a Canadian licence might jeopardize their non-resident status for taxation purposes. In fact, a Canadian driver's licence represents only a minor tie with Canada which should not, in the absence of other ties, affect non-resident status.

However, it is the responsibility of each province or territory to determine whether a person living outside Canada can continue to hold a valid provincial driver's licence. Our research indicates that provincial policies vary widely. For further information, contact the relevant authority listed below:

ALBERTA
Alberta Registries
Direct Customer Service
9th Floor South
10365-97th Street
Edmonton, Alberta
T5J 3W7
Canada
Tel: 403-427-2185
Fax: 403-422-4286

BRITISH COLUMBIA
Motor Vehicle Branch
2631 Douglas St.
Victoria, B.C.
V8T 5A3
Canada
Tel: 250-387-6824
Fax: 250 356 7369

MANITOBA
Division of Driver and Vehicle Licensing
1075 Portage Ave.
Winnipeg, Manitoba
R3G 0S1
Canada
Tel: 204-945-6850
Fax: 204-945-0652

NEW BRUNSWICK
New Brunswick
Department of Transportation
Motor Vehicle Branch
P.O. Box 6000
Fredericton, N.B.
E3B 5H1
Canada
Tel: 506-453-2810
Fax: 506-453-3076

NEWFOUNDLAND
Motor Registration Division
P.O. Box 8710
St. John's, Newfoundland
A1B 4J5
Canada
Tel: 709-729-2958
Fax: 709-729-6955

NORTHWEST TERRITORIES
Department of Transportation
Motor Vehicle Division
Box 1320
Yellowknife, NWT
X1A 2L9
Canada
Tel: 403-873-7406
Fax: 403-873-0120

NOVA SCOTIA
The Registry of Motor Vehicles
6061 Yonge Street
Halifax, Nova Scotia
B3J 2Z3
Canada
Tel: 902-424-5851
Fax: 902-424-0720

ONTARIO
Ministry of Transportation
Licensing Assistance Section
2680 Keele St., East Building
Downsview, Ontario
M3M 3E6
Canada
Tel: 416-235-2999
Toll Free: 1-800-387-3445 (from within Canada)
Fax: 416-235-4414

PRINCE EDWARD ISLAND
Highway Safety Division
P.O. 2000
Charlottetown, Prince Edward Island
C1A 7N8
Canada
Tel: 902-368-5200
Fax: 902-368-6269

QUEBEC
Driver's Licence Division
Information Department
SAAQ 333 Blvd. Jean Lesage
P.O. Box 19600
Quebec, P.Q.
G1K 8J6
Canada
Tel: 418-643-7620
Fax: 418-643-2009

SASKATCHEWAN
Saskatchewan Govt. Ins.
2260 11th Avenue
Regina, Saskatchewan
S4N 2N7
Canada
Tel: 306-775-6900
Fax: 306-352-5220

YUKON
The Yukon Government
Motor Vehicles
Box 2703
Whitehorse, Yukon
Y1A 2C6
Canada
Tel: 403-667-5315
Fax: 403-393-6220

9

Goods and Services Tax Refund for Visitors to Canada

If you make your permanent home outside Canada, you can get back some of the Goods and Services Tax (GST) you pay while visiting here. As long as you are not a resident or deemed resident (e.g. Armed Forces) of Canada, you may claim a refund of the GST (along with Manitoba and Quebec provincial sales taxes) you pay on accommodations occupied for less than one month on a visit to Canada. You can obtain the same refunds on tax paid on eligible goods you take home.

The basic rules are as follows:

You qualify for a tax refund if:
* you are not a resident of Canada;
* your total refund claim is for a minimum of CAN $14 for each tax you are claiming;
* you have your original receipts;
* for eligible goods, each individual receipt has to show a minimum of CAN $3.50 for each tax you are claiming.

Accommodation qualifies for refund if:
* you paid for it;
* you paid tax on the accommodation;
* the receipts show the number of nights of accommodation.

Goods qualify for a refund if:
* you paid tax on the goods;
* you bought the goods to use outside Canada;
* you remove the goods from Canada within 60 days of purchasing them.

There is no refund for tax you pay on:
- meals and beverages
- wine, liquor, beer and other alcoholic beverages
- tobacco products
- transportation such as air, train, bus or car rental
- services such as dry cleaning, shoe repairs, auto repairs, entertainment, etc.
- rental of campsites, tents and houseboats
- cruise ships or train berths
- automotive fuels
- goods consumed or left in Canada

Copies of the Revenue Canada pamphlet "Goods and Services Tax Refund for Visitors", which includes the necessary application form, can be obtained from:

Revenue Canada
Visitor Rebate Program
Summerside Tax Centre
Summerside, P.E.I.
C1N 6C6
Canada
Tel: Toll-free from inside Canada (1-800-668-4748)
TDD 1-800-465-5770
From outside Canada 902-432-5608

10

Canada Pension Plan and Old Age Security

CANADA PENSION PLAN (CPP)

The Canada Pension Plan (CPP) came into effect on January 1, 1966 and became fully effective January 1, 1976. Premiums are paid to persons in retirement and to widows, widowers, orphans, the disabled and children of disabled contributors. The retirement pension is earnings-related and payable in addition to Old Age Security payments. There is also a death benefit which is payable to the estate of a contributor.

Contributions are required from employees, the self-employed and employers. These are required from individuals from age 18 to age 65 (or to age 70 if the individual continues to work and does not apply for his or her retirement pension).

Since January 1, 1978, a contributor may collect his or her retirement pension as early as age 60, subject to an actuarial adjustment, if he or she has wholly or substantially ceased working.

No benefit is payable unless you make an application in writing and payment of the benefit has been approved. Applications are made on a prescribed form (Application for Retirement Pension Canada Pension Plan) addressed to Human Resources Development Canada (see address below).

To be eligible for a retirement pension, you must have:
- contributed to CPP for at least one year
- reached the age of 60
- substantially ceased working, if under 65 years of age.

The amount of your retirement pension is calculated on the basis of your pensionable earnings. This amount may be determined by making an inquiry to

Human Resources Development Canada. In general terms, as long as you have contributed to the CPP for at least one year, you will be eligible for a retirement pension of some amount. As well, your surviving spouse or orphaned children may be eligible for a survivor's pension. You do not have to be resident in Canada to apply for or to receive this retirement pension.

Since January 1, 1996, CPP payments made to non-residents of Canada have been subject to non-resident withholding tax of 25%. The rate may be reduced where there is a tax treaty between Canada and your country of residence. Some non-residents with relatively modest amounts of income, substantially from Canadian sources, may be able to obtain a reduction of the non-resident tax.

Remember, your CPP benefits may also be subject to tax in your country of residence.

OLD AGE SECURITY (OAS)

OAS is payable in addition to CPP. It is a flat-rate pension, escalated quarterly according to any increase in the Canadian Consumer Price Index, and payable at age 65. Application for OAS may be made to Human Resources Development Canada (see address below).

In order to qualify for OAS payments while living outside of Canada, you must have resided in Canada for at least 20 years after your 18th birthday. The 20 years need not have been consecutive. The amount of your OAS pension may be less than the maximum, however, if certain conditions relating to the period or periods you have been resident in Canada are not met. A current pensioner who has not completed 20 years Canadian residency will continue to receive payments for six months after leaving Canada, whereupon payments will be suspended until the individual resumes residence in Canada.

Since January 1, 1996, OAS payments have been subject to non-resident withholding tax of 25%. The rate of tax may be reduced where there is a tax treaty between Canada and your country of residence. As in the case of CPP benefits, some non-residents with relatively modest amounts of income, substantially from Canadian sources, may be able to obtain a reduction of the non-resident tax.

Also effective January 1, 1996, OAS payments to non-residents became subject to a "recovery tax" or clawback designed to reduce payments to higher-income pensioners. Non-resident recipients of OAS must report their world income to Revenue Canada by submitting the OAS Return of Income, due April

30 of each year. Recovery tax will be applied at a rate of 11.25% of the amount by which your net income after certain allowable deductions exceeds $53,215 (this figure may change from year to year). OAS payments for the current year will be based on the previous year's income.

The recovery tax may be reduced or, in some cases eliminated, by a tax treaty between Canada and your country of residence. Only those who reside in countries which are "recovery tax exempt" (slightly less than half of the countries with which Canada has a tax treaty) are not required to report. For all other countries (including other tax treaty countries) the full amount of the OAS payment will be withheld if the report is not filed.

Once again, we hate to remind you, but any amount you do receive will be subject to non-resident withholding tax in Canada and may also be taxed in your country of residence.

By the same token, tax paid to Canada may qualify for a foreign tax credit in your country of residence.

SENIOR'S BENEFIT

The 1996 Federal Budget introduced the Senior's Benefit which is intended to take effect in the year 2001. It will replace the OAS, the Guaranteed Income Supplement, the age tax credit and the pension income tax credit.

Instead of receiving various forms of government payments and credits, the senior will receive a tax free payment which will be fully indexed. How much a person receives will depend on his or her income (family income, if married) in the prior year. For example, if a senior has income up to $40,000, they will receive the same as they now receive. If their income is over $78,000, all of their benefits will be eliminated. Seniors with incomes between $40,000 and $78,000, will benefit in varying degrees.

The Senior's Benefit is still a proposal and may or may not apply as first intended. We recommend potential recipients, be they residents or non-residents, to consider what impact (if any) it may have on their well deserved retirement plans.

FURTHER INFORMATION

For further information regarding CPP or OAS, contact:

Human Resources
Development Canada
65 William St. South
P.O. Box 2020
Chatham, Ontario
N7M 6B2
Canada
Tel: 519-436-3000

Customs and Excise

RETURNING TO CANADA

If you return to reside in Canada after an absence of at least one year, you will be entitled to import most of your personal and household effects free of customs duties. Revenue Canada Customs and Excise sets out the full rules relating to this privilege in its memorandum D2-3-2 (Appendix A: CRA 17) and provides a summary in the pamphlet "Moving Back To Canada". Here are the highlights.

Personal and Household Effects

Your personal and household effects include a wide range of furniture, furnishings, silverware, linen, jewellery, appliances, books, musical instruments, family heirlooms, antiques, private collections of coins, stamps or works of art, hobby tools and other hobby items, boats and the trailers that carry them, vacation trailers, private aircraft and motor vehicles. Houses, large trailers used as residences, and any goods used or to be used commercially do not qualify.

Special rules limit quantities of liquor and tobacco. Other government regulations may affect your ability to import special categories of goods such as firearms, explosives, pets, plants, fruits, vegetables, meats and meat products and endangered species.

$10,000 Limit

If you import any single item of personal or household effects, including an automobile, that was acquired after March 31, 1977 and is valued at more than

$10,000 on the date of importation, you will be required to pay regular duties on the excess amount.

Motor Vehicles

You may import motor vehicles intended for non-commercial use as part of your household effects. Since stringent Transport Canada safety and emission standards apply to all motor vehicles less than 15 years old, we strongly recommend that you contact Transport Canada at the following address if you plan to import a vehicle:

> **Road Safety and Motor Vehicles Regulation Directorate**
> **Transport Canada**
> 13th Floor, Canada Building
> 344 Slater St.
> Ottawa, Ontario
> K1A 0N5
> Canada
> Tel: 613-998-2174

You should also check with your province or territory regarding sales tax regulations and with Customs authorities in the country from which you will be exporting the vehicle.

Ownership, Possession and Use Requirements

If you have been residing outside Canada for at least one year, but less than five years, your personal and household effects must have been in your ownership, possession and use for at least six months before you return to Canada to resume residence. If you have resided outside of Canada for at least five years, you do not have to meet the six-month requirement provided the goods were actually owned, possessed and used abroad by you (for any period of time) prior to the date of your return.

According to the Customs authorities:

"Ownership" means that the former resident has acquired, by purchase or other means, the legal right to have the goods as personal property and to exercise control over their use and disposition. Leased goods do not qualify.

"Possession" means that the former resident has, in person, physically accepted the goods.

"Use" requires the putting into action or service of goods for the purposes for which they are designed or intended.

Absence Requirements

The number of years you have been living abroad is based on the anniversary date of your departure. If you establish yourself as a resident of another country for a period of at least one year, you may make return visits to Canada (as a non-resident visitor) without jeopardizing your eligibility to import household effects duty-free at the time of your final return to Canada. However, if you do not establish yourself as a resident of another country (for example, if you take an extended vacation or world cruise) you will be able to import your household effects duty-free only if you are absent for a period of at least one year, without having returned to Canada during that time.

Listing Goods To be Imported

Before returning to Canada you must prepare a list in duplicate of all the goods you plan to import, showing the value, make, model and serial number where applicable. For household items of a general nature (e.g. kitchen utensils) you may provide a group listing and overall value. The list must be divided into two sections — goods that you are bringing with you, and goods that are to follow.
This list must be presented to the customs inspector when the former resident first arrives in Canada, even if no goods are being imported at that time. Only eligible goods which were declared and listed as "goods to follow" on the original list may be imported duty-free at a later date.

Shipping Goods To Canada

Try to ensure that your personal and household effects arrive in Canada at the same time or after you do. Goods will be held at Customs for only 40 days before being treated as unclaimed.

If it is necessary to ship goods in advance of your own return, you cannot take advantage of your duty-free privilege until you actually return to resume residence in Canada. You may, however, make arrangements to have your effects placed in "bonded storage" with a private service in Canada. Items can remain in bonded storage for a maximum of two years and such arrangements can be expensive. When you arrive in Canada to effect Customs clearance of the goods, only those items which met all of the ownership, possession and use requirements *before* their shipment to Canada may be imported duty-free.

Time spent in transit or in storage abroad or in Canada cannot be included when calculating the six-month period of possession or use.

If you are a non-resident of Canada for tax purposes, remember that household or personal effects shipped to Canada could be seen as a residential tie with this country, possibly affecting the date when you re-establish residency for tax purposes.

Disposal of Goods

If within one year of their importation into Canada, you sell or give away any of the goods you brought into Canada duty-free, you will be liable for all applicable duties. After one year, however, you are free to dispose of the goods without restriction.

FURTHER INFORMATION

For further information contact one of the following regional Customs Offices. Offices in other Canadian cities are listed in the telephone book under "Government of Canada Customs and Excise".

Customs Office   Tel: 403-292-4660
3033 - 34th Avenue, S.E.
Bay 32
Calgary, Alberta
T1Y 6X2
Canada

Customs Office   Tel: 604-666-0545
333 Dunsmuir Street
Vancouver, B.C.
V6B 5R4
Canada

Customs Office   Tel: 204-983-6004
Federal Building
269 Main Street
Winnipeg, Manitoba
R3C 1B3
Canada

Customs Office   Tel: 902-426-2911
Ralston Building
1557 Hollis Street
P.O. Box 3080
Station Parklane Centre
Halifax, Nova Scotia
B3J 3G6
Canada

Customs Office   Tel: 416-973-8022
P.O. Box 10, Station "A"
2nd Floor, 1 Front Street W.
Toronto, Ontario
M5W 1A3
Canada

Customs Office   Tel: 514-283-9900
400 d'Youville Square
Montreal, Quebec
H2Y 3N4
Canada

Death and Taxation

WILLS

Whether you venture abroad, or, after reading all of this, opt to live out your days in Canada, it is essential that you ensure the smooth administration of your affairs should you die or become disabled. As a first step, you need a will. To cite only the most basic advantages, a will allows you to choose the executors who will administer your estate and, within certain legal limitations, your beneficiaries. If you die without a will, these matters will be decided according to prescribed legal formulae which may result in ongoing state involvement in your affairs. We strongly recommend that you seek appropriate legal advice in making these decisions and drawing up the necessary documents.

Canadians who plan to live abroad should also prepare for the possibility they may die abroad. You would be well advised to seek legal counsel in every jurisdiction where you reside, have assets or other connections to determine the precise legal consequences of your demise. You may, for example, need to have a will in more than one jurisdiction.

Your death will also have tax consequences. Your estate or heirs may be responsible for inheritance tax outside of Canada. If you die as a non-resident for Canadian tax purposes, you should be aware that the various tax deferred transfers to a spouse do not apply. As a result, your taxable Canadian property will be deemed to be disposed of at fair market value on the date of your death. Your executor will be required to file a Canadian tax return to report this gain and pay the resulting tax.

Non-residents for tax purposes may be concerned that maintaining a will in a province of Canada would constitute a significant residential tie with Canada.

In fact, such a document would be viewed as a minor tie only, necessary for the administration of your property.

POWERS OF ATTORNEY

When you visit your lawyer, you should also inquire about the benefit of giving powers of attorney to the person you wish to manage your affairs in the event you are no longer able to do so yourself. While some jurisdictions recognize powers of attorney for both property and financial affairs and for personal care, you will need legal advice in each place where you reside, have assets or other connections to determine whether powers given in one jurisdiction will be valid in another.

Appendix

Revenue Canada / Revenu Canada

APPLICATION BY A NON-RESIDENT OF CANADA FOR A REDUCTION IN THE AMOUNT OF NON-RESIDENT TAX REQUIRED TO BE WITHHELD

- As a non-resident, it may be beneficial for you to elect under section 217 of the Canadian *Income Tax Act* to pay tax at the same rate as residents of Canada on your Canadian-source pensions or other benefits (as described under "Types of elective income" below). If you choose this option, you have to file an income tax return within 6 months of the end of the taxation year reporting all your elective income.

- Based on the information you provide on this application, we at Revenue Canada will determine if the election may benefit you. If it is beneficial, we will authorize your Canadian payer(s) to reduce the amount of non-resident tax to be withheld from your payments. Any reduction in non-resident withholding tax will apply from the date we authorize it. A reduction will not apply to payments before this date. To receive a reduction, you have to apply each year.

- If we approve this application, you will have to file your income tax return under section 217 within six months of the end of the taxation year. Otherwise you will have to pay the whole amount of the tax that your payer(s) should have withheld. If you file your return late, we will not process it.

- If you have questions about the section 217 election or this application, call the International Tax Services Office, toll-free, at 1-800-267-3395 (in Canada or the United States) or (613) 952-2344 (outside North America - you can call collect).

- Send this application to: International Tax Services Office, Revenue Canada, Ottawa ON K1A 1A8.

Types of elective income

1. Canada Pension Plan (CPP), or Quebec Pension Plan (QPP) benefits
2. Old Age Security (OAS) pension and supplement
3. Superannuation or pension benefits including registered pension plan (RPP) benefits *
4. Retiring allowance *
5. Death benefits
6. Benefits under the *Unemployment Insurance Act*
7. Registered supplementary unemployment benefits

8. Registered retirement savings plan (RRSP) payments *
9. Registered retirement income fund (RRIF) payments
10. Deferred profit-sharing plan payments *
11. Alimony
12. Transitional assistance benefits to persons employed in the making of products to which the Canada-United States Agreement on Automobile Products applies
13. Benefits under the *Labour Adjustment Benefits Act*
14. Retirement compensation arrangements

* Do not use this application for amounts 3, 4, 8, or 10 that you are transferring to your RRSP or RPP. Instead, use Form NRTA1, *Authorization for Non-Resident Tax Exemption*.

Applicant identification

Name _____   Social insurance number (SIN) _____

Address _____

Telephone number _____   Taxation year for this application _____

Date of birth (day, month, year) _____   Date of departure from Canada _____

Spouse's name _____   Spouse's SIN _____

Pension or other benefits from Canadian sources

Indicate the type of elective income for which you are making this application, and provide the information we request. See "Types of elective income" above.

Estimated gross annual amount (CAN$)

CPP or   QPP benefits (do not include death benefits)   Account number _____   _____

CPP or   QPP death benefits   Account number _____   _____

OAS   Account number _____   _____

Other type of income _____   Plan number _____   _____

☐ Annuity   ☐ Lump sum   RRIF minimum amount $_____

Payer's name _____

Address _____

Other type of income _____   Plan number _____   _____

☐ Annuity   ☐ Lump sum   RRIF minimum amount $_____

Payer's name _____

Address _____

Other type of income _____   Plan number _____   _____

☐ Annuity   ☐ Lump sum   ☐ RRIF minimum amount $_____

Payer's name _____

Address _____

Add all above amounts, and enter the total on line A of page 2.   Total _____

NR5 E (96/08)
Printed in Canada

(Ce formulaire existe aussi en français.)

Canada

We will use the information you provide below to establish the amount of any non-resident tax reduction. Please answer all questions, so we can quickly process your application. If you do not answer all the questions, we may reject your application.

World income information	Estimated gross annual amount (CAN$)
A. Enter the total amount shown at the bottom of page 1	A _____
B. Estimated other Canadian-source income for which you have to file a Canadian tax return (e.g., taxable income from employment, business, capital gains, bursaries, scholarships)	B _____
C. Estimated Canadian-source investment income (e.g., interest, dividends, net rental income)	C _____
D. Estimated income from sources outside Canada (e.g., income from employment, business or property, pensions, social security, capital gains, interest, dividends, royalties)	D _____
E. Total estimated world income for the year * (Total of amounts on lines A, B, C, and D)	E _____

  * If there are changes to your estimated world income for the year, you should file
    an amended application no later than 30 days after these changes occur.

Non-refundable tax credit information

Please respond to the following questions.

1. If you are married or have a common-law spouse, are you supporting your spouse?   Yes ☐   No ☐

   A common-law spouse is a person of the opposite sex with whom you live in a common-law relationship for any continuous period of a least 12 months, or with whom you live in a common-law relationship and who is the natural or adoptive parent of your child.

   If you answered *yes*, go to question 3.

2. Are you single, divorced, separated, or widowed, and supporting a relative who, on December 31, will be   Yes ☐   No ☐
   under 19, except for a relative who has a mental or physical disability.

   If you claim a person here, you cannot claim that person again in section 3 below.

3. Do you support a disabled dependent relative who, on December 31, will be 18 years old or older, and who   Yes ☐   No ☐
   has a physical or mental infirmity?

4. During the year, will you be paying tuition fees for yourself or will you be a full-time student?   Yes ☐   No ☐

   If *yes*, please provide the following information:
   • amount of your tuition fees, for courses you will take in the year, to attend a university or a college; $ _____
   • number of months in the year that you will be enrolled full-time in a qualifying educational program
     at a Canadian university, college, or a school offering job retraining courses or correspondence courses, or a
     university outside of Canada; and   _____
   • amount of any scholarships, fellowships, or bursaries you will receive in the year. $ _____

5. Are you disabled?   Yes ☐   No ☐

   Your disability has to markedly restrict your living activities and has to last, or be expected to last, for a continuous period of at least 12 months. If you are claiming this tax credit, you will have to submit, with your income tax return, a properly completed Form T2201, *Disability Tax Credit Certificate*.

Dependant information
If you have answered *yes* in sections 1, 2, or 3 above, please provide the information requested here (attach a list if you need more space).

Dependant's name _____

Residential address _____

Relationship to you _____ Date of birth (day, month, year) _____

Estimated annual world income (CAN$) _____ Nature of disability, if any _____

Certification
I, _____ , certify that the information given on this form is, to the best of my knowledge, correct and complete. I understand that I will have to pay the full non-resident withholding tax on my elective income if Revenue Canada approves this application, and I do not file an income tax return under section 217 of the Canadian *Income Tax Act* within six months of the end of the tax year for which this application is made.

_____   _____
                Non-resident's signature   Date

Printed in Canada

Revenue Revenu
Canada Canada

NR6
REV. 12/94

UNDERTAKING TO FILE AN INCOME TAX RETURN BY A NON-RESIDENT RECEIVING RENT FROM REAL PROPERTY OR RECEIVING A TIMBER ROYALTY

FOR TAXATION YEAR 19 ____

- Use this form if you are a non-resident receiving rent from real property or a timber royalty, and if you want an agent to be able to elect to deduct and remit tax at the applicable rate on the net amounts available (which may be a reasonable estimate) to you.

- You should forward one completed copy of this form, if you are the non-resident or a non-resident member of a partnership, to the Canadian agent, who will file it at the International Taxation Office, 2540 Lancaster Road, Ottawa ON K1A 1A8.

- Both you and your agent must sign this undertaking. Attach an official copy of a power of attorney (when applicable), to prove the signature made on your behalf is valid.

- It is the responsibility of the agent to file an NR4 information return.

- We need a separate undertaking for each taxation year. A taxation year is, in the case of an individual, a calendar year (January 1 to December 31). In the case of a corporation, estate, or trust, a fiscal period is not necessarily the calendar year.

- The agent should file this undertaking on or before the first day of each taxation year, or when the first rental payment is due. Agents have to withhold non-resident tax on the gross rental payments until they receive written notification from the Department authorizing them to withhold non-resident tax on the net rental income.

- If you, as the non-resident, fail to fulfil your obligations as specified in the undertaking, the agent has to pay to the Receiver General of Canada the full amount (i.e., on the gross amount) that would otherwise have been required to be remitted in the year. We calculate the required amount at the statutory rate of 25% (unless reduced to a lesser rate by the provisions of a bilateral tax treaty), minus the amount already remitted for the year.

- An incomplete form will not constitute a valid undertaking. However, if the agent does not have a remittance account number, we will assign one.

- Rent on real property includes crop-sharing proceeds.

- For more information, see Information Circular 77-16R4, *Non-Resident Income Tax*, or contact the International Taxation Office at 1-800-267-3395 (within Canada) or 1-613-526-6537 (outside Canada).

Note: The period for filing the return of income referred to in this undertaking is limited to six months from the end of the taxation year for which

Name of non-resident (if individual, surname first) (print)	Date of birth — Day Month Year
Given names	Fiscal year-end — Day Month Year
Address of non-resident	Individual I.D. number — T.I.N. or S.I.N.
Country of residence	Corporation number

* For corporations, estates, and trusts, please enter the fiscal year-end.

Address of rental properties	* * Gross rents	* * Expenses	* * Net income
Total ▶			

* * Please provide a breakdown of expenses. For each non-resident who is a member of a partnership, report only their share of the gross rents, expenses, and net income. Also, note that the capital cost allowance is deductible only after you file the prescribed income tax return.

Name of Canadian agent (print)	Remittance account number
Address of Canadian agent	Date the first rental payment is due
City	Postal code	Area code and telephone number ( )

Undertaking by non-resident

For internal use

I **hereby undertake** to file the prescribed income tax return for the above-noted year within six months of the end of the taxation year, and to include all rents from my real property and timber royalties, and to pay any additional tax owing. (Note: A separate income tax return must be filed for each non-resident who is a member of a partnership.)

_____   _____
Date   Signature of non-resident

Undertaking by agent

I **hereby undertake**, if the non-resident fails to file a return and pay the tax according to the above undertaking, to pay to the Receiver General the full amount that I would otherwise have been required to remit in the year, minus the amounts that I have remitted in the year.

_____   _____
Date   Signature of agent

Printed in Canada   Form authorized by the Minister of National Revenue.   (Français au verso)

Revenue **Revenu**
Canada Canada

APPLICATION FOR REFUND OF NON-RESIDENT TAX WITHHELD
- Seend copy 1 to: Revenue Canada, International Tax Services Office, 2204 Walkley Road, Ottawa ON K1A 1A8
- See the back of copy 2 for instructions.

NR7-R CONTROL NUMBER
_____

Name of applicant (print)

Address - Number, street, and apartment number

City, country, and postal code

Details of payment and tax withheld

Amount of payment from which tax to be refunded was withheld

$ _____ ☐ U.S. ☐
(specify if other than Canadian currency)

Amount of tax withheld (___ %) $ _____
                        Rate

Date of payment |__|__| |__|__| |__|__|
                   D   M   Y

Amount of tax payable (___ %) $ _____
                        Rate

Amount of refund applied for $ _____ ☐ U.S. ☐
                              (specify if other than Canadian currency)

Beneficial owner is:

☐ the holder of a letter of exemption _____ issued under article XXI of the Canada-United States Income Tax
Identification no.

☐ the holder of a *Certificate of Exemption* _____ in force on the date of payment, issued under subsection 212(14) of the *Income Tax*
Number

☐ entitled to the lower rate of ____ % as a resident of and taxable in _____
Name of country

☐ other (specify)

Type of payment non-resident tax was withheld from:

☐ Interest paid in Canadian currency   ☐ Interest paid in foreign currency   ☐ Dividends

☐ Other (specify) _____

Type of security (indicate, if applicable): ☐ Bond ☐ Debenture ☐ Note ☐ Mortgage ☐ Hypothec ☐ Similar obligation ☐ Discount obligation ☐ Share

Name of security _____ CUSIP No. _____
(see explanation on back of copy 2)

Certificate _____ Date of issue _____

Is the above security a part of a security-lending ☐ Yes ☐ No If *yes*, please provide a copy of the lending agreement.
Note: We may delay processing this application, or we may reject it if you do not answer this question.

Name of registered owner at date of record _____

Name of beneficial owner _____

Address _____
Number, street, and apartment number   City, country, and postal code

Note: • Attach a sworn statement giving the name of the beneficial owner If, on the date of payment, the security was registered in a name other than that of the exempt non-resident owner or other person entitled to the refund.
• Attach a photocopy of the *Certificate of Exemption* If the owner of the security held a certificate that was in force on the date of payment.

Name of payer or agent who withheld non-resident tax _____

Certification

I certify that the information contained above and in any documents attached is correct and complete.

_____ _____ _____
Name of authorized person (print)   Position or office   Area code and telephone number

_____ _____
Signature of authorized person   Date

Certificate of tax withheld

I _____
(Name and address of payer or disbursing agent)

certify that the non-resident tax in the sum of $ _____ ☐ U.S. ☐ was withheld from
(specify if other than Canadian currency)

_____
(Name of registered owner)

and remitted under Account Number _____

and included in $ _____ ☐ U.S. ☐ remitted on _____
Total amount of remittance (specify if other than Canadian currency)   Date of remittance

for _____ _____
Type of payment   Name of security

_____ _____ _____
Name of authorized person (print)   Position or office   Area code and telephone number

_____ _____
Signature of authorized person   Date

NR7-R E (96)
Printed in Canada

Copy 1 International Tax Services Office

(Ce formulaire existe aussi en français.)

Instructions

- Complete this form to the end of the Certification area.

- Attach copy 3 of the NR4 Supplementary slip to copy 1 of this form. If you do not have the supplementary slip, the payer or disbursing agent has to complete the *Certificate of tax withheld* area of this form.

  Note: You are responsible for having the payer or disbursing agent fully complete the "Certificate of tax withheld" area. If there is missing or incomplete information, we may delay processing the application, and we may return it to you unprocessed.

- Send copy 1 of this form to Revenue Canada, International Tax Services Office, 2204 Walkley Road, Ottawa ON K1A 1A8, no later than two years after the end of the calendar year in which the tax was remitted.

- Keep copy 2 for your records.

- The CUSIP number identifies a specific publicly traded security. If applicable, enter it in the space provided on the front of this form.

- A securities lending arrangement is an arrangement where the owner of a security transfers or lends a security to an arm's-length person with the expectation that, at or after a specified time, the borrower will transfer or return to the lender a security identical to that originally transferred or lent.

Note

- We will issue refunds in a foreign currency only if the tax was remitted in that currency. We use the exchange rate that applies on the date we issue the refund cheque. As a result, the amount refunded may differ from the amount requested.

- The NR7-R control number printed on the front of this form appears on the refund cheque.

- Amounts of less than $2 are not refundable.

- Should your application be approved, your refund cheque will be forwarded to the address as indicated in the "name of applicant" area of this form.

Revenue   Revenu
Canada   Canada

DETERMINATION OF RESIDENCY STATUS (Leaving Canada)

- Use this form if you plan to leave or have left Canada, either permanently or temporarily. Revenue Canada will determine if you are a resident of Canada for income tax purposes.

- Mail one completed copy of this form for each taxation year in question to the International Tax Services Office, 2204 Walkley Road, Ottawa ON K1A 1A8. If you prefer, you can send the form by fax to 613-941-2505.

- If you need help completing this form, you can get Interpretation Bulletin IT-221R2, *Determination of an Individual's Residence Status*, or call the International Tax Services Office at the following numbers:

  Calls from within the Ottawa area 952-3741
  Calls from other areas in Canada and the United States 1-800-267-5177
  Calls from outside Canada and the United States (we accept collect calls)   (613) 952-3741

- Please attach any necessary additional information to this form and refer to **Additional information** on page 4.

1.

Surname	Usual first name and initial	Social insurance number or temporary taxation number	Taxation year
			19

Address while outside Canada	Telephone number

Mailing address (if different from above)	Citizenship

Do you want us to change our records to show this as your mailing address? ☐ Yes ☐ No	In what country will you live?

2.

Date of departure - provide: day/month/year	How many months or years do you expect to be living outside Canada?

3. Which of the following applies to you?

☐ You usually live in another country and you were temporarily living in Canada for _____ days in the year, but will leave, or have left Canada during the year. (We will calculate the number of days if you give us the dates you were, or will be, in Canada.)

☐ You usually live in another country, but enter and leave Canada on the same day to work, shop, or study.

☐ You usually live in Canada, but you leave Canada during the day to work, shop, or study in another country, and return to Canada the same day.

☐ None of the above.

4. Indicate why you are leaving Canada by selecting one of the following:

☐ Employment   ☐ Spouse of an individual leaving Canada
☐ Retirement   ☐ Child or grandchild of an individual leaving Canada
☐ Studying or conducting research   ☐ None of the above. Please specify.
☐ Self-employment   _____
☐ Professional-improvement leave   _____

5. If you are the spouse, dependent child, or dependent grandchild of an individual who has left Canada, or will be leaving, please indicate whether your spouse, parent, or grandparent, after he or she has left Canada, will be a :

☐ Factual resident of Canada   ☐ Deemed resident of Canada   ☐ Non-resident of Canada
   If you do not know the residency status of your spouse, parent, or grandparent, please have that individual also complete Form NR73, *Determination of Residency Status (Leaving Canada)*, and submit it with this request.

If you are the spouse of a person leaving Canada:

Are you, or were you, a resident of Canada in the current year, prior to leaving Canada?   ☐ Yes   ☐ No
Were you a resident of Canada in a previous year?   ☐ Yes   ☐ No
Will you live with your spouse at any time in the year?   ☐ Yes   ☐ No

If you are a dependent child or grandchild of a person leaving Canada, select one of the following that applies to you:

☐ You are under 18 years old at any time during the year.
☐ You are 18 or older and you are dependent because of a mental or physical disability.
What will your net world income be for the year? _____

NR73 E (96)   (Ce formulaire existe aussi en français.)   Canada

6. Please complete this area if you will be employed while you live abroad.

Select the situation that applies to you.

☐ You are a missionary.

How many years will you be living outside Canada? _____

Are you a Canadian citizen or landed immigrant? ☐ Yes ☐ No

Will you be employed by a Canadian religious organization while you are outside Canada? ☐ Yes ☐ No

Will you file a Canadian income tax return for each year you are living outside Canada and report your world income? ☐ Yes ☐ No

☐ You are a member of the Canadian Forces.

(a) ☐ You are an ambassador, a high commissioner, an agent-general of a province or territory of Canada, or an officer or servant (employee) of Canada or of a province or territory of Canada.

(b) ☐ You are an employee or officer of a Canadian Crown corporation, either federal or provincial, where

☐ the corporation is designated as an agent of Canada

☐ the employees of the corporation have been given the status of servants of Canada

☐ none of the above apply. Please explain. _____

If either (a) or (b) apply,

Will you receive a representation allowance for the year? ☐ Yes ☐ No

Were you a factual resident or a deemed resident of Canada immediately before your appointment or employment by Canada, the province, the territory, or the Crown corporation? ☐ Yes ☐ No

☐ You are performing services as an employee, co-operant, advisor, contractor, or sub-contractor under a prescribed international development assistance program of the Government of Canada that is financed with Canadian funds. Please specify.

_____

Were you a factual resident or a deemed resident of Canada at any time during the three months before the day you started your services abroad? ☐ Yes ☐ No

☐ You are a member of the overseas Canadian Forces school staff.

Will you choose to file a Canadian income tax return each year, reporting your world income? ☐ Yes ☐ No

Were you living in the province of Quebec before your departure? ☐ Yes ☐ No

☐ You are an employee of an organization other than those described above.

Provide your employer's name and address. _____

Do you foresee a return to Canada because of a contract with an employer, or because you have a specific date to report back to work in Canada? ☐ Yes ☐ No

If you have a contract with your employer, please attach a copy of the contract.

If you do not have a contract with your Canadian employer or a return date to Canada specified by your employer, will your job be kept available for you upon your return to Canada? ☐ Yes ☐ No

7. Which of the following ties will you have in Canada while living in another country? Tick (✓) those that apply.

☐ Your spouse or common-law spouse will remain in Canada. Please provide the name, citizenship, and current address of your spouse or common-law spouse. If you are legally separated, this item will not apply to you.

_____

☐ You will leave a child or a grandchild in Canada who is dependent on you for support. Please provide the child's name, age, citizenship, and current address, as well as the name and address of the school the child attends and the grade in which the child is enrolled. _____

☐ You will continue to support a person in Canada who lives in a dwelling (a house, apartment, trailer, room, suite, etc.) that you occupied and maintained before your departure.

☐ You will continue to own a dwelling in Canada.

☐ You will sublet the dwelling in Canada that you rented for the period of your absence from Canada and you intend to renew the lease of such a dwelling when it expires.

☐ You will maintain a dwelling in Canada suitable for year-round occupancy by:

☐ keeping the dwelling vacant;

☐ renting the dwelling at non-arm's length (i.e. rented to a relative)

☐ renting the dwelling at arm's length. Please provide details with respect to the terms of the lease, termination clause, etc. _____

☐ You will keep (by storing or renting out) your furniture, furnishings, appliances, utensils, etc., in Canada.

☐ You will have personal possessions in Canada, such as your clothing (essentially your wardrobe), personal items, pets, etc.

☐ You will keep vehicles in Canada that are registered in Canada.

☐ You will keep your Canadian driver's licence.

☐ You will continue to renew your Canadian driver's licence when it expires.

☐ You will maintain eligibility for provincial or territorial hospitalization and medical insurance coverage for more than three months after you leave Canada. To find out whether you will be eligible for provincial or territorial medical coverage while living outside Canada, contact the provincial or territorial health authorities where you live.

☐ You will keep memberships in Canadian social or recreational organizations. Please list these memberships. _____

☐ You will keep memberships in professional associations in Canada that depend on Canadian residency. Please list these memberships. _____

☐ You will keep bank accounts in Canada. Please explain why you are keeping these accounts. _____
☐ You will use credit cards from Canadian financial institutions.
☐ You will have investments in Canada. Please describe these investments. _____
☐ You will keep a seasonal residence in Canada. (e.g. a cottage, chalet, etc.)
☐ You or your spouse will receive Child Tax Benefit payments, while living outside Canada. For more information about Child Tax Benefits, contact Human Resources Development Canada at 1 800 387-1193.

☐ You will have a telephone service in Canada. Even if it is not listed, provide the address for your telephone service and indicate if it is a personal or business service.

☐ You will use personal stationery and business cards with a Canadian address. Provide the address you will use. _____

☐ You will use post office boxes and/or safety deposit boxes in Canada. Provide the addresses for these boxes _____

☐ You will be involved with and have responsibilities in partnerships, corporate or business relationships, or endorsement contracts in Canada. Please specify. _____

☐ You will have other ties with Canada. Please describe them. _____

☐ None of the items in this section will apply to you.

8. Do you intend to return to Canada to live?   ☐ Yes   ☐ No

Please provide details of your long-term career goals.
_____
_____
_____

9. You will make return visits to Canada.   ☐ Yes   ☐ No

If yes, state the number of return visits you will make each year, and expected aggregate duration of your stay in Canada. _____

10. The following questions about your residential ties in another country will help us provide an opinion on your residency status.

a) If your spouse (or common-law spouse) will not remain in Canada, please provide:
Spouse's name: _____ Citizenship: _____
Spouse's current address: _____

Spouse's date of departure (Day/month/year): _____

b) If you have dependent children and your children will not remain in Canada, please provide the child's name, age, citizenship and current address, as well as the name and address of the school your child attends and the grade in which the child is enrolled. _____

c) If you have dependent children who will not remain in Canada, please provide:
Children's date of departure (Day/month/year): _____
Number of months your children expect to live outside Canada: _____
d) If you support individuals, other than through a charitable organization, provide the names and current addresses of these people and financial details of your support. _____

e) Describe the dwelling in which you will live in the other country. Include details such as address, type, size, and whether you rent or own the dwelling. If you rent the dwelling, provide the length of the time you have agreed to be a tenant. _____

f) Describe the personal possessions (clothing, furniture, personal items, pets, etc) you will have in the other country. _____

g) If you have a driver's licence issued in a country other than Canada, please state for which country it is issued, the expiry date, and whether you will renew it. _____

h) If applicable, provide the name of the insurer of your medical/hospitalization coverage while living outside Canada and the length of the coverage.

i) List the professional, social or recreational organizations in which you will be a member in countries other than Canada.

j) Describe the investments you will have in countries other than Canada. Include details of chequing and savings accounts, pension and retirement plans, property, and shares in companies you will have in these countries. Explain why these investments are kept outside Canada.

k) Provide details of other consumer relationships, such as lines of credit and credit cards, you will have in other countries.

l) Provide the address for your telephone service in other countries, even if it is not listed, and indicate if it is a personal or business service.

m) Provide the address you use for personal stationery and business cards in other countries, if applicable.

n) Provide the addresses for post offices boxes and/or safety deposit boxes that you use in other countries, if applicable.

o) Provide details of your involvement and responsibilities in any partnerships, corporate or business relationships, and endorsement contracts you have in other countries.

p) List the countries, other than Canada, you have visited in this calendar year, the length of time spent in each country, and the reason for visiting those countries. Include the dates of entry and departure for each country visited.

q) Are you considered to be a resident of another country?   ☐ Yes   ☐ No

If yes, we may ask you to provide a letter from that government stating that you are a resident of that country for the year in question, and that you are subject to tax in that country as a resident. We may also ask you to provide proof of your income subject to tax in the other country.

11.

Certification

We use this form as a starting point to obtain the facts we need to provide an opinion on your residency status. Please contact us if your situation changes as your residency status could also change.

I, _____ (please print) _____ , certify that the information given on this form is, to the best of my knowledge, correct and complete.

_____   _____
Date   Signature

Additional information

Has your intention to live outside Canada on a permanent basis changed since you first left Canada? _____
If yes, when? _____
Please provide details. _____

■✦■ Revenue Revenu
      Canada Canada

OVERSEAS EMPLOYMENT TAX CREDIT
CALENDAR YEAR _____

Step I – Must be fully completed by the employer
Employer certification

I,_____ (authorized officer), certify that _____ (employee's full name),

social insurance number _____, was employed by_____ (employer's full name)
throughout a **period of more than 6 consecutive months** (the **"qualifying period"**) that began before the end of the calendar
year and included any part thereof. *

The employer has met the requirements of subsection 122.3(2) of the *Income Tax Act* as a specified employer and is one of the
following (check one):

☐ a person resident in Canada;

☐ a partnership in which persons resident in Canada or corporations controlled by persons resident in Canada own
   interests which exceed 10% of the fair market value of all interests in the partnership; or

☐ a corporation that is a foreign affiliate of a person resident in Canada.

The employee, during that qualifying period extending from _____ to _____ :

(1) was employed, **other than** for performing services under international development assistance program of the
Canadian International Development Agency (CIDA);

and

(2) throughout that period performed **all or substantially all (90% or more)** of the duties of employment **outside Canada** in
connection with a contract under which the employer carried on a business outside Canada conducting one of the
following activities outlined in clause 122.3(1)(b)(i) (A),(B), or (C) of the Income Tax Act (check one):

☐ the exploration for or exploitation of petroleum, natural gas, minerals, or other similar resources;

☐ any construction, installation, or agricultural or engineering activity; or

☐ an activity performed under contract with the United Nations. (For 1994 and subsequent calendar years only)

or

☐ for the purpose of obtaining, on behalf of the employer, a contract to undertake any of the above activities.

Please provide details: e.g., country, name of the project.

_____

_____

If a waiver on withholding had been requested with respect to this credit, please provide the name of the Tax Services Office

where the waiver request was processed: _____

The employer also undertakes to provide to Revenue Canada, on request, any necessary information to substantiate the
accuracy of the information on this form.

Date _____ 19 _____   _____   _____
                              Signature of authorized officer   Employer's business account number

                                                                  (_____)
                                                                  Telephone number

* Note: If the qualifying period extends over more than one calendar year, you must complete this form for each of the years.

T626 E (96)   (Ce formulaire existe aussi en français.)   **Canadä**

Step II – Calculation of employment income

1. Number of days in the qualifying period referred to in Step I that are in this calendar year and during which you were resident in Canada `620`

2. Gross salary, wages, and other remuneration for the period referred to in A . . . . $ _____

3. Deduct: Employment deductions related to amount B:

4.   Sales expenses . . . . $ _____

5.   Travelling expenses . . . . _____

6.   Annual union or professional dues . . . . _____

7.   RPP contributions . . . . _____

8.   Other deductions (please specify) . . . . _____

9.   **Total** . . . . ▶ $ _____

10. Net salary, wages and remuneration for the period referred to in A (amount B minus amount C) . . . . `621` $ _____

Note: You should apportion employment deductions partly related to the period referred to in A in the same ratio as the number of days relates to 365.

Step III – Calculation of credit limits

11. Enter the number of days in A above _____ X $80,000 . . . . = $ _____
                          divided by 365

12. Enter the amount in D above $_____ X 80% . . . . = $ _____

13. Net income for the year (line 236 of T1 return) . . . . $ _____

14. Add: Forward-averaging withdrawal (Form T581) included in calculating
     taxable income for the taxation year _____

Notes: If the amount on line 5 of Form T581 is positive, enter the amount from line 6 of that form on line 14 above. If the amount on line 5 of Form T581 is negative, enter any positive amount from line 7 of that form on line 14 above. If line 7 of Form T581 is also negative, enter nil on line 14 above.

15. Subtotal (lines 13 and 14) . . . . $ _____

16. Deduct: Any deduction for net capital losses of other years (line 253 of T1 return) . . . . . $ _____

17.   Amounts for shares deductible under paragraph 110(1)(d.2) or 110(1)(d.3) . . . . _____

18.   Employee home relocation loan deductible under paragraph 110(1)(j) . . . . _____

19.   Capital gains deduction (line 254 of T1 return) . . . . _____

20.   Payments of income deductible under paragraph 110(1)(f) . . . . _____

21.   **Total** of line 15 minus lines 16 to 20 . . . . $ _____ ▶ $ _____

Step IV – Calculation of basic federal tax (see Schedule 1, *Federal Tax Calculation*)

22. Enter taxable income (line 260 of T1 return) . . . . $ _____

23. On the first _____ tax is . . . .

24. On the remaining _____ tax at ___% is _____

25. **Total** (lines 23 and 24) . . . . $ _____

26. Add: Tax adjustments
     (see line 500 of guide) . . . . _____

27. **Total** (lines 25 and 26) . . . . ▶ $ _____

28. Subtract: Total non-refundable tax credits
     (line 350 of T1 return) . . . . _____

29. **Total** . . . . $ _____ H

30. Subtract: Overseas employment tax credit (note c)
     (amount I from step V below) . . . . _____

31. **Total** . . . . $ _____

32. Subtract: Federal dividend tax credit
     (see line 502 of guide) . . . . _____

33. **Total** . . . . $ _____ ▶

34. Subtract: Minimum tax carry-over (see line 504 of guide) . . . . _____

35. Basic federal tax (enter this amount on line 506 on Schedule 1 of T1 return) . . . . ▶

Notes: a) A foreign tax paid on income subject to an overseas employment tax credit must be excluded in calculating any foreign tax credit to which you may be entitled.

    b) If you are otherwise entitled to a foreign tax credit, the amount on line 30 must be added to the federal tax plus any dividend tax credit in the multiplier (on Schedule 1) of the foreign tax credit calculation.

    c) The amount on line 30 must be added to basic federal tax on line A of the individual surtax calculation (on Schedule 1).

    d) A claim for the overseas employment tax credit may result in the application of minimum tax. You should also complete Form T691, *Calculation of Minimum Tax*, to determine if minimum tax is payable.

Step V – Calculation of overseas employment tax credit

36. Enter the lesser of E and F $_____ X amount H $_____ . . . . `635` _____
                             divided by amount G $_____

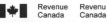 Revenue Revenu
Canada Canada

T2061
Rev. 95

ELECTION BY AN EMIGRANT TO DEFER DEEMED DISPOSITION OF PROPERTY AND CAPITAL GAINS THEREON

FOR DEPARTMENTAL USE ONLY

- For use by an individual other than a trust (taxpayer), to elect under subparagraph 128.1(4)(b)(iv) of the Income Tax Act to defer the deemed disposition of capital property (which would otherwise be deemed disposed of) owned by the taxpayer on the date the taxpayer ceased to be a resident of Canada.

- Where the taxpayer is an individual other than a trust, the following properties are not deemed to have been disposed of and no election is required:

  (i) property that would have been taxable Canadian property (under subsection 248(1) of the Income Tax Act), if the taxpayer had not been resident in Canada at any time in the year.

  (ii) property that is described in the inventory of a business carried on by the taxpayer in Canada at the time of disposition or deemed disposition.

  (iii) a right to receive specified periodic payments such as pension benefits, retirement benefits and other annuity benefits and payments from a registered retirement savings plan, registered retirement income fund or deferred profit sharing plan.

- One copy of this election is to be filed with the taxpayer's Income Tax Return on or before the day on or before which the return for the year in which the taxpayer ceased to be resident in Canada is required to be filed.

- Security acceptable to the Minister for the payment of any tax the payment of which is deferred by the election must be provided and should be submitted not later than the due date for filing this election. The taxpayer should contact the Collections Section of the local Tax Services Office to determine the security necessary.

- Property subject to this election, shall be deemed to be taxable Canadian property until it is disposed of or until the taxpayer next becomes resident in Canada, whichever occurs first.

- Additional information may be obtained from the current version of Interpretation Bulletin IT-451, entitled "Deemed disposition and acquisition on ceasing to be or becoming resident in Canada."

Name of Taxpayer in Full (Print)	
Present Address	
Address While Resident in Canada	
Date Canadian Residence Ceased	(Day, Month, Year)	Canadian Social Insurance Number

Particulars of Property to Which this Election Applies

Description	Adjusted Cost Base	Fair Market Value at Date Canadian Residence Ceased
	$	$

- Attach schedule if space is insufficient.

CERTIFICATION

I, _____ , certify that the information given on this form is, to the best of my knowledge, correct and
complete. (Please print)

_____ _____ _____
Date (Signature of authorized person) (Position or office)

Printed in Canada   Form authorized by the Minister of National Revenue   (Français au verso)

I✦I Revenue   Revenu
     Canada   Canada

T2061A
Rev. 95

ELECTION BY AN EMIGRANT TO REPORT DEEMED DISPOSITIONS OF *TAXABLE CANADIAN PROPERTY* AND CAPITAL GAINS AND/OR LOSSES THEREON

FOR DEPARTMENTAL USE ONLY

- For use by an individual other than a trust (taxpayer), who ceased at any time in the year to be a resident of Canada, to elect under paragraph 128.1(4)(d) of the Income Tax Act to recognize the deemed disposition of any property that:
  - (i) would be taxable Canadian property if the taxpayer had been resident in Canada at no time in the taxpayer's last taxation year that began before the particular time or
  - (ii) is described in the inventory of a business carried on by the taxpayer in Canada at the particular time.

- Taxable Canadian property is property described in subsection 248(1) of the Income Tax Act.

- One copy of this election is to be filed with the taxpayer's Income Tax Return on or before the day on or before which the return for the year in which the taxpayer ceased to be resident in Canada is required to be filed.

- The capital gain or loss arising from the elected deemed dispositions and the calculation of the capital gains deduction and the cumulative net investment loss are reported respectively on Schedule 3 of the Income Tax Return, either or both Forms T657 and T657A and Form T936 which are to be filed with the taxpayer's Income Tax Return for the year in which the taxpayer ceased to be resident in Canada.

- Additional information may be obtained from the current version of Interpretation Bulletin IT-451, entitled "Deemed disposition and acquisition on ceasing to be or becoming resident in Canada."

Name of Taxpayer in Full (Print)		
Present Address		
Address While Resident in Canada		
Date Canadian Residence Ceased	(Day, Month, Year)	Canadian Social Insurance Number

Particulars of Property to Which this Election Applies

Description	Adjusted Cost Base	Fair Market Value at Date Canadian Residence Ceased
	$	$

- Attach schedule if space is insufficient.

CERTIFICATION

I, _____ , certify that the information given on this form is, to the best of my knowledge, correct and
complete.   (Please print)

Date	(Signature of authorized person)	(Position or office)

Printed in Canada   Form authorized by the Minister of National Revenue   (Français au verso)

REQUEST BY A NON-RESIDENT OF CANADA FOR A CERTIFICATE
OF COMPLIANCE RELATED TO THE
DISPOSITION OF TAXABLE CANADIAN PROPERTY

Revenue Canada / Revenu Canada

T2062(E)
Rev. 95

- For use by a non-resident of Canada to provide notice of (a) the disposition of, or (b) the proposed disposition of, certain *taxable Canadian property.* *Taxable Canadian property* is property described in paragraph 115(1)(b) of the *Income Tax Act.*
- For information concerning residency status in Canada, refer to the current release of Interpretation Bulletin IT 221, *Determination of an Individual's Residency Status,* or contact the International Tax Services Office at 952-3741 (calls from within the Ottawa area), 1-800-267-5177 (calls from other areas in Canada and the United Steates) or 613-952-3741 (calls from outside Canada and the United States). We accept collect calls from outside Canada and the United States.
- Copies 1 to 4 of this request must be filed at the Tax Services Office for the area in which the property is located.
- **The notice for a disposition under subsection 116(3) must be sent by registered mail not later than 10 days after the date of disposition.**

Check (✓) purpose for this notice

- ☐ Proposed disposition: attach a copy of the offer to purchase.
- ☐ Completed disposition: attach a copy of the agreement of sale and the statement of adjustments or a copy of the filed T2057 or T2058 election forms and the transfer agreement where a section 85 election is applicable.

- ☐ Gifts of property inter-vivos: attach documentation to support fair market value.

Provide full address including as applicable street address, post office box, city, state, country and mail code.
(Refer to item 5 on the reverse of copy 5 for details concerning the requested identification numbers.)

Last name of non-resident (print)	First name & initial of non-resident (print)	Date of birth D M Y	Date of departure from Canada D M Y
Present address of non-resident		(Canadian) Social Insurance Number or TTN	
		Non-resident Individual, Corporation or Business Account Number	
Person to contact for information – Name and address		Telephone	
Purchaser – Name and address			
	Telephone	Purchaser Identification Number	

1. Have you previously filed a T2062 or T2062A in the current calendar year?   ☐ YES ☐ NO
   If "YES", specify the Tax Services Office(s) where the request(s) were filed and indicate the name and address of the purchaser(s).

2. Is the disposition subject to an election under section 85?   ☐ YES ☐ NO
   If "YES", indicate the date of filing the section 85 election form and the Tax Services Office where the election form was filed.

3. Do you hold or contemplate holding a mortgage as a result of the disposition?   ☐ YES ☐ NO

4. Have you received any income, including rents, royalties or lease payments, from the property?
   ☐ YES, income was received from the property (complete the following).
   ☐ Non-resident tax was withheld
       Indicate name and address of person who withheld the tax
   ☐ Non-resident tax was not withheld
       Specify the period(s) that income was received from the property _____ to _____   (Attach income statements that indicate amount(s) of gross income.)
       (day, month, year)   (day, month, year)
   ☐ NO, income was not received from the property.

5. Do you have any outstanding balances for taxes, including income or excise taxes, custom duties, or the Goods & Services Tax (GST)?   ☐ YES ☐ NO
   If "YES", specify the identification or account number(s) related to the outstanding balance for taxes.

6. Indicate when and where you last filed a Canadian income tax return, if applicable:
   Year _____ City _____ Province _____

7. Is the disposition to a person by way of gift of property inter-vivos or to a person with whom you are not dealing at arm's length?   ☐ YES ☐ NO
   If "YES" and the disposition is at less than fair market value enter the fair market value at the time of disposition in Column (4) below.

PARTICULARS OF PROPERTY

(1) Date or Proposed Date of Disposition	(2) Vendor's Acquisition Date	(3) Description - Refer to item 3 on the reverse of Copy 5	(4) Estimated or Actual Amount of Proceeds of Disposition	(5) Adjusted Cost Base	(6) Gain or (Loss) Column (4) Less Column (5)
			$	$	$
			Net Gain or (Loss)		$
			(1990 and subsequent years - 33 1/3%)		$

USE A SEPARATE LINE FOR EACH TYPE OF PROPERTY– ATTACH A SCHEDULE IF SPACE IS NOT SUFFICIENT

Attachments: The following, if applicable, must accompany this request. Check (✓) which have been attached.

- ☐ Offer to Purchase or Purchase Agreement.
- ☐ Sales Agreement, Statement of Adjustments or Transfer Agreement.
- ☐ Calculation of Adjusted Cost Base.
- ☐ Copy of section 85 election form T2057 or T2058.
- ☐ List of name and addresses of all members where the property is held as joint tenancy, tenancy-in-common or co-ownership.
- ☐ Cheque or money order payable to the Receiver General.
- ☐ Evidence that security has been provided.
- ☐ **A T2062A which is being filed simultaneously with**
- ☐ Schedule(s) where space is insufficient.
- ☐ **Documentation to support fair market value in respect of a section 85 election, a gift inter-vivos or a on-arm's length**

CERTIFICATION

I, _____ , certify that the information given on this form is, to the best of my knowledge, correct and complete.
   Print Name

Date _____   (Signature of authorized person) _____   (Position or office) _____

FOR DEPARTMENTAL USE ONLY

Subsidiary Ledger Account Number		Amount of Payment	

Form acceptable to the Minister of National Revenue

COPY 1 – Revenue Canada – T1, T2 and T3 Vendor's File (Permanent Correspondence)

INFORMATION

- The notice under subsection 116(3) must be sent by registered mail not later than 10 days after the date of disposition.
- Sections, subsections, paragraphs and subparagraphs referred to in this form are sections, subsections, paragraphs and subparagraphs of the *Income Tax Act.*
- If a request is filed with respect to a proposed disposition pursuant to subsection 116(1) and the completed disposition complies with the requirements of subparagraphs 116(3)(d), (e) and (f), a separate request is not required to be filed pursuant to subsection 116(3) in respect of the completed disposition.
- A separate request is required for each disposition or proposed disposition. However, where several properties are disposed of, or are proposed to be disposed of, to the same purchaser at the same time, only one request is required as notice of the entire disposition.
- A separate T2062 must be filed by each person indicating an interest in a joint tenancy, tenancy in common or co-ownership.
- Where a T2062 and a T2062A are required in respect of a disposition to the same purchaser the forms must be filed together.
- Copies 1 to 4 of this request must be filed at the Tax Services Office for the area in which the property is located.

EXPLANATIONS AND INSTRUCTIONS

(1) A certificate of compliance is issued once a payment as or on account of tax is paid or security acceptable to the Minister is submitted in respect of the disposition. Final settlement of the tax liability is made when your Canadian income tax return is filed.

(2) Dispositions or proposed dispositions of Canadian Resource Property, Canadian Real Property (other than capital property), Canadian Timber Resource Property and/or Recapture on Depreciable Taxable Canadian Property are to be reported on   form T2062A. Dispositions of life insurance policies in Canada are to be reported on form T2062B.

(3) "Description" of property – include the following details:

    (a) **Real Estate** – street address, city or town, plan number, lot number, registration number, municipal value and use of property (e.g. personal residence, rental or business property).

    (b) **Shares of Stock** – number and class of shares, certificate numbers, name of corporation and par value.

    (c) **Partnerships** – name, address and identification number of partnership.

    (d) **Trusts** – name and address, if any, of trust; otherwise name(s) and address(es) of trustee(s).

(4) Outlays and expenses related to the sale of *taxable Canadian property,* including real estate commissions, brokerage fees, and legal and notary fees, may not be claimed at the time of filing the T2062. These amounts may be claimed when filing your Canadian income tax return.

(5) Use applicable identification number(s) when filing your Canadian income tax return and on all correspondence with the Department.

    (Canadian) Social Insurance Number (SIN) – is only applicable if an individual was formerly a resident or a deemed resident of Canada.

    Non-resident Individual, Corporation or Business Account Number – is the number indicated on a notice of assessment, which is issued if a Canadian income tax return was filed in a previous year.

(6) Additional information may be obtained from current release of:

    Information Circular:

    IC 72-17 – Procedures concerning the disposition of *taxable Canadian property* by non-residents of Canada - section 116

    Interpretation Bulletins:

    IT 171 – Non-resident individuals - Taxable income earned in Canada

    IT 176 – Taxable Canadian Property - Interests in and Options on Real Property and Shares

    IT 419 – Meaning of arm's length

> **NOTE:** Completion of this information will serve as notification for the person named herein, to act as your authorized representative with respect to matters concerning the filing of this request.

Printed in Canada

■◆■ Revenue   Revenu
Canada   Canada

REQUEST BY A NON-RESIDENT OF CANADA FOR A CERTIFICATE   T2062A(E)
OF COMPLIANCE RELATED TO THE DISPOSITION OF CANADIAN RESOURCE PROPERTY,   Rev. 95
CANADIAN REAL PROPERTY (OTHER THAN CAPITAL PROPERTY), CANADIAN TIMBER
RESOURCE PROPERTY AND/OR DEPRECIABLE TAXABLE CANADIAN PROPERTY

- For use by a non-resident of Canada to provide notice of (a) the disposition of, or (b) the proposed disposition of "Canadian resource property, Canadian real property (other than capital property), Canadian timber resource property and/or depreciable taxable Canadian property".
- For information concerning residency status in Canada, refer to the current release of Interpretation Bulletin IT-221, *Determination of an Individual's Residency Status*, or contact the International Tax Services Office at 952-3741 (calls from within the Ottawa area), 1-800-267-5177 (call from other areas in Canada and the United States) or 613-952-3741 (calls from outside Canada and the United States). We accept collect calls from outside Canada and the United States.
- Copies 1 to 4 of this request must be filed at the Tax Services Office for the area in which the property is located.
- The notice for a disposition under subsection 116(3) must be sent by registered mail not later than 10 days after the date of disposition.

Check (✓) purpose for this notice

☐ Proposed disposition: attach a copy of the offer to purchase.
☐ Completed disposition: attach a copy of the agreement of sale and statement of adjustments or a copy of the filed T2057 or T2058 election forms and the transfer agreement where a section 85 election is applicable.
☐ Gifts of property inter-vivos: attach documentation to support fair market value.

Provide full address including as applicable street address, post office box, city, state, country and mail code.
(Refer to item 5 on the reverse of copy 5 for details concerning the requested identification numbers.)

Last name of non-resident (print)	First name & initial of non-resident (print)	Date of birth			Date of departure from Canada		
		D	M	Y	D	M	Y

Present address of non-resident	(Canadian) Social Insurance Number or TTN
	Non-resident Individual, Corporation or Business Account Number

Person to contact for information Name and address	Telephone

Purchaser – Name and address		
	Telephone	Purchaser Identification Number

1. Have you previously filed a T2062A or T2062 in the current calendar year?   ☐ YES   ☐ NO
   If "YES", specify the Tax Services Office(s) where the request(s) were
   filed and indicate the name and address of the purchaser(s). _____

2. Is the disposition subject to an election under section 85?   ☐ YES   ☐ NO
   If "YES", indicate the date of filing the section 85 election form and the
   Tax Services Office where the election form was filed. _____

3. Do you hold or contemplate holding a mortgage as a result of the disposition?   ☐ YES   ☐ NO

4. Have you received any income, including rents, royalties or lease payments, from the property?
   ☐ YES, income was received from the property (complete the following).
       ☐ Non-resident tax has been deducted.
          Indicate name and address of person who withheld the tax _____
       ☐ Non-resident tax has not been deducted.   (Attach income statements that indica
          Specify the period(s) that income was received from the property _____ to _____   amount(s) of gross income.)
                                                              (day, month, year)   (day, month, year)
   ☐ NO, income was not received from the property.

5. Do you have any outstanding balances for taxes, including income or excise taxes, custom duties, or
   the Goods & Services Tax (GST)?   ☐ YES   ☐ NO
   If "YES", specify the identification or account number(s) related to the outstanding balance for taxes.

6. Indicate when and where you last filed a Canadian income tax return, if applicable:
   Year _____   City _____   Province _____

7. Is the disposition to a person by way of gift of property inter-vivos or to a person with whom you are not dealing at arm's length? ☐ YES   ☐ NO
   If "YES" and the disposition is at less than fair market value enter the fair market value at the time of disposition in Column (4) below.

- COMPLETE THE APPLICABLE INFORMATION FOR DISPOSITION(S) OF REAL PROPERTY (OTHER THAN CAPITAL PROPERTY) AND RECAPTURE ON DISPOSITION OF DEPRECIABLE PROPERTY AND/OR TIMBER RESOURCE PROPERTY.
- USE A SEPARATE LINE FOR EACH TYPE OF PROPERTY - ATTACH A SCHEDULE IF SPACE IS NOT SUFFICIENT.
- CALCULATE THE PAYMENT REQUIRED ON ACCOUNT OF TAX FOR RESOURCE PROPERTIES ON T2062A SCHEDULE 1.

PARTICULARS OF PROPERTY

(1) Date or Proposed Date of Disposition	(2) Vendor's Acquisition Date	(3) Description - Refer to item 3 on the reverse of Copy 5	(4) Estimated or Actual Amount of Proceeds Disposition or Cost Amount - Refer to Item 5 on the	(5) Undepreciated Capital Cost or Cost Amount - Refer to Item 5 on the	(6) Income or (Loss) Column (4) Less Column (5)
			$	$	$
			Income or (Loss)	$	
	Payment required per the applicable Part 1 Federal Tax Rate (For resource property, obtain amount from Form T2062A Schedule 1)			$	

USE A SEPARATE LINE FOR EACH TYPE OF PROPERTY– ATTACH A SCHEDULE IF SPACE IS NOT SUFFICIENT.
Attachments: The following, if applicable, must accompany this request. Check (✓) which have been attached.

☐ Offer to Purchase or Purchase Agreement.   ☐ Cheque or money order payable to the Receiver General.
☐ Sales Agreement, Statement of Adjustments or Transfer Agreement. ☐ Evidence that security has been provided.
☐ Calculation of Adjusted Cost Base.   ☐ A T2062 which is being filed simultaneously with
☐ Copy of section 85 election form T2057 or T2058.   ☐ T2062A Schedule 1.
☐ List of name and addresses of all members where the property is held as joint tenancy, tenancy-in-common or co-ownership.
☐ Documentation to support fair market value in respect of a section 85 election, a gift inter-vivos or a non-arm's length transfer at less than fair market value.

━━━━━━━━━━ CERTIFICATION ━━━━━━━━━━
I, _____ , certify that the information given on this form is, to the best of my knowledge, correct and complete.
        Print Name

_____   _____   _____
        Date   (Signature of authorized person)   (Position or office)

━━━━━━━━━━ FOR DEPARTMENTAL USE ONLY ━━━━━━━━━━

Subsidiary Ledger Account Number		Amount of Payment	

Form acceptable to the Minister of National Revenue

COPY 1 – Revenue Canada – T1, T2 and T3 Vendor's File (Permanent Correspondence)

INFORMATION

- **The notice under subsection 116(3) must be sent by registered mail not later than 10 days after the date of disposition.**
- Sections, subsections, paragraphs and subparagraphs referred to in this form are sections, subsections, paragraphs and subparagraphs of the *Income Tax Act*.
- A separate request is required for each disposition or proposed disposition. However, where several properties are disposed of, or are proposed to be disposed of, to the same purchaser at the same time, only one request is required as notice of the entire disposition.
- A separate T2062A must be filed by each person indicating an interest in a joint tenancy, tenancy in common or co-ownership.
- Where a T2062A and a T2062 are required in respect of a disposition to the same purchaser the forms must be filed together.
- **Copies 1 to 4 of this request must be filed at the Tax Services Office for the area in which the property is located.**

EXPLANATIONS AND INSTRUCTIONS

(1) A disposition of Canadian real property (other than capital property) includes any interest or option in respect of such property whether or not such property is in existence. A disposition of Canadian timber resource property includes any interest or option in respect of such property.

(2) A certificate of compliance is issued once a payment as or on account of tax is paid or security acceptable to the Minister is submitted in respect of the disposition. Final settlement of the tax liability is made when a Canadian income tax return is filed.

(3) "Description" of property – include the following details:

    (a) **Depreciable Property, Real Property (other than capital property) and/or Limber Resource Property** – street address, city or town, plan number, lot number, registration number, serial number and use of property (rental, lease or business); a written description and the applicable class of asset per schedule II of the Income Tax Regulations.

    (b) **Resource Property** – well location and legal description.

(4) **Outlays and expenses related to the sale of *taxable Canadian property*, including real estate commissions, brokerage fees, and legal and notary fees, may not be claimed at the time of filing the T2062A. These amounts may be claimed when filing your Canadian income tax return.**

(5) **Column 4** - For dispositions of depreciable property, the amount to be entered is the lesser of: the estimated or actual proceeds of disposition or capital cost. For dispositions of timber resource property and real property (other than capital property), the amount to be entered is the actual proceeds of disposition.
Column 5 - For dispositions of depreciable property and timber resource property, the amount to be entered is the "undepreciated capital cost." For dispositions of real property (other than capital property), the amount to be entered is the "cost amount."

(6) The disposition or proposed disposition of other *taxable Canadian property*, including the gain on the disposition of depreciable property, are to be reported on Form T2062.

(7) Use applicable identification number(s) when filing your Canadian income tax return and on all correspondence with the Department.

    (Canadian) Social Insurance Number (SIN) – is only applicable if an individual was formerly a resident or a deemed resident of Canada.

    Non-resident Individual, Corporation or Business Account Number – is the number indicated on a notice of assessment, which is issued if a Canadian income tax return was filed in a previous year.

(8) Additional information may be obtained from current release of:

    Information Circular:

    IC 72-17 – Procedures concerning the disposition of *taxable Canadian property* by non-residents of Canada - section 116

    Interpretation Bulletins:

    IT 171 – Non-resident individuals - Taxable income earned in Canada

    IT 176 – Taxable Canadian Property - Interests in and Options on Real Property and Shares

    IT 419 – Meaning of arm's length

> **NOTE:** Completion of this information will serve as notification for the person named herein, to act as your authorized representative with respect to matters concerning the filing of this request.

Printed in Canada

BACK OF COPY 5

I✦I Revenue   Revenu
      Canada   Canada

**DESIGNATION OF A PROPERTY AS A PRINCIPAL RESIDENCE
BY AN INDIVIDUAL (OTHER THAN A PERSONAL TRUST)**

- Use this form to designate a property as a principal residence and to calculate the capital gain for 1996 if you:
  - disposed of, or were considered to have disposed of, your principal residence, or any part of it; or
  - granted someone an option to buy your principal residence, or any part of it.

- Attach one copy of this form to your 1996 income tax return **only** if you have to report a capital gain.

- If you designate the property as your principal residence for **all the years** in which you owned it, there is no capital gain.

  Note
  If you were not a resident of Canada for the entire time you owned the designated property, contact your tax services office. Your period of non-residence may reduce or eliminate the availability of the principal residence exemption.

- If you disposed of, or were considered to have disposed of, a property for which you or your spouse filed Form T664 or T664(Seniors), *Election to Report a Capital Gain on Property Owned at the End of February 22, 1994*, use this form to calculate the capital gain for 1996 if:
  - the property was your principal residence for 1994; or
  - you are designating the property in this form as your principal residence for any taxation year.

- You may be entitled to a reduction as a result of the capital gains election. To calculate this reduction, use Form T2091(IND)-WS, *Principal Residence Worksheet for 1996*. You can get this form from your tax services office.

- The term **spouse** used throughout this form applies to a legally married spouse and, for 1993 and the following years, a common-law spouse as defined in the glossary of the income tax guide called *Capital Gains*.

- For more information about designating a principal residence and what qualifies as a principal residence, see Interpretation Bulletin IT-120, *Principal Residence*, and the chapter called "Principal Residence" in the income tax guide called *Capital Gains*.

──────────── **Designation** ────────────

For the purpose of this form, the **acquisition date** is the date on which you last acquired or reacquired the property, or December 31, 1971, whichever is later. However, if you or your spouse filed Form T664 or T664(Seniors), you or your spouse are not considered to have disposed of and immediately reacquired the property as a result of that election.

Note: If the property was designated as a principal residence for the purpose of filing Form T664 or T664(Seniors), you have to include those previously designated taxation years as part of your principal residence designation.

Description of property designated: _____

I, _____, hereby designate the property described above to have been my principal residence for
         (print name)

the following taxation years ending after the **acquisition date**:

a) _____
        (specify which taxation years after 1971 and before 1982)

b) _____
        (specify which taxation years after 1981)

For those years before 1982, I confirm that I have not designated any other property as my principal residence.

For those years after 1981, I also confirm that neither I, my spouse (who was not separated and living apart from me throughout the year under a judicial separation or written separation agreement), nor any of my children (who were under 18 and unmarried throughout the year), designated any other property as a principal residence. For any taxation year after 1981 for which I am designating the property and throughout which I was under 18 and unmarried, I also confirm that neither my mother, father, nor any of my brothers and sisters (who were under 18 and unmarried throughout the year), designated any other property.

Signature	Date

Information needed to calculate the capital gain

Number of taxation years for which the property is designated as a principal residence:

- Before 1982 (as per designation above) .... _____   1
- After 1981 (as per designation above) .... + _____   2
- Total number of years designated (line 1 **plus** line 2) .... = _____   3

Number of taxation years ending after the **acquisition date** in which you owned the property (jointly with another person or otherwise):

- Before 1982 .... _____   4
- After 1981 .... + _____   5
- Total number of years owned (line 4 **plus** line 5) .... = _____   6

Proceeds of disposition or deemed disposition .... _____   7
Outlays and expenses related to the disposition .... _____   8
Adjusted cost base at the time of disposition (if you or your spouse filed Form T664 or T664(Seniors) for this property, do not take into consideration any increase to the adjusted cost base as a result of that election) ..... _____   9
Adjusted cost base on December 31, 1981 .... _____   10
Fair market value on December 31, 1981 .... _____   11
Adjustments to the cost base made after 1981 (e.g., capital expenditures) .... _____   12

T2091(IND) E (96)   (Ce formulaire existe aussi en français.)   **Canadä**

Calculation of the capital gain

Part 1

Proceeds of disposition or deemed disposition (line 7)	13
Adjusted cost base at the time of disposition (line 9)	14
Outlays and expenses (line 8) +	15
Line 14 **plus** line 15 = ▶ −	16
Capital gain before principal residence exemption (line 13 minus line 16) =	17
Amount from line 17	18
Line 3 **plus** 1 (one year is granted by law) x	19
Multiply line 18 by line 19 =	20
Line 6 ÷	21
Divide line 20 by line 21 = ▶ −	22
Net capital gain from Part 1 (line 17 **minus** line 22; if negative, enter "0") =	23

Part 2

Complete Part 2 **only** if the property disposed of is one of two or more properties that qualify as principal residences a family member owned on December 31, 1981, and continuously thereafter until its disposition. You will find a definition of family in the chapter called "Principal Residence" in the income tax guide called *Capital Gains*. **In all other cases**, do not complete Part 2 and enter the amount from line 23 above on line 53 in Part 3 below.

a) Pre-1982 gain – If you designated the property as a principal residence for all the years you owned it
   before 1982, do not complete lines 24 to 31 and enter "0" on line 32.

Fair market value on December 31, 1981 (line 11)	24
Adjusted cost base on December 31, 1981 (line 10) −	25
Pre-1982 gain before principal residence exemption (line 24 minus line 25) =	26
Amount from line 26	27
Line 1 **plus** 1 (one year is granted by law) x	28
Multiply line 27 by line 28 =	29
Line 4 ÷	30
Divide line 29 by line 30 = ▶ −	31
Pre-1982 gain (line 26 **minus** line 31; if negative, enter "0") =	32

b) Post-1981 gain – If you designated the property as a principal residence for all the years you owned it
   after 1981, enter "0" on line 44 and complete area d) below.

Proceeds of disposition or deemed disposition (line 7)	33
Fair market value on December 31, 1981 (line 11). If the fair market value of the property on December 31, 1981, is more than the amount on line 33, enter "0" on line 44 and complete areas c) and d) below	34
Adjustments made to the cost base after 1981 (line 12) +	35
Outlays and expenses (line 8) +	36
Add lines 34 to 36 = ▶ −	37
Post-1981 gain before principal residence exemption (line 33 minus line 37) =	38
Amount from line 38	39
Line 2 x	40
Multiply line 39 by line 40 =	41
Line 5 ÷	42
Divide line 41 by line 42 = ▶ −	43
Post-1981 gain (line 38 **minus** line 43; if negative, enter "0") =	44

c) Post-1981 loss

Fair market value on December 31, 1981 (line 11)	45
Proceeds of disposition or deemed disposition (line 7) −	46
Post-1981 loss (line 45 minus line 46; if negative, enter "0") =	47

d) Net capital gain from Part 2

Pre-1982 gain, if any (line 32)	48
Post-1981 gain, if any (line 44) +	49
Line 48 **plus** line 49 =	50
Post-1981 loss, if any (line 47) −	51
Net capital gain from Part 2 (line 50 **minus** line 51; if negative, enter "0") = ▶	52

Part 3

Total capital gain (If you completed Part 2, enter the amount from line 23 or line 52, **whichever is less**.
Otherwise, enter the amount from line 23) — 53

Complete Part 4 **only** if you or your spouse filed Form T664 or T664(Seniors) for this property. In all other cases, enter the amount from line 53 on line 029 of Schedule 3, *Capital Gains (or Losses) in 1996*.

Part 4

Total capital gain before reduction (line 53)	54
Reduction as a result of the capital gains election (line 66 of Form T2091(IND)-WS) −	55
Capital gain (line 54 **minus** line 55; if negative, enter "0") =	56

Enter the amount from line 56 on line 029 of Schedule 3, *Capital Gains (or Losses) in 1996*.

Information Circular 72-17R4

Subject: Procedures Concerning the Disposition of Taxable Canadian Property by Non-Residents of Canada - Section 116.

Date: April 24, 1992

This circular cancels and replaces Information Circular No. 72-17R3 dated May 8, 1987.

Contents   Page

General information
1. Under section 116 of the *Income Tax Act* (the Act), non-resident vendors (from now on referred to as vendors) who dispose of certain types of taxable Canadian property (see item 2 below), have to notify Revenue Canada , Taxation about the disposition either before they dispose of the property or after they dispose of it. In addition, before we at Revenue Canada, Taxation can issue a certificate of compliance to the vendor, we have to receive either an amount to cover the tax owing, or appropriate security for any gain the vendor may realize at the time the property is disposed of. We will credit any payments or security the vendor provides to the vendor's account, and make the final settlement of tax when we assess the vendor's income tax return for the year.

If the vendor does not comply with the section 116 requirements, which the vendor must do so before receiving the certificate of compliance, the purchaser of the property may deduct or withhold a specified amount from the proceeds of the disposition to cover any tax which the vendor owes.

2. (a) The types of taxable Canadian property (referred to in item 1 above) are the types of property, or an interest therein, described in paragraph 115(1)(b) of the Act excluding subparagraphs 115(1)(b)(iv),(viii) and (ix). They may be described as follows:

    (i)   real property situated in Canada (mortgages and hypothecs are not considered to be an interest in real property);

    (ii) other capital property used to carry on business (other than property used or held by an insurer to carry on an insurance business) in Canada;

    (iii) capital property of an insurer that in the year is used or held by the insurer to carry on an insurance business in Canada;

    (iv) shares of corporations that reside in Canada, other than public corporations;

    (v)   an interest in a partnership, if at any time during the 12 months immediately before the disposition, 50% or more of the fair market value of all the partnership property (including the amount of any money of the partnership on hand) consisted of:
    A. property that would be "taxable Canadian property," as described in paragraph 115(1)(b) of the Act;
    B. a Canadian resource property, as defined by paragraph 66(15)(c) of the Act;
    C. a timber resource property as defined by paragraph 13(21)(d.1) of the Act; or
    D. an income interest in a Canadian resident trust;

    (vi) a capital interest in a Canadian resident trust (other than a unit trust); and

    (vii) a unit of a Canadian resident unit trust (other than a mutual fund trust).

    (b) Certain types of taxable Canadian property fall into the category of excluded property as defined in subsection 116(6) and, as such, are not subject to the requirements of section 116. The disposition of excluded properties by a non-resident person may result in tax payable under subsections 2(3) and 115(1). Excluded property consists of:

    (i)   property described in subparagraph 115(1)(b)(ix);

    (ii) a share of capital stock of a public corporation, or an interest therein;

    (iii) a unit of a mutual fund trust;

(iv) a bond, debenture, bill, note, mortgage, hypothec or similar obligation; and

(v) property prescribed by Regulation 810 to be excluded property.

(c) Regulation 810 excludes:

(i) property of a non-resident insurer that is a qualified insurance corporation;

(ii) an option on property referred to in (b) (i) to (iv) and (c)(i) and (ii) above, whether or not the property exists;

(iii) an interest in a property referred to in (b) (i), (iii), and (iv) and (c)(i) and (ii) above.

(d) Section 116 specifies that non-residents notify us when they dispose or propose to dispose of a life insurance policy in Canada, a Canadian resource property, or depreciable property that is or would be taxable Canadian property if they disposed of it. After February 20, 1990, property (other than capital property) that is real property situated in Canada, including any interest in or option on the property (whether or not such property exists) and a timber resource property or any interest in or option on the property, are also subject to the provisions of section 116.

3. Section 116 will apply when the vendor is a non-resident or considered to be a non-resident under the Act (e.g., subsection 250(5)). The purchaser's domicile or country of residence is not relevant in determining if section 116 applies. The purchaser may be either a Canadian resident or a non-resident. Section 116 applies at the time the disposition occurs. Thus, if a vendor is contemplating selling the property to which section 116 applies, and the vendor is a Canadian resident before the property is disposed of, but will be a non-resident when the property is finally disposed of, section 116 will apply.

Notification process

4. If a vendor chooses to submit a Notice of Proposed Disposition under section 116, the vendor should send the notice at least 30 days before the property is actually disposed of to give us enough time to review the transaction and verify that the vendor's payment or security is adequate. If possible, we will issue the certificate of compliance before the actual date the vendor disposes of the property. The vendor should send us the Notice of Actual Disposition, as required by subsection 116(3), by registered mail, not later than 10 days after the date the property was disposed of.

5. Because no forms have been prescribed for the purposes of notification by vendors under section 116, vendors may notify us by letter when they dispose of

property. To review the disposition, we often need additional documentation to support the proceeds or proposed proceeds of disposition, real estate appraisals, business equity valuations or the calculations used to determine the adjusted cost base. The Department has available a series of T2062 forms which list the documentation or information we need for specific types of situations. If a vendor is notifying us by letter, we also need to see all the necessary documentation to support the gain reported along with the following information:

(a) the vendor's name and address;

(b) the complete name and address of the proposed or actual purchaser;

(c) a description that will enable the Minister to identify the property;

(d) the estimated or actual amount of the proceeds of disposition; and

(e) the vendor's adjusted cost base at the time the notice was filed.

To ensure that the payment is properly posted, it is important that the vendor clearly state in a letter that he or she is making a section 116 Notice of Disposition. In addition, the names of the vendor and purchaser must be indicated, along with the vendor's Canadian social insurance number, corporate account number or non-resident account number, if one is available.

6. If possible, vendors should use the appropriate T2062 forms to notify us about section 116 dispositions rather than reporting transactions by letter. The T2062 forms outline the procedures to follow for reporting the transaction, calculating the gain, the required payment on account of tax, and the information essential to enable us to issue the certificate as soon as possible. Using these forms reduces delays and often expedites the processing of the notice. Vendors can obtain the T2062 forms from any district office.

7. If the facts and amounts stated on the Notice of the Proposed Disposition agree with the facts and amounts of the actual disposition, the vendor does not have to send us a notice regarding the actual disposition.

8. We only require notice of the actual disposition (in accordance with subsection 116(3)) if the vendor did not file a Notice of a Proposed Disposition, or if the circumstances of the proposed disposition differ from those of the actual disposition. The vendor should send us the notice of the actual disposition, by registered mail, within 10 days from the day the transaction was completed, in accordance with subsection 116(3) of the Act.

Sometimes a vendor has to file a second notice. This occurs if the actual purchaser is a person other than the proposed purchaser, the actual proceeds of disposition are more than the estimated proceeds, or the actual adjusted cost base of the property immediately before the disposition is less than the reported adjusted cost base. As soon as we receive the second notice along with any required additional payment on account of tax or acceptable security, we will issue a certificate of compliance (Form T2068) in accordance with subsection 116(4) of the Act.

9. We need the vendor's Canadian social insurance number, corporate account number, or non-resident account number to ensure that any payment the vendor makes agrees with the information on the vendor's income tax return for the year.

10. When there is more than one vendor, each one must file a separate form indicating his or her interest in the property. For partnership dispositions, it is our policy to accept one Notice of Disposition filed on behalf of all partners. However, along with the notice, we need a complete listing of the non-resident partners who are disposing of the property together with their Canadian and foreign addresses, Canadian social insurance numbers, corporate account numbers or non-resident account numbers, how much each partner owns, and their portion of the payment or security. We will then issue one certificate of compliance and attach a list of the above information. The partnership is responsible for providing the relevant information to each affected partner. Each partner's tax liability will be determined when we assess each partner's income tax return for the year.

11. The vendor should complete the applicable form and send it with the required payment on account of tax or acceptable security to the district office serving the area in which the property is located. If the properties are located in several areas and more than one district office is affected, the vendor should send the notice to the district office that serves the area where the majority of the properties are located.

Appropriate forms

12. Vendors should use Form T2062 to notify us about an actual or proposed disposition of taxable Canadian property (other than depreciable property or excluded property) as described in item 2 above. If the property is not depreciable property (see item 14 below for definition of depreciable property) such as personal use property (e.g., a property in the country consisting of land, building, and equipment), vendors should send only one T2062 form. We will only issue one certificate of compliance.

13. Vendors should use Form T2062A to declare proposed or actual dispositions of properties identified in paragraph 2(d) above. Except as otherwise noted, the notification process for Form T2062A is outlined in items 4 to 11 above.

14. In some cases, vendors may have to file a T2062 form and a T2062A form for one disposition. When vendors dispose of depreciable taxable Canadian property, they should use a T2062 form to declare the gain or loss on the land and building. The recapture of capital cost allowance or terminal loss should be reported on Form T2062A.

Depreciable property is property for which a taxpayer is entitled to claim capital cost allowance, which is deductible when calculating income from business or property. A T2062 form and a T2062A form for depreciable property should be filed even if capital cost allowance has not been claimed. We will then issue two certificates of compliance.

15. Non-resident vendors should use Form T2062A Schedule 1 to determine the balances in the various "pools" and the payment on account of tax (if any) when they dispose of Canadian resource properties. To support the amounts reported, vendors should submit Form T2062A along with any other supporting documents. Vendors cannot use unrelated outlays and expenses and losses carried forward from previous years to reduce the balance in the "pools" and thus lower the amount subject to payment on account of tax.

16. Life insurance companies should use Form T2062B and Form T2062B Schedule 1 to report the disposition of life insurance policies in Canada on behalf of a vendor. In these instances, the insurer requests a letter of authorization from the vendor in order to establish an agency relationship. The insurer then submits a copy of this letter with Form T2062B and the appropriate payment on account of tax to the Department. After we have verified the payment, we will issue a certificate of compliance (Form T2068) to the insurer and the vendor.

Technical applications
17. A "disposition" for capital gains purposes is defined in paragraph 54(c) of the *Income Tax Act* as including "any transaction or event that entitles a taxpayer to proceeds of disposition of property." Therefore, the disposition of real property normally occurs at the time the deed, in properly executed form, is delivered to the purchaser. This is usually the closing date. If the disposition is in the form of a vendor's agreement for sale, then the disposition normally

occurs when the properly executed agreement for sale is delivered to the person acquiring the property.

18. The term "proceeds of disposition" is defined in paragraph 54(h) of the Act.

19. If the disposition is not at arm's length, proceeds will
be considered to be equal to fair market value in accordance with subsection 116(5.1), if the consideration is less than the fair market value.

20. The adjusted cost base reported on Forms T2062, T2062A, T2062B must be calculated in accordance with the relevant sections of the *Income Tax Act* and the *Income Tax Application Rules*. If we estimate that the adjusted cost base differs from the amount reported by the vendor, we may take the position that the vendor has not reported the information required, and we will then withhold the certificate until the vendor has given us the correct information.

21. The rules for determining whether a disposition of a life insurance policy in Canada has occurred, as well as the amount of the proceeds and the adjusted cost base are set out in section 148 of the Act.

Real estate appraisals or business equity valuations
22. To reduce delays, we may request copies of the vendor's financial statements for the previous year, as these are usually not readily available in the district offices. These statements will be used by the Department's Business Equity Valuation Units or Real Estate Appraisal Sections to review the taxpayer's reported values.

23. (a) If we find that we must do a detailed real estate appraisal or business equity valuation, we will try to establish an "estimated value" on which any required payment on account of tax may be based. If the non-resident wishes to make the payment based on this "estimated value," we will issue the certificate of compliance to enable the taxpayer to complete the transaction without having to wait for the results of the appraisal or valuation, which usually takes several months.
   (b) Once the business equity valuation or real estate appraisal has been completed, any changes in the values will be discussed with the vendor or the vendor's representative. The values established as a result of the appraisal or equity valuation should be used when the vendor files a return of income for the year in which the disposition occurs.

(c) If the valuation or appraisal is finalized in the vendor's favour before the income tax return for the year in which the disposition occurs may be filed, the vendor may request a refund of any excess payment on account of tax. The request must be made in writing to the district office that processed the section 116 notice.

Tax treaty exemptions

24. The Department allows vendors to claim an exemption under a specific tax treaty at the time they file the Notice of Disposition. Vendors must state the applicable Article (paragraph) of the particular treaty which Canada has with their country of residence.

To expedite the processing of the exemption, the necessary documentation to support the claim should be submitted along with the request. The documentation which is acceptable must be based on the particular tax treaty under which the exemption is claimed, such as proof of residency, or that the gain has or will be reported in the vendor's country. Tax officials, in some countries, will supply the necessary certification required to claim the exemption.

25. The United States Department of the Treasury, Internal Revenue Service will provide certification for corporations, exempt organizations and individuals. Requests for certification should be sent to the appropriate service centre. The Department of the Treasury, Publication 686, *Certification for Reduced Tax Rates in Tax Treaty Countries*, outlines the certification process.

26. We need at least 30 days to make the necessary determination. Section 116 does not provide for treaty exempt status. It is important that the vendors supply the necessary documentation to support their claim. If the Department and the vendor cannot agree as to whether the exemption of a particular tax convention applies, the vendor must provide the required payment or security before we can issue a certificate of compliance. A letter of undertaking is not considered acceptable security. Once the matter is resolved, the vendor may request a refund or release of security based on the final decision.

27. The granting of exemptions at the time of notification of disposition is departmental policy, and as such is discretionary. We will issue a certificate of compliance indicating that the disposition is treaty exempt. However, we will only issue the certificate of compliance, in this instance, if all other outstanding debts with the Department have been satisfied.

28. For the purpose of paragraph 9, Article XIII of the Canada-United States Income Tax Convention, the reduction of the capital gain for properties held since before January 1, 1972 and disposed of after December 31, 1984, is calculated by using a ratio based on the number of months in that period over the total number of months since January 1, 1972 to the date of disposition. This is so because capital gains in Canada became taxable after 1971, and it is reasonable to view the monthly accrual of such gains as only taking place after 1971.

The Median Rule described in ITAR 26(3) of the Act applies when calculating the gain, otherwise subject to tax, for the purposes of paragraph 9, Article XIII of the Convention.

If the vendor is an individual, ITAR 26(3) would be subject to any election made previously by that individual under ITAR 26(7) of the Act.

Inventory of land
29. Before February 20, 1990, inventory of land was excluded from section 116 requirements. For dispositions affected by this legislative revision, we have a discretionary exemption policy for certain vendors who operate a business involving inventory of land. To qualify, the vendor must satisfy the Department that:

    (a) property transactions of this kind have been previously reported on income account; and/or

    (b) the vendor is making regular instalment payments.

If at the time of filing the Notice of Disposition, the vendor and the Department disagree as to the nature of the transaction, i.e., whether proceeds are on account of income or capital, the request for exemption will be referred to the International Audit Section in the applicable district office. Before this submission, the vendor will have to supply any necessary supporting documentation or representation as to why the nature of the transaction should be in respect of capital rather than income.

If we are satisfied that the vendor meets the established criteria, and has no outstanding tax liabilities, we will issue a certificate of compliance stating "qualified business exemption."

Section 85 elections
30. If a vendor notifies us of a disposition that is subject to an election in respect of a transfer according to section 85 of the Act, we will not issue the

requested certificate unless the prescribed section 85 election Form T2057 or Form T2058 has been submitted along with Form T2062 or Form T2062A.

31. In addition to submitting the completed Forms T2057 and T2058, the transferor and transferee must send all the information specified on these forms and provide supporting documentation, such as business equity valuations, real estate appraisals or calculations, showing how the reported values were determined.

Security or payments on account of tax
32. The objective of obtaining a payment on account of tax or security on the disposition of property, as described in item 2 above, is to protect the revenues of the Crown that are generated by taxes which may be exigible on the income and capital gains realized by vendors on these dispositions at the time a return of income for the year is assessed. Refer to item 38 below for procedures for providing security.

33. The amount subject to a payment on account of tax under section 116 is the amount by which the estimated amount of proceeds of disposition exceeds the adjusted cost base at the time the notice of the proposed disposition is sent (paragraph 116(2)(a)), or the amount by which the actual proceeds of disposition exceeds the adjusted cost base immediately before the disposition (paragraph 116(4)(a)). Outlays and expenses to the extent that they were incurred for the purpose of making the disposition are not taken into account. These amounts are allowable when calculating the gain on the disposition to report on the income tax return for the year in which the disposition occurred.

34. For a certificate of compliance to be issued, the required payment on account of tax or security on the disposition or proposed disposition of property, as described in item 2(a) above, is a flat rate of 33 1/3% of the excess of the proceeds of disposition over the adjusted cost base of the property (i.e., 33 1/3% of the total capital gain). Form T2062 is the appropriate form to use to report these dispositions.

35. For a certificate of compliance to be issued under subsection 116(5.2), for either an actual or a proposed disposition, a payment on account of tax or security acceptable to the Minister must be provided. Refer to item 2(d) above for a description of the properties. The amount subject to a payment on account of tax from the disposition of the above types of property recognizes the fact that those amounts are fully included in income. Therefore, the non-resident federal tax rates must be used for individuals, and 38% for corporations, less

the Federal Tax Abatement, plus the 3% corporation surtax, if the income generated is from a business. The Federal Tax Abatement does not apply to the recapture of capital cost allowance resulting from a disposition when the income is from property.

36. Non-resident federal tax rates for individuals can be found in the current issue of the *General Tax Guide and Return for Non-Residents and Deemed Residents of Canada*. Tables A and B, or Schedule 1, "Detailed Tax Calculation," included in the guide package should be used. The rates in this guide include the federal surtax, which must be considered in determining the payment on account of tax. A copy of this guide can be obtained from any district office, or from the International Taxation Office.

37. The Department's policy is as follows regarding payments on account of tax or security for the disposition of depreciable taxable Canadian property, and any resulting capital gains and recapture or terminal loss of capital cost allowance:

  (a) when the correct amount subject to recapture of capital cost allowance can be determined, or if no capital cost allowance has ever been claimed, the required payment on account of tax is determined as follows:

    (i) 33 1/3% of the total capital gain on the land and building. The amount determined should be reported on Form T2062;

    (ii) the applicable individual or corporate non-resident federal tax rates, as referred to in items 35 and 36 above, must be applied to determine the payment on account of tax on the amount of recapture because this amount will be fully taxable when the vendor files a return of income for the year in which the disposition occurred. Recapture of capital cost allowance should be reported on Form T2062A.

  (b) When the amount of recapture of capital cost allowance or terminal loss cannot be determined at the time of disposition or proposed disposition, or an agreement of the amount for the purposes of the notice cannot be reached with the Department, the required payment on account of tax is determined as follows:

    (i) 33 1/3% of the total capital gain on the land and building. The amount determined should be reported on Form T2062;

    (ii) the non-resident federal tax rates should be applied on the estimated recapture based on the assumption that the full capital cost allowance was claimed from the time of purchase to the date of disposition. Every attempt should be made to resolve the matter before filing an income tax return for the year the disposition occurred. This procedure will attempt to ensure that a sufficient payment is provided to cover any amount subject to recapture. The final settlement of tax will be made when the return of income, for the year in which the disposition occurs, is assessed. Form T2062A should be used for the notification.

This procedure will only be used after all efforts to determine the correct amount subject to recapture of capital cost allowance have been exhausted, and it is imperative that the certificate of compliance be issued. Income tax returns for previous years should be made available to support the recapture reported or the terminal loss claimed.

38. As an alternative to immediate payment of the tax, we may accept security for the tax as an interim arrangement. In such a case, the vendor should contact the Chief of Collections at the district office concerned, to negotiate the security that the Department is prepared to accept.

Certificate of compliance
39. We will issue the certificate of compliance at the earliest possible date once we have received and validated the necessary information, and have received acceptable payment or security.

40. We will issue a copy of the certificate of compliance to both the vendor and the purchaser. The certificate protects both the vendor and the purchaser from any further tax liability in respect of the **particular notice** filed for that particular disposition.

41. We will issue a (Form T2064) certificate of compliance for a proposed disposition in accordance with subsection 116(2) of the Act if the conditions of subsection 116(1) are met, and the required payment on account of tax or acceptable security is provided.

42. We will issue a certificate of compliance (Form T2064 or Form T2068 for proposed or actual dispositions respectively) in accordance with subsection 116(5.2) of the Act, provided that the vendor has paid any required amount on account of tax, or provided acceptable security for the properties described in item 2(d) above.

Purchaser's liability

43. If the vendor does not comply with the requirements of subsections 116(2) and 116(4), the purchaser may become liable under subsection 116(5) to pay a specified amount of tax on behalf of the vendor. The purchaser is then entitled to withhold a specified amount of tax from the proceeds of disposition. The required amount must be remitted to the Receiver General 30 days after the end of the month in which the property was acquired.

The purchaser is liable, and is entitled to withhold and remit 33 1/3% for dispositions occurring after 1989 of either:

    (a) the cost of the property acquired by the purchaser; or

    (b) if a certificate has been issued, the amount by which the cost of the property acquired by the purchaser exceeds the certificate limit fixed by a proposed disposition.

Note: For dispositions occurring after April 27,1989 and before 1990, the rate is 30%.

Purchaser liability assessments are not subject to any time restrictions. Therefore, we may issue an assessment at any time we become aware that section 116 has not been adhered to.

44. The circumstances under which a purchaser may become liable are:

    (a) when we do not issue a certificate of compliance (Form T2064 or Form T2068) under either subsection 116(2) or 116(4) of the Act, for a proposed or actual disposition of taxable Canadian property; or

    (b) when we issue a certificate of compliance for a proposed disposition under subsection 116(2) of the Act, and the cost to the purchaser of the property is more than the amount specified in the certificate of compliance Form T2064 (the estimated proceeds of disposition), and the vendor did not notify the Department or did not comply with the requirements under subsections 116(3) and 116(4) of the Act. Refer to item 8 above.

45. Once we have issued a certificate of compliance under subsection 116(4) of the Act, the purchaser does not have to pay tax in respect of the particular disposition for which the particular certificate of compliance was issued.

46. For dispositions of properties described in item 2(d) above, the purchaser is entitled to withhold and remit, and may become liable under the provisions of subsection 116(5.3) of the Act to pay to the Department, on behalf of the

vendor, an amount equal to 50% of the amount by which the purchase price of the property exceeds the amount fixed in the certificate of compliance, if any, issued under subsection 116(5.2). The required amount must be sent to the Receiver General 30 days after the end of the month in which the property was acquired.

47. The purchaser's liability for tax under subsection 116(5) or 116(5.3) does not extend to a mortgagee who acquired a property by foreclosure, unless the transactions of mortgage and foreclosure were used as a device to sell the property. When the mortgagee is not liable under section 116 to pay tax, and we receive a request to do so, we will issue a letter to that effect.

48. If a mortgagee exercises a power of sale based on the terms of the mortgage rather than foreclosing, title to the property passes directly from the mortgagor to a third party purchaser. Thus the provisions of subsections 116(5) or (5.3) of the Act apply when a property is sold pursuant to a power of sale, and the vendor (mortgagee) must comply with section 116.

49. Any tax remittances payable by the purchaser are due within 30 days after the end of the month in which the property was acquired. The purchaser should give particulars of the transaction, identify the remittances, and specify that the payment concerned pertains to subsections 116(5) or 116(5.3) of the *Income Tax Act*. The full name and address of the vendor and the purchaser should be indicated.

50. Any purchaser who fails to remit or pay an amount required under subsections 116(5) or (5.3) may be assessed a penalty under the authority of subsection 227(10.1), calculated under the provisions of subsection 227(9). Subsection 227(9) provides for a penalty of 10% of the amount required for the first failure and a 20% penalty for second and subsequent failures. Subsection 227(9.3) provides for the levying of interest on the payment or remittance required by subsections 116(5) or (5.3).

51. For penalty and interest in respect of the 1985 and following taxation years, the Minister has the discretion to waive or cancel all or any portion of any penalty or interest if it is found that the penalty or interest resulted from circumstances beyond the control of the purchaser.

52. The purchaser incurs no obligation to pay tax if, after reasonable inquiry, there was no reason to believe the vendor was a non-resident of Canada. There is a question as to what constitutes "reasonable inquiry." Our position is that

the purchaser must take prudent measures to confirm the vendor's residence status. We will review each case on an individual basis whenever a purchaser assessment is being considered. The purchaser may become liable if, for any reason, we believe the purchaser could have or should have known that the vendor was a non-resident. We will not make inquiries on behalf of a purchaser in this regard.

Filing a tax return — Refund of excess payment
53. The final settlement of tax on the disposition of properties is made when the vendor's income tax return is assessed. The return should be filed for the taxation year in which the disposition took place. After the return is filed, any excess payment is refunded or provision is made for the release of security once the established debt has been satisfied.

54. For individuals, the income tax return is due on April 30 of the year following the year in which the disposition occurred. For corporations, the return is due six months after the end of the taxation year in which the disposition took place. Trust returns are due 90 days after the end of the trust's taxation year in which the disposition took place. Returns that are filed late are subject to interest and applicable penalties. Copies of the income tax returns and the related guides can be obtained from any district office. Individuals should request the income tax return for "non-residents and deemed residents."

55. These returns must be filed at the:
    International Taxation Office
    875 Heron Road
    Ottawa, Canada
    K1A 1A8

Any questions concerning the assessment of the return should also be sent to this address.

56. Delays in processing a vendor's income tax return occur for many reasons. However, if the proper information is provided at the time of filing, the return will be processed as quickly as possible.

Vendors should ensure that:
    (a) the information area is completed in detail,
    (b) their Canadian social insurance number, corporate account number or non-resident account number is entered as requested;

(c) the tear-off information slip attached to the certificate of compliance should be enclosed. This information slip is invaluable in tracing payments, security or exemptions in respect of the disposition. This is particularly important for non-residents who do not have the identification in (ii) above; and

(d) if, for any reason, circumstances have changed and the amount reported on the vendor's income tax return differs substantially from the amount reported for the disposition, a note should be attached to the income tax return along with the appropriate documentation. This will greatly reduce any delays.

57. For the 1985 and following years, the Minister has the discretion to assess the individual returns and testamentary trust returns that are filed more than three years after the end of the taxation year in which the disposition occurred in order to issue refunds or to reduce taxes payable. This discretion may be exercised where the request is in writing and the Minister is satisfied that the refund would have been issued or tax payable reduced had the returns been filed on time.

Misallocated or lost payments
58. We make every effort to ensure that a payment made for a section 116 disposition is matched to the income tax return filed. Since many non-residents do not have account numbers, this is often difficult. If vendors follow the instructions for filing income tax returns in items 53 to 57 above, this problem will be alleviated.

59. If vendors are not credited with the proper amount, they should contact:
Non-Resident Correspondence
T1 Revenue Accounting
International Taxation Office
Ottawa, Canada
K1A 1A8

Vendors should also provide the following information:
(a) a brief description of the disposition;
(b) the date of the payment;
(c) the district office that processed the notice; and
(d) a photocopy of the front and back of the cancelled cheque. This is most important

60. Multiple-member partnerships are particularly subject to misallocation of a single payment made on behalf of the many partners. We will issue one certificate of compliance with a list of all non-resident partners, their addresses as provided, their Canadian social insurance numbers, corporate account numbers, or non-resident account numbers, and if no account identification is available, we will provide a number in the S/L XXXXXXX format. It is imperative that each member of the partnership receive the relevant information to ensure the efficient processing of his or her income tax returns. It is important to note that the assignment of the S/L number is temporary until such time as the applicable return is assessed. All assessed returns are assigned an account number that should be used in all future dealings with the Department. For more information concerning partnerships refer to item 10 above.

General comments
61. Section 116 does not apply to a deemed disposition on death under subsection 70(5). However, the executor acting on behalf of a non-resident decedent must file an income tax return for the year of death, and pay any tax that may be necessary on the deemed disposition.

62. Section 116 does not apply to property that is transferred or distributed on or after death and as a consequence thereof.

63. If compensation is received for damages to property, consideration must be given as to whether any part of the compensation involves a transfer of title or an interest therein to which section 116 would apply. It is unlikely that a transfer of title or an interest therein has taken place when compensation has been paid to the owner of real estate for damages claimed in a tort action. However, when such a payment is made according to a contractual arrangement between the parties, the terms of the contract should be examined to determine whether title or an interest in the real property has been received in exchange for the compensation.

64. Our position regarding amalgamations and section 116 of the Act is discussed in the relevant paragraph of Interpretation Bulletin IT-474R. This bulletin states that the section 116 procedures do not have to be complied with for the deemed disposition of shares on an amalgamation to which subsection 87(4) of the Act applies.

65. Sections 116 and 212(2) both apply to levy a withholding tax in those cases when a non-resident disposes of shares of a Canadian corporation in a

non-arm's length transaction. The amount subject to withholding tax under subsection 212(2) is calculated in accordance with section 212.1. To eliminate double taxation, the Department will accept a calculation of proceeds of disposition of the shares, for purposes of section 116, which includes a reduction for the section 212.1 deemed dividend.

Vendors should submit a letter of explanation and a copy of the section 212.1 calculation along with Form T2062, when requesting a certificate of compliance in these cases.

66. Under the Doctrine of Sovereign Immunity, the Government of Canada may grant exemption from tax on certain Canadian-source investment income paid or credited to the government of a foreign country. Capital gains on the disposition of taxable Canadian property may be eligible for this exemption, subject to the conditions described in the relevant paragraph of Information Circular 77-16R3. When the vendor of taxable Canadian property is a foreign government, we may give the purchaser, upon request, written authorization not to pay tax in accordance with subsection 116(5) as long as we have substantiated that the property is, in fact, whollyowned by that government. The request should be sent to:

> Revenue Canada, Taxation
> 875 Heron Road
> Ottawa, Ontario
> K1A OL8

> Attention: Provincial and International Relations Division

67. The disposition of mineral rights in Canada is considered to be a disposition of a Canadian resource property, and as such, is subject to the requirements of subsection 116(5.2). In the case of a delay rental agreement, the bonus portion (bonus consideration) is subject to the provisions of subsection 116(5.2). The annual delay rental is subject to withholding tax under paragraph 212(1)(d) of the Act.

68. The disposition of a principal residence by a non-resident owner may be exempt from tax by virtue of paragraphs 40(2)(b) or (c) of the Act. When the gain on a principal residence is either partially or entirely exempt by these paragraphs, the non-resident should submit a Notice of Disposition (Form T2062) with a letter attached outlining the calculation of the expected amount of any capital gain on the disposition. A payment or security must be provided for the non-exempt portion before we can issue the certificate of compliance

indicating the "principal residence exemption (amount) and principal residence non-exempt portion (amount)." If the entire gain is exempt, we will issue a certificate of compliance indicating "principal residence - exempt."

69. Section 115.1 allows a non-resident person or partnership (vendor) and a purchaser to jointly elect, subject to the Minister's approval, to defer taxation of a gain or income according to a prescribed tax treaty, by filing the prescribed election T2024 form. These dispositions may also be subject to the provisions of section 116. In these instances, the T2024 form should be filed along with the applicable Notice of Disposition Form T2062, Form T2062A, or both, at the district office serving the area where the property is located. The requirement for security or payment on account of tax may be waived when a non-resident's request for relief under a treaty provision has been accepted by the Canadian competent authority.

Interpretation Bulletin IT-120R4

Subject: *Income Tax Act*
              Principal Residence

Date: March 26, 1993

Reference: Subsection 40(2) and paragraph 54(g) (also sections 45, 54.1,
              110.6, 116 and 216, subsections 13(7), 40(4), 40(5), 40(6), 40(7),
              70(6), 73(1), 107(2), 107(2.01), 107(4) and 252(1) and paragraph
              104(4)(a) of the Act and Part XXIII of the Regulations)

Application
This bulletin replaces and cancels Interpretation Bulletin IT-120R3 dated
February 16, 1984. Current revisions are indicated by vertical lines.

Summary
This bulletin discusses the principal residence exemption which eliminates or
reduces for income tax purposes a gain on the disposition of a principal
residence. In order to qualify for designation as a taxpayer's principal residence
for a taxation year, the property must be owned by the taxpayer. Joint
ownership with another person qualifies for this purpose. The residence
generally must be inhabited in the year by the taxpayer or certain family
members. For taxation years after the 1981 year, only one property per family
unit can be designated as a principal residence.

If the land on which a housing unit is situated is not in excess of 1/2 hectare, it
usually qualifies as part of a principal residence. In some cases, land in excess
of 1/2 hectare may qualify, if established to be necessary for the use and
enjoyment of the housing unit as a residence.

A principal residence may be located on farm land. The taxpayer has a choice
of two methods for determining what portion of a gain realized on a disposition
of a farm property can be eliminated by the principal residence exemption.

A complete or partial change in the use of a property from principal residence
to income-producing, or vice-versa, results in a deemed disposition at fair
market value. A taxpayer may be able to elect that the deemed disposition on a
complete change in use does not apply. A property covered by such an election
can qualify as a principal residence for up to 4 years, or possibly longer in the
case of a work relocation.

The above topics are discussed more fully below, as well as other topics relating to the principal residence exemption.

Discussion and Interpretation
Topics Discussed and Their Applicability
1. Various topics concerning the principal residence exemption are discussed under the headings listed below. *It should be noted from these headings that some of the topics are not relevant for all taxpayers. For example, a resident of Canada who owns only one housing unit which is situated in Canada on land of 1/2 hectare or less and which has been used since its acquisition strictly as his or her residence, will usually find that 20 to 45 below have no particular relevance.*

Qualification as a Principal Residence

2. In order for a property to qualify as a taxpayer's principal residence for any particular taxation year, the requirements in paragraph 54(g) of the Income Tax Act must all be satisfied. The basic requirements are described in 3 to 6 below.

3. A housing unit or leasehold interest in a housing unit can qualify as a principal residence. Also, a share of the capital stock of a co-operative housing corporation, if acquired for the sole purpose of obtaining the right to inhabit a housing unit owned by that corporation, can qualify.

4. The property must be owned in the taxation year by the taxpayer. The meaning of "ownership of property" for this purpose is discussed in the current version of IT-437. The taxpayer's ownership of the property qualifies under paragraph 54(g) whether such ownership is "jointly with another person or otherwise". These words include sole ownership, joint tenancy, tenancy-in-common and co-ownership.

5. The housing unit must be ordinarily inhabited in the taxation year by the taxpayer or by the spouse, former spouse or a child of the taxpayer. Alternatively, an election under subsection 45(2) or (3) must be in force for the year (see 32 and 35 below, respectively).

6. The property must be designated by the taxpayer as his or her principal residence for the taxation year and no other property may have been so designated by the taxpayer for that year. Furthermore, where the taxpayer is designating the property as his or her principal residence for a taxation year that is subsequent to the 1981 year, no other property may have been designated as the principal residence of any member of the taxpayer's family unit for that year. For this purpose, the "family unit" includes, in addition to the taxpayer:
- (a) the taxpayer's spouse throughout the year, unless the spouse was throughout the year living apart from, and was separated pursuant to a judicial separation or written agreement from, the taxpayer;
- (b) the taxpayer's children, except those who were married persons or 18 years of age or older during the year; and

(c) where the taxpayer was neither a married person nor 18 years of age or older during the year, the taxpayer's mother and father, as well as the taxpayer's brothers and sisters who were neither married persons nor 18 years of age or older during the year.

7. A property transferred by a taxpayer (transferor) to his or her spouse or to a spousal trust under the rollover provisions of subsection 70(6) (for a transfer on death) or subsection 73(1) (for an inter vivos transfer) may qualify as a principal residence of the spouse or spousal trust for taxation years ending after the transfer, as well as for taxation years prior to the transfer in which the property qualified as a principal residence of the transferor. For a discussion on this topic see the current version of IT-366.

Note: If proposed amendments to the Income Tax Act contained in Bill C-92 (which received first reading by the House of Commons on November 26, 1992) are enacted, a property could qualify as a principal residence of any trust, and not just a spousal trust, for the years in which the property was owned by the trust, provided certain conditions have been met. This change in the law would apply for property dispositions occurring after 1990. For more information, see Form T2091.

Meaning of "Housing Unit"
8. The term "housing unit" includes a house, an apartment in a duplex, apartment building or condominium, a cottage, a mobile home, a trailer or a houseboat.

Meaning of "Co-operative Housing Corporation"
9. The term "co-operative housing corporation" means an association, incorporated subject to the terms and conditions of the legislation governing such incorporation and formed and operated for the purpose of providing its members with the right to inhabit, by reason of ownership of shares therein, a housing unit owned by the corporation. To qualify as a principal residence, a share in such a corporation must have been acquired by a taxpayer solely to obtain the right to inhabit a housing unit owned by the corporation.

Ownership of a Property by Spouses
10. Where there is a gain on the disposition of a property owned by a taxpayer and his or her spouse in one of the forms of ownership described in 4 above, both spouses will have a gain on the disposition. If one of the spouses designates the property as his or her principal residence for any taxation year after the 1981 taxation year, the other spouse should consider so designating

the same property because, in accordance with the rule described in 6 above, no other property can be designated as a principal residence of that other spouse for that year. For the 1981 and prior taxation years, there was no such restriction and one of the spouses could designate a property (or an interest therein) owned by that spouse while the other spouse could designate another property (or an interest therein) owned by that other spouse.

Partnership Property

11. A housing unit, a leasehold interest therein, or a share of the capital stock of a co-operative housing corporation can be a partnership asset. The partnership is not a taxpayer and cannot use the principal residence exemption on the disposition of such a property. However, a member of the partnership could use the principal residence exemption to reduce or eliminate the portion of any gain on the disposition of the property which is allocated to that partner pursuant to the partnership agreement, provided that the other requirements of paragraph 54(g) are met (e.g., the partner resided in the partnership's housing unit for the years in question).

Meaning of "Ordinarily Inhabited"

12. The question of whether a housing unit is "ordinarily inhabited" in a taxation year by a taxpayer or by the spouse, former spouse or a child of the taxpayer must be resolved on the basis of the facts in each particular case. Where a housing unit is occupied by such a person for only a short period of time in the year (e.g., a seasonal residence occupied during a taxpayer's vacation or a house sold early or bought late in the year), it is the Department's view that the person ordinarily inhabits the housing unit in the year, provided that the principal reason for owning the property is not for the purpose of gaining or producing income. Where a taxpayer receives incidental rental income from a seasonal residence, the property is not considered to be owned principally for the purpose of gaining or producing income.

Designation of a Property as a Principal Residence (Form T2091)

13. Section 2301 of the Regulations provides that any designation of a property as a principal residence for one or more taxation years shall be made in the taxpayer's income tax return for the taxation year in which he or she has disposed of the property or granted an option to another person to acquire the property. Form T2091, which is available at any local taxation office, may be used for this purpose. However, in accordance with the Department's practice, Form T2091 need not be completed and filed with the taxpayer's income tax return unless a taxable capital gain on the disposition of the property remains after using the principal residence exemption **but before claiming any capital**

gains deduction under section 110.6 (see note below regarding a proposed amendment to the capital gains deduction rules). Note that where a taxpayer using the principal residence exemption to eliminate a gain on the disposition of a property is not, in accordance with the above-mentioned practice, required to complete and file Form T2091, a designation of such property is still considered to have been made by the taxpayer for the years in question as far as the limitations discussed in 6 above are concerned. Also note that where a property is transferred by a taxpayer (transferor) to his or her spouse or to a spousal trust, a designation of the property as the principal residence of the transferor for one or more years may be relevant in order for the property to qualify for designation at a later date as the principal residence of the spouse or spousal trust for those same years. Further particulars on the transfer of a principal residence to a spouse or spousal trust, including comments on the manner and timing of filing these designations, are contained in the current version of IT-366.

Note: If proposed amendments to the Income Tax Act contained in Bill C-92 (which received first reading by the House of Commons on November 26, 1992) are enacted, the capital gains deduction (which is a deduction in calculating taxable income) would generally not be available for any portion of a taxable capital gain on the disposition of real property that is attributable to the period after February 1992. Any portion of the taxable capital gain that is attributable to the period before March 1992 would still be eligible for the capital gains deduction to the extent allowed by section 110.6. (The calculation of the portion of the gain attributable to each of these two periods would be by means of a simple proration based on the number of months in each period.)

Calculation of Gain on Disposition of a Principal Residence — The Principal Residence Exemption

14. The principal residence exemption contained in paragraph 40(2)(b) provides that a taxpayer's gain otherwise determined on the disposition (or deemed disposition) of any property that was the taxpayer's principal residence at any time after its acquisition date, is reduced by the portion of that gain which is calculated under the following formula:

$$\underline{A} \times C$$
$$B$$

where

A is 1 + the number of taxation years ending after the acquisition date for which the property was the taxpayer's principal residence and during which the taxpayer was resident in Canada,

B is the number of taxation years ending after the acquisition date during which the taxpayer owned the property, and

C is the gain otherwise determined on the disposition.

The "acquisition date" is defined to be the later of December 31, 1971 and the date on which the taxpayer last acquired or reacquired the property or is deemed to have last acquired or reacquired it. For the meaning of "resident in Canada", see the current version of IT-221. The word "during" in reference to a taxation year means "at any time in" rather than "throughout the whole of" the taxation year.

More Than One Residence in a Taxation Year

15. While only one property may be designated under paragraph 54(g) as a taxpayer's principal residence for a particular taxation year, the formula in paragraph 40(2)(b) recognizes that the taxpayer can have two residences in the same year, i.e., where one residence is sold and another acquired in the same year. The effect of the "one plus" in the formula above is to treat both properties as a principal residence in such a year, even though only one of them may be designated as such for that year.

Construction of a Housing Unit on Vacant Land

16. Where a taxpayer acquires land in one taxation year and constructs a housing unit on it in a subsequent year, the property may not be designated as a principal residence for the years that are prior to the year in which the taxpayer, his spouse, former spouse or child commences to ordinarily inhabit the housing unit. Such prior years (when the taxpayer owned only the vacant land or the land with a housing unit under construction) would not be included in the numerator "A" in the formula in 14 above. However, all years, commencing with the year in which the taxpayer acquired the vacant land, would be included in the denominator "B". Therefore, it is possible that when the property is later disposed of, only part of the gain otherwise determined will be eliminated by the principal residence exemption.

Example

A taxpayer acquired vacant land for $25,000 in 1983, constructed a housing unit on it costing $75,000 and started to ordinarily inhabit the housing unit in 1986, and disposed of the property for $150,000 in 1992. The principal residence exemption would reduce the $50,000 gain otherwise determined ($150,000 — $100,000) by only $40,000, computed as follows:

$$\frac{1 + 7 \ (1986 \ to \ 1992)}{10 \ (1983 \ to \ 1992)} \times \$50,000 = \$40,000 \ exempt \ portion \ of \ gain.$$

Property Owned on December 31, 1981
17. A taxpayer is allowed to designate a property as his or her principal residence for any taxation year prior to the 1982 year even if another property has been designated as the principal residence of another member of the family unit for that year. However, as indicated in 6 above, a taxpayer may not designate a property as his or her principal residence for any taxation year after the 1981 year if another property has been designated as the principal residence of any other member of the family unit for that year. Where a taxpayer disposes of a property which he or she has owned (whether jointly with another person or otherwise) continuously since before 1982 and the property cannot be designated as the taxpayer's principal residence for one or more years after the 1981 year because of the above-mentioned rule, a transitional provision in subsection 40(6) places a limitation on the amount of gain (if any) on the disposition. Schedule A at the end of this bulletin provides examples which illustrate how the rule in subsection 40(6) works.

Property Acquired from a Trust
18. Where
- a personal trust has distributed a property to a beneficiary in satisfaction of all or any part of the beneficiary's capital interest in the trust in circumstances to which the rollover provision in subsection 107(2) applies and subsection 107(4) (see below) does not apply, and
- the beneficiary later disposes of the property, for purposes of claiming the principal residence exemption, the beneficiary is deemed by subsection 40(7) to have owned the property since the trust last acquired it. The following illustrates the effect of this deemed ownership provision in subsection 40(7).

Example

A trust acquired a residential property on October 1, 1986 for $75,000. On August 10, 1989, the property was distributed to Mr. X in satisfaction of his capital interest in the trust. Under the provisions of subsection 107(2),

Mr. X was deemed to have acquired the property on a rollover basis at a cost equal to its $75,000 cost amount to the trust. Mr. X lived in the residence from October 15, 1986 until he disposed of the property on May 30, 1992 for $125,000, incurring no costs in connection with the disposition. Subsection 40(7) deems him to have owned the property from October 1, 1986 rather than from August 10, 1989. His gain on the disposition of the property after using the principal residence exemption is nil. That is, the $50,000 gain otherwise determined is fully eliminated by the amount calculated under the formula in 14 above, which is as follows:

$$\underline{A} \times C = \underline{1 + 7\ (1986\ to\ 1992)} \times \$50,000.$$
$$B \qquad\quad 7\ (1986\ to\ 1992)$$

Mr. X's gain is nil because the property has qualified for and been designated as his principal residence for all of the relevant years. However, if neither Mr. X nor his spouse, former spouse or child had ordinarily inhabited the residence until it was distributed by the trust to Mr. X on August 10, 1989, then the gain after using the principal residence exemption would be $14,286, since the $50,000 gain otherwise determined would be reduced by only $35,714, calculated as follows:

$$\underline{A} \times C = \underline{1 + 4\ (1989\ to\ 1992)} \times \$50,000.$$
$$B \qquad\quad 7\ (1986\ to\ 1992)$$

A spousal trust may generally be described as an inter vivos or testamentary trust created by a taxpayer under which the taxpayer's spouse is entitled to receive all the trust's income arising before the spouse's death and no one else may receive or use any of the trust's income or capital before the spouse's death. Since a spousal trust is a type of personal trust, the subsection 107(2) rollover provision and subsection 40(7) deemed ownership provision, as described and illustrated above, both generally apply where the spousal trust distributes a property to the spouse who is the beneficiary of the trust. There are exceptions, however, to these general rules:

(a) The subsection 40(7) deemed ownership provision does not apply where a post-1971 spousal trust distributes a property to a person other than the spouse and subsection 107(4) prevents a subsection 107(2) rollover from occurring. The precise meaning of what is referred to above as a "post-1971" spousal trust is contained in paragraph 104(4)(a).

Note: There are some proposed amendments to subsection 107(4) and paragraph 104(4)(a) contained in Bill C-92, which received first reading by the House of Commons on November 26, 1992.

(b) Where a spousal trust has distributed a property to the spouse who is its beneficiary in circumstances to which subsection 107(2) applies, if the property qualifies as its principal residence (see 7 above and the current version of IT-366) for a taxation year, the spousal trust can instead make an election under subsection 107(2.01). Under this election the trust would be deemed, just before the distribution to the spouse, to have disposed of and reacquired the property at fair market value. This could be done, for example, in order for the spousal trust to use the principal residence exemption to eliminate or reduce the gain on the property to that point in time. The cost of the property to the spouse (beneficiary) would be that same fair market value, and he or she would not be deemed by subsection 40(7) to have owned the property during the period of time in which it was held by the trust prior to the distribution.

Note: If proposed amendments to the Income Tax Act contained in Bill C-92 (which received first reading by the House of Commons on November 26, 1992) are enacted, the subsection 107(2.01) election would be available to any personal trust and not just a spousal trust. This change, which would be as a consequence of the general extension of the principal residence exemption to all personal trusts as mentioned in the note at the end of 7 above, would have application for trust distributions occurring after 1990. For more information, see the T3 Guide and Trust Return.

Loss on Disposition of a Residence

19. A property which is used primarily as a residence, i.e., for the personal use and enjoyment of those living in it, or an option to acquire a property which would, if acquired, be so used, is "personal-use property". Therefore, a loss on the disposition of such a property or option is deemed to be nil by virtue of subparagraph 40(2)(g)(iii).

Land Contributing to the Use and Enjoyment of the Housing Unit as a Residence

20. Subparagraph 54(g)(v) provides that the principal residence of a taxpayer for a taxation year shall be deemed to include, except where the property consists of a share of the capital stock of a co-operative housing corporation, the land upon which the housing unit stands and any portion of the adjoining land that can reasonably be regarded as contributing to the taxpayer's use and

enjoyment of the housing unit as a residence. Evidence is not usually required to establish that 1/2 hectare of land or less, including the area on which the housing unit stands, contributes to the taxpayer's use and enjoyment of the housing unit as a residence. However, where a portion of that land is used to earn income from business or property, such portion will not usually be considered to contribute to such use and enjoyment. Where a taxpayer claims a portion of the expenses related to the land (such as property taxes or mortgage interest) in computing income, the allocation of such expenses for this purpose is normally an indication of the extent to which the taxpayer considers the land to be used to earn income.

Land in Excess of 1/2 Hectare
21. Where the total area of the land upon which a housing unit is situated exceeds 1/2 hectare, the excess land is deemed by subparagraph 54(g)(v) not to have contributed to the use and enjoyment of the housing unit as a residence and thus will not qualify as part of a principal residence, except to the extent that the taxpayer establishes that it was necessary for such use and enjoyment. The excess land must clearly be necessary for the housing unit to properly fulfil its function as a residence and not simply be desirable. Land in excess of 1/2 hectare could be so necessary where the size or character of a housing unit together with its location on the lot make such excess land essential to its use and enjoyment as a residence or where the location of a housing unit requires such excess land in order to provide the taxpayer with access to and from public roads. Other factors which may in some cases be relevant in determining whether land in excess of 1/2 hectare is necessary for the use and enjoyment of the housing unit as a residence are severence or subdivision restrictions and minimum lot sizes (see 22 below). In all cases, however, it is a question of fact as to how much, if any, of the excess land is necessary for the use and enjoyment of the housing unit as a residence.

22. A property used for residential purposes may be affected by a law or regulation of a municipality or province requiring a minimum lot size for a residential site. A legally imposed minimum lot size, for residential use, exceeding 1/2 hectare that was in effect on the date the property was acquired by the taxpayer, is generally considered to be the minimum amount of land necessary for the use and enjoyment of the housing unit as a residence throughout the period that the property is continuously owned by the taxpayer after that acquisition date. However, where a portion of the minimum lot size is not used for residential purposes but rather for income-producing purposes, such portion is usually not considered to be necessary for the use and enjoyment of the housing unit as a residence.

Disposition of Bare Land in Excess of 1/2 Hectare

23. Where a taxpayer's housing unit is situated on land in excess of 1/2 hectare and part or all of that excess land is severed from the property and sold, the land sold is generally considered not to be part of the principal residence unless the housing unit can no longer be used as a residence due to the land sale. If the housing unit can still be so used, such a sale indicates that the land sold was not necessary for the use and enjoyment of the housing unit as a residence. However, where circumstances or events beyond the taxpayer's control cause a portion of the land to cease to be necessary for the use and enjoyment of the housing unit as a residence (e.g., a minimum lot size requirement in effect at the date of acquisition is subsequently relaxed) and the taxpayer then sells such unnecessary excess land, the Department considers it to have been "necessary" until the time of its sale.

Disposition of Part of a Principal Residence

24. Where only a portion of a property qualifying as a taxpayer's principal residence is disposed of, such as in the type of situation described in the last sentence of 23 above or as a result of the granting of an easement or the expropriation of land, the taxpayer may designate the property as his or her principal residence in order to use the principal residence exemption for the portion of the property disposed of. It is important to note that such a designation is made on the entire property (including the housing unit) that qualifies as the principal residence and not just on the portion of the property disposed of. Accordingly, when the remainder of the property is subsequently disposed of, it too will be recognized as the taxpayer's principal residence for the taxation years for which the above-mentioned designation was made. No other property may be designated by the taxpayer (or, after the 1981 taxation year, by any of the other persons in the family unit as described in 6 above) as a principal residence for those years.

Disposition of a Property Where Only Part of It Qualifies as a Principal Residence

25. In some cases, only a portion of a property that is disposed of for a gain will qualify as a principal residence (see 20 to 22 above). If the taxpayer designates such qualifying portion of the property as his or her principal residence, it will be necessary to calculate the gain on it separately from the gain on the remaining portion of the property which does not qualify as a principal residence. This is because the gain on the portion of the property designated as the principal residence may be reduced or eliminated by the principal residence exemption, whereas the gain on the remaining portion of the property results in

a taxable capital gain (for which a capital gains deduction may be available under section 110.6; see, however, the note at the end of 13 above). In allocating the proceeds of disposition and adjusted cost base of the total property between the two portions, consideration must be given to any kind of restriction on the severability of any part of the property, including the portion that does not qualify as the principal residence, imposed by a law or regulation of a province or municipality and in effect at the date of disposition or at the date of acquisition.

Example

A property with a residence on it has a total area of fifteen hectares consisting mostly of scrub land. At all relevant times the legally imposed minimum lot size for a residential property in the area is ten hectares and thus the land considered to be necessary for the use and enjoyment of this particular housing unit as a residence is ten hectares. However, the portion of the total value of the property, as of the dates of purchase and sale, attributed to the excess five hectares would be relatively low because such excess land would have no intrinsic value of its own and could never have been severed and sold separately.

The comments in this paragraph do not apply if the property includes land used in a farming business (see instead 26 to 29 below).

Principal Residence on Land Used in a Farming Business
26. Where the taxpayer is an individual who disposes of land used in a farming business carried on by him or her at any time and such land includes property that was at any time the taxpayer's principal residence, paragraph 40(2)(c) provides that any gain on the disposition of the land may be calculated using either one of two methods described in the following paragraphs.

27. *First Method*: The taxpayer may regard the land as being divided into two portions: the principal residence portion and the remaining portion, part or all of which was used in the farming business. The proceeds of disposition and adjusted cost base of the total land must be allocated on a reasonable basis between the two portions in order to determine the gain for each. The gain otherwise determined for the principal residence portion may be reduced or eliminated by the principal residence exemption (based on the formula in 14 above), whereas the gain on the remainder of the land results in a taxable capital gain (see, however, 30 below). For purposes of determining what portion of the proceeds of disposition of the total land may reasonably be

allocated to the principal residence, the Department's usual practice is to accept
the **greater of**

    (a) the fair market value, as of the date of disposition of the land, of 1/2
          hectare of land estimated on the basis of comparable sales of similar
          farm properties in the same area (the fair market value of more than
          1/2 hectare could be used to the extent that such excess land was
          necessary for the use and enjoyment of the housing unit as a residence
          — see 21 and 22 above), and

    (b) the fair market value, as of the date of disposition of the land, of a
          typical residential building site in the same area.

Whichever basis is chosen, (a) or (b), for allocating a portion of the proceeds of
disposition of the total land to the principal residence, the same basis should be
used to allocate a portion of the adjusted cost base of the total land to the
principal residence (in this case the fair market value used in (a) or (b) above
would be as of the date of the acquisition of the land). Schedule B at the end of
this bulletin provides an example which illustrates the use of the first method
(please note that although the first method provided for in paragraph 40(2)(c)
pertains only to the land, values for the residential and farm buildings are also
included in this example).

28. *Second Method*: The taxpayer may elect under subparagraph 40(2)(c)(ii) to
compute the gain on the disposition of the total land (including the property
that was the principal residence) without making the allocations described
above or using the principal residence exemption formula in 14 above. With
regard to this election, section 2300 of the Regulations requires that a letter
signed by the taxpayer be attached to the income tax return filed for the
taxation year in which the disposition of the land took place. The letter should
contain the following information:

    (a) a statement that the taxpayer is electing under subparagraph
          40(2)(c)(ii) of the Income Tax Act;

    (b) a statement of the number of taxation years ending after the
          acquisition date for which the property was the taxpayer's principal
          residence and during which the taxpayer was resident in Canada (for
          the meanings of "acquisition date", "resident in Canada" and
          "during", see 14 above); and

    (c) a description of the property sufficient to identify it with the property
          designated as the taxpayer's principal residence.

Under this election, the gain otherwise determined for the total land is
decreased by the total of $1,000 plus $1,000 for each taxation year in (b) above.
Schedule B at the end of this bulletin provides an example which illustrates the
use of the second method (please note that although the second method

provided for in paragraph 40(2)(c) pertains only to the land, values for the residential and farm buildings are also included in this example).

29. When the second method is used, the exemption of $1,000 per year, which is to allow for the fact that a portion of the total land pertains to the principal residence rather than the farm, is not reduced where part of the residence itself is used to earn income (e.g., there could be an office in the house which is used in connection with a business). However, any gain or capital cost allowance recapture pertaining to the portion of the residence so used to earn income (either or both of which can occur, for example, where the use of such portion of the residence is changed back from income-producing to non-income-producing — see 36 and 40 below) cannot be reduced by the $1,000 per year exemption.

30. Where an individual has a taxable capital gain from the disposition of a farm property, a section 110.6 capital gains deduction (which is a deduction in calculating taxable income) may usually be claimed. Further particulars on this topic are contained in the chapter on Capital Gains in the Farming Income Tax Guide.

Complete Change in Use from Principal Residence to Income-Producing
31. When a taxpayer has completely converted a principal residence to an income-producing use, he or she is deemed by paragraph 45(1)(a) to have disposed of the property (both land and building) at fair market value ("FMV") and reacquired it immediately thereafter at the same amount. Any gain otherwise determined on this deemed disposition may be eliminated or reduced by the principal residence exemption. The taxpayer may instead, however, defer recognition of any gain to a later year by electing under subsection 45(2) to be deemed not to have made the change in use of the property. This election is made by means of a letter to that effect signed by the taxpayer and filed with the income tax return for the year in which the change in use occurred. If the election is rescinded in a subsequent taxation year, there is a deemed disposition and reacquisition at FMV (with the above-mentioned tax consequences) on the first day of that subsequent year. If capital cost allowance ("CCA") is claimed on the property, the election is considered to be rescinded on the first day of the year in which that claim is made. It is the Department's usual practice to accept a late-filed election provided that no CCA has been claimed on the property since the change in use has occurred and during the period in which the election remains in force.

32. A property can qualify under paragraph 54(g) as a taxpayer's principal residence for up to four taxation years during which a subsection 45(2) election remains in force, even if the housing unit is not ordinarily inhabited during those years by the taxpayer or by the spouse, former spouse or a child of the taxpayer. However, the taxpayer must be resident, or deemed to be resident, in Canada during those years for the full benefit of the principal residence exemption to apply (see the numerator "A" in the formula in 14 above). It should also be noted that the rule described in 6 above prevents the designation for any particular year of more than one property by the taxpayer or, after 1981, any other member of the family unit. Thus, a designation for the same year of one property by virtue of a subsection 45(2) election being in force and another property by virtue of the taxpayer ordinarily inhabiting it would not be permitted.

Example

Mr. A and his family lived in a house for a number of years until September 30, 1985. From October 1, 1985 until March 31, 1990 they lived elsewhere and Mr. A rented the house to a third party. On April 1, 1990 they moved back into the house and lived in it until it was sold in 1992. Mr. A designates the house as his principal residence for the 1986 to 1989 taxation years inclusive by virtue of the subsection 45(2) election, which he filed with his 1985 income tax return, having been in force for those years. (He is able to make this designation because no other property has been designated by him or a member of his family unit for those years.) He designates the house as his principal residence for all the other years in which he owned it by virtue of his having ordinarily inhabited it during those years, including the 1985 and 1990 years. Having been resident in Canada at all times, Mr. A's gain on the disposition of the house is therefore completely eliminated by the principal residence exemption.

Any income in respect of a property (e.g., the rental income in the above example), net of applicable expenses, must be reported for tax purposes. However, for taxation years covered by a subsection 45(2) election, CCA should not be claimed on the property (see 31 above).

33. Section 54.1 removes the above-mentioned four-year limitation for taxation years covered by a subsection 45(2) election if all of the following conditions are met:

(a) the taxpayer does not ordinarily inhabit the housing unit during the years covered by the election because the taxpayer's or spouse's place of employment has been relocated,

(b) the employer is not related to the taxpayer or spouse,

(c) the housing unit is at least 40 kilometres farther from such new place of employment than is the taxpayer's subsequent place or places of residence, and

(d) the taxpayer resumes ordinary habitation of the housing unit during the term of such employment by such employer or before the end of the taxation year immediately following the taxation year in which such employment terminates, or the taxpayer dies during the term of such employment.

Two corporations that are members of the same corporate group, or are otherwise related, are not considered to be the "same employer".

Complete Change in Use from Income-Producing to Principal Residence

34. When a taxpayer has completely changed the use of a property (for which an election under subsection 45(2) is not in force) from income-producing to a principal residence, he or she is deemed by paragraph 45(1)(a) to have disposed of the property (both land and building), and immediately thereafter reacquired it, at FMV. This deemed disposition can result in a taxable capital gain (for which a section 110.6 capital gains deduction may be available; see, however, the note at the end of 13 above). The taxpayer may instead defer recognition of the gain to a later year by electing under subsection 45(3) that the above-mentioned deemed disposition and reacquisition under paragraph 45(1)(a) does not apply. This election is made by means of a letter to that effect signed by the taxpayer and filed with the income tax return for the year in which the property is ultimately disposed of or earlier if a formal "demand" for the election is issued by the Department.

35. Similar to the treatment for a subsection 45(2) election (see 32 above), a property can qualify as a taxpayer's principal residence for up to four taxation years covered by a subsection 45(3) election (such years would in this case be prior to the change in use), in lieu of fulfilling the "ordinarily inhabited" requirement. As in the case of a subsection 45(2) election, residence or deemed residence in Canada during the years covered by the subsection 45(3) election is necessary for the full benefit of the principal residence exemption to apply, and the rule described in 6 above prevents the designation for any particular year of more than one property by the taxpayer or, after 1981, any other member of the family unit.

Example

Mr. X bought a house in 1984 and rented it to a third party until mid-1990. He and the other members of his family unit then lived in the house until it was sold in 1992. Mr. X has been resident in Canada at all times. He designates the house as his principal residence for the 1990 to 1992 taxation years inclusive by virtue of his having ordinarily inhabited it during those years. He also designates the house as his principal residence for the 1986 to 1989 years inclusive (i.e., the maximum 4 years) for which his subsection 45(3) election, which he files with his 1992 income tax return, is in effect. (He is able to make this designation because no other property has been designated by him or a member of his family unit for those years.) However, his gain on the disposition of the house in 1992 cannot be fully eliminated by the principal residence exemption because he cannot designate the house as his principal residence for the 1984 and 1985 years.

Any income in respect of a property (e.g., the rental income in the above example), net of applicable expenses, must be reported for tax purposes. However, for taxation years covered by a subsection 45(3) election, CCA should not be claimed on the property by the taxpayer, the taxpayer's spouse or a trust under which the taxpayer or the spouse is a beneficiary. Such a CCA claim would, by virtue of subsection 45(4), nullify the subsection 45(3) election as if it had never been made.

Partial Changes in Use
36. When a taxpayer has partially converted a principal residence to an income-producing use, paragraph 45(1)(c) provides for a deemed disposition of the portion of the property so converted (such portion is usually calculated on the basis of the area involved) for proceeds equal to its proportionate share of the property's FMV. Paragraph 45(1)(c) also provides for a deemed reacquisition immediately thereafter of the same portion of the property at a cost equal to the very same amount. Any gain otherwise determined on the deemed disposition is usually eliminated or reduced by the principal residence exemption. If the portion of the property so changed is later converted back to use as part of the principal residence, there is a second deemed disposition (and reacquisition) thereof at FMV. A taxable capital gain attributable to the period of use of such portion of the property for income-producing purposes (for which a section 110.6 capital gains deduction may be available; see, however, the note at the end of 13 above) can arise from such a second deemed disposition or from an actual sale of the whole property subsequent to the original partial change in

use. An election under subsection 45(2) or (3) cannot be made where there is a partial change in use of a property as described above.

37. The above-mentioned deemed disposition rule applies where the partial change in use of the property is substantial and of a more permanent nature, i.e., where there is a structural change. This occurs, for example, with the conversion of the front half of a house into a store, the conversion of a portion of a house into a self-contained domestic establishment for earning rental income (a duplex, triplex, etc.) or alterations to a house to accommodate separate business premises. In these and similar cases, the taxpayer reports the income and may claim the expenses pertaining to the altered portion of the property (i.e., a reasonable portion of the expenses relating to the whole property) as well as CCA on such altered portion.

38. It is the Department's practice to not apply the deemed disposition rule, but rather to consider that the entire property retains its nature as a principal residence, where all of the following conditions are met:
   (a) the income-producing use is ancillary to the main use of the property as a residence,
   (b) there is no structural change to the property, and
   (c) no CCA is claimed on the property.
These conditions can be met, for example, where a taxpayer carries on a business of caring for children in his or her home, rents one or more rooms in the home or has an office or other work space in the home which is used in connection with his or her business. In these and similar cases, the taxpayer reports the income and may claim the expenses (other than CCA) pertaining to the portion of the property used for income-producing purposes. Certain conditions and restrictions are placed on the deductibility of expenses relating to an office or other work space in an individual's home (if the income is income from a business, see the current version of IT-514). In the event that the taxpayer commences to claim CCA on the portion of the property used for producing income, the deemed disposition rule is applied as of the time at which the income-producing use commenced.

Change in Use Rules Regarding CCA, Deemed Capital Cost and Recapture
39. When the taxpayer completely or partially changes the use of a property from principal residence to income-producing, subsection 13(7) provides for a deemed acquisition of the property or portion of the property so changed that is depreciable property. For purposes of claiming CCA, the deemed capital cost of such depreciable property is its FMV as of the date of the change in use unless that FMV is greater than the cost of such depreciable property. In the latter

case, the deemed capital cost is determined by a formula which essentially limits it to the actual cost plus the taxable part of the gain on the depreciable property but only to the extent that a capital gains deduction is not claimed to offset such taxable part of the gain. The formula is as follows:

C + R(FMV - [C + rE])

where

C   is the cost of the depreciable property,

FMV is the FMV of the depreciable property as of the date of the change in use,

E   is the amount of capital gains deduction claimed under section 110.6 to offset the taxable portion of the excess of FMV over C (if a portion of the gain is attributable to a period of time after February 1992, see the note at the end of 13 above),

R   is the capital gains inclusion rate in effect in the year of the change in use, and

r   is the reciprocal of R (i.e., R x r = 1).

Example

Mr. A completely converted his house to a rental property in January 1992, at which time its cost and FMV were $60,000 and $100,000, respectively (the cost and FMV of the land are ignored in this example as they are not taken into account under subsection 13(7)). The principal residence exemption reduced Mr. A's $40,000 gain otherwise determined by $10,000 to $30,000 (the house did not qualify as his principal residence for all of the years in which he resided in it because Mrs. A had designated a cottage as her principal residence for some of those years). The 3/4 capital gains inclusion rate in effect for 1992 resulted in a taxable capital gain of $22,500 to Mr. A. In calculating taxable income, he claimed a corresponding capital gains deduction of $22,500 under section 110.6. The deemed capital cost of Mr. A's house at the time of its change in use to a rental property was calculated as follows:

C + R(FMV - [C + rE])
= $60,000 + 3/4 of ($100,000 - [$60,000 + 4/3 of $22,500])
= $60,000 + 3/4 of ($100,000 - [$60,000 + $30,000])
= $60,000 + 3/4 of ($100,000 - $90,000)
= $60,000 + 3/4 of $10,000
= $60,000 + $7,500
= $67,500.

To summarize, the change in use of the principal residence to a rental property in January 1992 resulted in a potentially taxable amount of $30,000, i.e., 3/4 of Mr. A's $40,000 gain otherwise determined. $7,500 of this amount was exempted from taxation by means of the principal residence exemption, i.e., 3/4 of the above-mentioned $10,000 reduction to the gain otherwise determined. The remaining $22,500 of the $30,000 potentially taxable amount was reported as a taxable capital gain but was then, in effect, exempted from taxation by means of the capital gains deduction (if a portion of the gain had been attributable to a period of time after February 1992, see the note at the end of 13 above). In determining the deemed capital cost of the house as a rental property for purposes of claiming CCA, the formula permitted the $7,500 to be added to the $60,000 cost of the house, but did not permit the $22,500 to be added.

In the case of a complete change in use of a property from principal residence to income-producing, a subsection 45(2) election will cause subsection 13(7), as described above, not to apply. However, if the election is rescinded in a subsequent taxation year (e.g., by claiming CCA on the property), a subsection 13(7) deemed acquisition of depreciable property will occur on the first day of that subsequent year. A subsection 45(2) election cannot be made, and thus such an election cannot cause subsection 13(7) not to apply, where there is only a partial change in use of a property from principal residence to income-producing. However, subsection 13(7) would have no particular relevance and would not be applied to a partial change in use where conditions (a) to (c) in 38 above have been met, including the condition not to claim CCA on the portion of the property used to earn income.

40. When a taxpayer completely or partially changes the use of a property from income-producing to principal residence, there is a deemed disposition at FMV, by virtue of subsection 13(7), of the portion of the property so changed that is depreciable property. This can result in a recapture of CCA previously claimed on the property. A subsection 45(3) election cannot be used to defer such a recapture, caused by the operation of subsection 13(7), of CCA claimed for taxation years prior to those covered by that election (the claiming of CCA during the years covered by the subsection 45(3) election is prohibited — see 35 above).

Principal Residence Outside Canada
41. A property that is located outside Canada can, depending on the facts of the case, qualify as a taxpayer's principal residence (see the requirements in 2 to 6

above). A taxpayer who is resident in Canada and owns such a qualifying property outside Canada during a particular taxation year can designate the property as a principal residence for that year in order to use the principal residence exemption (see 14 above for the meanings of "resident in Canada" and "during"). Should a non-resident of Canada who owns a property outside Canada become resident in Canada, the provisions of the Income Tax Act normally apply to deem that person to acquire the property on the date of immigration to Canada at fair market value, thereby ensuring that any unrealized gain on the property accruing to that date will not be taxable in Canada. Thereafter, the comments in the first two sentences of this paragraph may apply.

Non-Resident Owner of a Principal Residence in Canada
42. A property in Canada owned in a particular taxation year by a non-resident of Canada may qualify as his or her principal residence for that year. That is, the property would qualify if the housing unit were ordinarily inhabited in that year (see 12 above) by the non-resident or by the spouse, former spouse or a child of the non-resident (see 5 above) or if an election under subsection 45(2) or (3) were in force for that year (see 32 and 35 above), provided that the property met the other requirements of paragraph 54(g). However, it should be noted that the use of the principal residence exemption is limited by reference to the number of taxation years ending after the acquisition date during which the taxpayer was resident in Canada (see 14 above for the principal residence exemption formula and the meanings of "acquisition date", "resident in Canada" and "during"). Therefore, the non-resident may not be able to use the principal residence exemption for all the years for which the property qualifies as his or her principal residence. That is, the principal residence exemption can benefit the non-resident only for those taxation years in which he or she was at some time resident in Canada (the benefit is increased, however, by the extra year discussed in 14 and 15 above, or the extra $1,000 discussed in 28 above). As a result of this limitation, even in a case where the property qualifies as the non-resident's principal residence for all the years in which he or she owned it, a disposition of the property could result in a taxable capital gain resulting from the gain accruing in some or all of those years.

43. In spite of the limitation mentioned in 42 above in connection with the principal residence exemption, an election under subsection 45(2) or (3) could allow the non-resident individual owning a property in Canada to defer a taxable capital gain which would otherwise result from a deemed disposition of the property on a change in its use (see 31 and 34 above).

44. Where the non-resident has rented a property in Canada in a particular taxation year for which an election under subsection 45(2) or 45(3) is in effect, CCA should not be claimed on the property (see 31 and 35 above, respectively). This restriction on CCA applies where an election is made to report the rental income under section 216 (that election is discussed in the current version of IT-393).

Disposition of a Principal Residence in Canada by a Non-Resident Owner
45. Where a non-resident wishes to obtain a certificate under section 116 of the Income Tax Act for a property in Canada which he or she proposes to dispose of or has disposed of within the last 10 days, a prepayment on account of tax must be made or security acceptable to the Department must be given before the certificate will be issued. Form T2062, Notice by a Non-resident of Canada Concerning the Disposition or Proposed Disposition of Taxable Canadian Property, or a similar notification, must be filed in connection with a request for a section 116 certificate. Further particulars regarding the above are contained in the current version of Information Circular 72-17. Where part or all of any gain otherwise determined on the disposition of the property by the non-resident is or will be eliminated by the principal residence exemption, the amount of prepayment on account of tax to be made or security to be given may be reduced accordingly. An application for such a reduction should be made by means of a letter signed by the taxpayer and attached to the completed Form T2062 or similar notification. Such letter should contain a calculation of the portion of the gain otherwise determined that is or will be so eliminated by the principal residence exemption.

Other Publications

I   Interpretation Bulletins

Current version of
IT-221   *Determination of an Individual's Residence Status*
IT-437   *Ownership of Dwelling Property*
IT-366   *Principal Residence — Transfer to Spouse, Spouse Trust or Certain Other Individuals*
IT-393   *Election re Tax on Rents and Timber Royalties — Non-Residents*
IT-514   *Work Space in Home Expenses*

II   Information Circulars

Current version of

72-17   *Procedures Concerning the Disposition of Taxable Canadian Property by Non-Residents of Canada — Section 116*

III   Tax Guides

Current version of

* *Capital Gains Tax Guide* (see comments regarding Principal Residence)
* *Farming Income Tax Guide* (see comments regarding Capital Gains — Principal Residence)
* *T3 Guide and Trust Return* (see comments regarding Principal Residence)

If you have any comments regarding the matters discussed in this bulletin, please send them to:

Director, Technical Publications Division
Legislative and Intergovernmental Affairs Branch
Revenue Canada Taxation
875 Heron Road
Ottawa, Ontario
K1A 0L8

Schedule A — Illustration of the Rule in Subsection 40(6) (see above)

Where a taxpayer disposes of a property which he or she has owned (whether jointly with another person or otherwise) continuously since before 1982, the rule in subsection 40(6) provides that the gain calculated under the usual method, using the principal residence exemption formula in above, cannot be greater than the maximum total net gain determined under an alternative method. Under the alternative method, there is a hypothetical disposition on December 31, 1981 and reacquisition on January 1, 1982 of the property at fair market value ("FMV"). The maximum total net gain determined under the alternative method is then calculated as follows:

pre-1982 gain + post-1981 gain - post-1981 loss = maximum total net gain

where

the **"pre-1982 gain"** is the gain (if any), as reduced by the principal residence exemption formula in 14 above, that would result from the hypothetical disposition at FMV on December 31, 1981,

the **"post-1981 gain"** is the gain (if any), as reduced by the principal residence exemption formula in 14 above without the "1 +" in the numerator "A" in that formula, that would result from the hypothetical acquisition at FMV on January 1, 1982 and the subsequent actual disposition, and

the **"post-1981 loss"** is the amount of any loss that has accrued from December 31, 1981 to the date of the actual disposition, i.e., the excess (if any) of the FMV on December 31, 1981 over the proceeds from the actual disposition.

Example 1

Mrs. X acquired a house in 1975 for $50,000. She and her husband lived in it until February 1988 when she sold it for $115,000, resulting in an actual gain of $65,000. Ever since the sale of the house in 1988, Mr. and Mrs. X have been living in rented premises. In filing her 1988 income tax return, Mrs. X designated the house as her principal residence for 1975 to 1988 inclusive, and thus her gain otherwise determined was completely eliminated by the principal residence exemption.

Mr. X acquired a lot in 1975 for $7,000 and built a cottage on it in 1979 for $13,000. Mr. and Mrs. X used the cottage as a seasonal residence in 1979 to 1992 inclusive. In the fall of 1992 Mr. X sold the cottage for $55,000, resulting in an actual gain of $35,000. In filing his 1992 income tax return, Mr. X designates the cottage property as his principal residence for 1979 to 1981 inclusive, as well as for 1989 to 1992 inclusive. He cannot designate the property as his principal residence for 1975 to 1978 inclusive because it was only a vacant lot and thus no one "ordinarily inhabited" it in those years (see 16 above); nor can he designate the property as his principal residence for 1982 to 1988 inclusive because of his wife's designation of the house as her principal residence for those years (see 6 above). As a result, not all of his $35,000 gain otherwise determined is eliminated by the principal residence exemption formula in 14 above. However, because the property has been owned by Mr. X continuously since before 1982, subsection 40(6) comes into play in computing his gain.

Assuming that the fair market value of the cottage on December 31, 1981 was $30,000, the calculations under subsection 40(6) in connection with Mr. X's gain on the cottage are as follows:

USUAL METHOD FOR CALCULATING GAIN

Gain otherwise determined ($55,000 - $20,000)	$35,000
Reduce by principal residence exemption:	
$\frac{1 + 7 \text{ (1979 to 1981 \& 1989 to 1992)}}{18 \text{ (1975 to 1992)}}$ x $35,000	15,556
Gain	$19,444

ALTERNATIVE METHOD — CALCULATION OF MAXIMUM TOTAL NET GAIN

Pre-1982 gain:

Gain otherwise determined ($30,000 - $20,000)	$10,000
Reduce by principal residence exemption:	
$\frac{1 + 3 \text{ (1979 to 1981)}}{7 \text{ (1975 to 1981)}}$ x $10,000	5,714
Gain	$ 4,286

Post-1981 gain:

Gain otherwise determined ($55,000 - $30,000)	$25,000
Reduce by principal residence exemption:	
$\frac{4 \text{ (1989 to 1992)}}{11 \text{ (1982 to 1992)}}$ x $25,000	9,091
Gain	$15,909

Post-1981 loss:

N/A $	NIL

Pre-1982 gain + post-1981 gain - post-1981 loss
= $4,286 + $15,909 - $Nil
= $20,195.

RESULT: The husband's gain remains at the $19,444 calculated under the usual method since that amount does not exceed the maximum total net gain of $20,195 calculated under the alternative method.

Example 2

Assume the same facts as in Example 1 except that the cottage was sold in 1992 for $35,000. The calculations under subsection 40(6) in connection with the husband's gain on the cottage are as follows:

USUAL METHOD FOR CALCULATING GAIN

Gain otherwise determined ($35,000 - $20,000)	$15,000
Reduce by principal residence exemption:	
$\frac{1 + 7 \text{ (1979 to 1981 \& 1989 to 1992)}}{18 \text{ (1975 to 1992)}} \times \$15,000$	6,667
Gain	$ 8,333

ALTERNATIVE METHOD — CALCULATION OF MAXIMUM TOTAL NET GAIN

Pre-1982 gain:

Gain otherwise determined ($30,000 - $20,000)	$10,000
Reduce by principal residence exemption:	
$\frac{1 + 3 \text{ (1979 to 1981)}}{7 \text{ (1975 to 1981)}} \times \$10,000$	5,714
Gain	$ 4,286

Post-1981 gain:

Gain otherwise determined ($35,000 - $30,000)	$ 5,000
Reduce by principal residence exemption:	
$\frac{4 \text{ (1989 to 1992)}}{11 \text{ (1982 to 1992)}} \times \$5,000$	1,818
Gain	$ 3,182

Post-1981 loss:

N/A	$ NIL

Pre-1982 gain + post-1981 gain - post-1981 loss
= $4,286 + $3,182 - $Nil
= $7,468.

RESULT: Although the husband's gain calculated under the usual method is $8,333, such gain cannot exceed the maximum total net gain of $7,468 calculated under the alternative method. Therefore, the gain is reduced to $7,468.

Example 3

Assume the same facts as in Example 1 except that the cottage was sold in 1992 for $28,000. The calculations under subsection 40(6) in connection with the husband's gain on the cottage are as follows:

USUAL METHOD FOR CALCULATING GAIN

Gain otherwise determined ($28,000 - $20,000)	$ 8,000
Reduce by principal residence exemption:	
$\dfrac{1 + 7\ (1979\ \text{to}\ 1981\ \&\ 1989\ \text{to}\ 1992)}{18\ (1975\ \text{to}\ 1992)}$ x $8,000	3,556
Gain	$ 4,444

ALTERNATIVE METHOD — CALCULATION OF MAXIMUM TOTAL NET GAIN

Pre-1982 gain:

Gain otherwise determined ($30,000 - $20,000)	$10,000
Reduce by principal residence exemption:	
$\dfrac{1 + 3\ (1979\ \text{to}\ 1981)}{7\ (1975\ \text{to}\ 1981)}$ x $10,000	5,714
Gain	$ 4,286

Post-1981 gain:

N/A	$ NIL

Post-1981 loss:

$30,000 - $28,000	$ 2,000

Pre-1982 gain + post-1981 gain - post-1981 loss
= $4,286 + $Nil - $2,000
= $2,286.

RESULT: Although the husband's gain calculated under the usual method is $4,444, such gain cannot exceed the maximum total net gain of $2,286 calculated under the alternative method. Therefore, the gain is reduced to $2,286.

Schedule B — Illustration of Calculation of Gain on Disposition of a Farm Property

Assume that a taxpayer resident in Canada has sold a 50 hectare farm. The taxpayer owned the farm and occupied the house on it from July 30, 1984 to June 15, 1992. The house and 1/2 hectare of the land have been designated as the taxpayer's principal residence for the 1984 to 1992 taxation years inclusive. The taxpayer's calculations of the gain on the disposition of the farm property, using the two methods permitted by paragraph 40(2)(c) of the Income Tax Act, are as follows:

FIRST METHOD (see 27 above)

	Principal Residence	Farm	Total Property
Proceeds of disposition			
Land	$ 10,000*	$ 90,000	$100,000
House	50,000		50,000
Barn		35,000	35,000
Silo		15,000	15,000
	$ 60,000	$140,000	$200,000
Adjusted cost base			
Land	$ 2,000*	$ 58,000	$ 60,000
House	20,000		20,000
Barn		11,000	11,000
Silo		4,000	4,000
	$22,000	$ 73,000	$ 95,000

Gain otherwise determined	$ 38,000	$ 67,000	$105,000
Less: Principal residence exemption	38,000	-	38,000
Gain	$ NIL	$ 67,000	$ 67,000

* Since the principal residence portion of the land is 1/100 of the total land (i.e., 1/2 hectare divided by 50 hectares), one way (as described in (a) above) of assigning values to the principal residence portion of the land would be to simply use $1,000 (i.e., 1/100 of $100,000) for the proceeds for such portion of the land and $600 (i.e., 1/100 of $60,000) for the adjusted cost base of such portion. Assume, however, that a typical residential site in the area, although less than 1/2 hectare in this example, had a fair market value of $10,000 as of the date of sale and $2,000 as of the date of acquisition. As indicated in 27(b) above, the Department would accept the taxpayer's use of the latter amounts, which in this case would result in a greater portion of the gain being eliminated by the principal residence exemption.

SECOND METHOD (see above)

Proceeds of disposition for total farm property	$200,000
Adjusted cost base for total farm property	95,000
Gain otherwise determined	$105,000
Less: Principal residence exemption using subparagraph 40(2)(c)(ii) election: $1,000 + (9 x $1,000)	10,000
Gain	$ 95,000

RESULT: In this example, the first method results in a lower gain to the taxpayer.

Interpretation Bulletin IT-221R2

Subject: *Income Tax Act*
            Determination of an Individual's Residence Status

Date: February 25, 1983

Reference: Section 2 (also sections 48, 114, 115, 212 and 250)

This Bulletin replaces and cancels IT-221R dated May 26, 1980 and is applicable to individuals leaving Canada after May 26, 1980 other than those individuals who are deemed by section 250 to have been resident in Canada throughout a taxation year (see 17 below). The Department's position with respect to individuals leaving Canada on or prior to that date is outlined in IT-221 dated May 26, 1975. The comments in IT-221 will also continue to apply where an employee leaves Canada after May 26, 1980 to fulfill a written contract entered into by his employer prior to July 24, 1979 to provide services outside Canada. Current revisions are designated by vertical lines.

1. The purpose of this bulletin is to explain the Department's position concerning the determination of an individual's residence status for income tax purposes.

General Comments
2. The term "resident" is not defined in the Income Tax Act. The Courts have held that an individual is resident in Canada for tax purposes if Canada is the place where he, in the settled routine of his life, regularly, normally or customarily lives. In making this determination, all of the relevant facts in each case must be considered.

LEAVING CANADA

3. Where an individual leaves Canada after May 26, 1980, the following factors will be taken into consideration in determining whether or not the individual will remain a resident of Canada for tax purposes while abroad:
    (a) permanence and purpose of stay abroad,
    (b) residential ties within Canada,
    (c) residential ties elsewhere, and
    (d) regularity and length of visits to Canada.

Permanence and Purpose of Stay Abroad
4. In order for an individual to become a non-resident of Canada, there must be a degree of permanence to his stay abroad. Where a Canadian resident is absent from Canada (for whatever reason) for less than 2 years, he will be presumed to have retained his residence status while abroad, unless he can clearly establish that he severed all residential ties on leaving Canada. If there is evidence that his return to Canada was foreseen at the time of his departure (e.g. a contract for employment upon return to Canada), the Department will presume that he did not sever all residential ties on leaving Canada.

5. Where an individual is absent from Canada for 2 years or longer, he will be presumed to have become a non-resident of Canada, provided that he satisfies the other requirements for non-resident status outlined in 6 to 12 below.

Residential Ties Within Canada
6. The primary residential ties of an individual are his
    (a) dwelling place (or places),
    (b) spouse and dependants, and
    (c) personal property and social ties.

7. An individual who leaves Canada, but ensures that a dwelling place suitable for year-round occupancy is kept available in Canada for his occupation by maintaining it (vacant or otherwise), by leasing it at non-arm's length, or by leasing it at arm's length with the right to terminate the lease on short notice (less than 3 months) will generally be considered not to have severed his residential ties within Canada.

8. If a married individual leaves Canada, but his spouse or dependants remain in Canada, the individual will generally be considered to remain a resident of Canada during his absence. An exception to this may occur where an individual and his spouse are legally separated and the individual has permanently severed all other residential ties within Canada. The residential ties of a single person are frequently of a more tenuous nature and, in the majority of cases, if such a person leaves Canada for 2 years or more and establishes a residence elsewhere, it is likely that he will be a non-resident of Canada during his absence, unless other important ties within Canada indicate that he is not. For example, where a single person is supporting someone in a dwelling maintained and occupied by him in Canada and, after his departure, he continues to support that person in the dwelling, he will not be considered to have severed his residential ties within Canada.

9. Generally speaking, an individual who leaves Canada and becomes a non-resident will not retain any residential ties in the form of personal property (e.g. furniture, clothing, automobile, bank accounts, credit cards, etc.) or social ties (e.g. resident club memberships, etc.) within Canada after his departure. Where such ties are retained within Canada, the Department may examine the reasons for their retention to determine if these ties are significant enough to conclude that the individual is a continuing resident of Canada while absent. Other ties that may also be relevant in this determination are the retention of

    (a) provincial hospitalization and medical insurance coverage,

    (b) a seasonal residence in Canada,

    (c) professional or other memberships in Canada (on a resident basis), and

    (d) family allowance payments.

Residential Ties Elsewhere

10. The Courts have held that

    (a) everyone must be resident somewhere, and

    (b) it is quite possible for an individual to be resident in more than one place at the same time for tax purposes.

Accordingly, where a resident of Canada goes abroad, but does not establish a permanent residence elsewhere, there is a presumption that he remains a resident of Canada. Also, the fact that an individual establishes a permanent residence abroad does not, in and by itself, mean that the individual has become a non-resident of Canada.

11. Where an individual is resident in Canada and, at the same time, resident in another country by its laws, reference should be had to any tax convention or agreement that Canada may have with the other country.

Regularity and Length of Visits to Canada

12. Where an individual leaves Canada and purports to become a non-resident, his tax status as a non-resident will not generally be affected by occasional return visits to Canada, whether for personal or business reasons. However, where such visits are more than occasional, particularly where the visits occur on a regular basis, this factor together with other residential ties that exist (as set out in 9 above) will be examined to determine whether they are significant enough in total to conclude that the individual is a continuing resident of Canada.

Date Non-Resident Status Acquired

13. The date on which a Canadian resident leaving Canada becomes a non-resident for tax purposes is generally the latest of the dates on which

(a) he leaves Canada,

(b) his spouse and/or dependants leave Canada (if applicable), or

(c) he becomes a resident of the country to which he is immigrating.

An exception to this will occur where the individual was resident in another country prior to entering Canada and he is leaving to re-establish his residence in that country. In this case, the individual will generally become a non-resident on the date he leaves Canada; even if, for example, his spouse remains temporarily behind in Canada to dispose of their dwelling place in Canada.

Tax Avoidance

14. The comments in this bulletin are intended only for the guidance of persons leaving Canada under ordinary circumstances. In cases where one of the main purposes of a person's absence from Canada is to avoid Canadian income taxes which would otherwise be payable, regard may be had to other factors.

ENTERING CANADA

Sojourners

15. An individual who sojourns (i.e. is temporarily present) in Canada for a total of 183 days or more in any calendar year is deemed by the Income Tax Act to be resident in Canada for the entire year. In order for this to occur, the individual must be a resident of another country during the 183 (or more) days in question. Thus, a resident of Canada who becomes a non-resident in the last half of a calendar year is not deemed to be a resident of Canada for the entire year. However, if having taken up residence in another country in the first half of a calendar year (or in a previous year), he returns often enough to have sojourned in Canada for a total of 183 days or more during the year (while non-resident), he would be deemed to be resident in Canada for the whole of the year.

Immigrants

16. Where an individual enters Canada, otherwise than as a sojourner, and establishes residential ties within Canada (see 6 to 9 above), he will generally be considered to have become a resident of Canada for tax purposes on the date he entered Canada.

DEEMED RESIDENTS OF CANADA

17. In addition to persons sojourning in Canada for a total of 183 days or more in any calendar year (see 15 above), subsection 250(1) ensures that any person, who is included in any one of the categories described in (a) to (e) below, is a resident of Canada by deeming him to be so, even if he would not be a resident under the general rules in this bulletin. These categories are

   (a) persons who were members of the Canadian Forces at any time in the year,

   (b) officers or servants of Canada or a province who were resident in Canada or deemed to be resident in Canada (e.g. — members of the Canadian Forces who have been serving abroad) immediately prior to their appointment or employment by Canada or the province,

   (c) individuals who perform services outside Canada under an international development assistance program of the Canadian International Development Agency described in Part 3400 of the Regulations to the Income Tax Act, provided they were resident in Canada at any time in the three month period prior to the day the services commenced,

   (d) persons who were, at any time in the 1980 and subsequent taxation years, members of the overseas Canadian Forces school staff who have filed their returns for the year on the basis that they were resident in Canada throughout the period during which they were such members, and

   (e) the spouse of a person described in (a) to (d) above, if living with that person during the year and if a resident of Canada in a previous year, and any dependent children of that person who were:

      (i) under 18 years of age at any time during the year, or

      (ii) 18 years of age or over throughout the year and dependent by reason of either physical or mental infirmity.

18. A person referred to in 17(a) to (e) above is deemed to be resident in Canada regardless of where he lives or performs his services. If, at a date in the year, he ceases to be a person so described, he will be deemed to be resident in Canada only to that date. Thereafter, his residency will depend on the factors outlined in 4 to 12 above.

Interpretation Bulletin IT-270R2

Subject: *Income Tax Act*
Foreign Tax Credit

Date: February 11, 1991

Reference: Section 126 (also sections 3, 4, 110.5, 115.1 and 127.5 and subsection 180.1(1.1))

Application
This bulletin cancels and replaces IT-270R dated July 9, 1984. Current revisions are indicated by vertical lines. The comments in this bulletin do not reflect any changes proposed in the Draft Amendments to the Income Tax Act and Related Statutes issued by the Minister of Finance on July 13, 1990. Any necessary changes will be subject of a Special Release.

Summary
This bulletin discusses the foreign tax credit, which is a deduction from Canadian tax otherwise payable, that may be claimed in respect of income or profits tax paid to a foreign country by a taxpayer. This credit must be calculated on a country-by-country basis and in general terms is limited to the lesser of the income and profits tax paid to the particular foreign country and the Canadian tax otherwise payable for the year on income from sources within that particular country. Other relevant Interpretation Bulletins are the current versions of IT-520, *Unused Foreign Tax Credits — Carryforward and Carryback,* IT-395, *Foreign Tax Credit — Capital Gains and Capital Losses on Foreign Property* (see 34 below), IT-194, *Foreign Tax Credit — Part-time Residents,* IT-451, *Deemed Dispositions and Acquisitions on Ceasing to be or Becoming Resident in Canada* (see 40 below) and IT-173, *Capital Gains Derived in Canada by Residents of the United States* (see 44 below).

The commentary below gives a detailed description of how to calculate the foreign tax credit and discusses the relevant terms used in this calculation and some of the situations that may be encountered in this area. Other than as discussed in paragraphs 40 and 44 to 46 below, the commentary pertains to a person resident in Canada throughout a taxation year. For comments relevant to a person who is resident in Canada for only part of a year, refer to the current version of the above-mentioned IT-194.

Discussion and Interpretation

1. Separate foreign tax credit calculations are required for "business-income tax" (subsection 126(2)) and "non-business-income tax" (subsection 126(1)) and, as indicated above, each calculation is required on a country-by-country basis.

2. Subject to the exceptions described in 3 to 5 and 42 and 43 below, the credits available to a taxpayer resident in Canada throughout a taxation year in respect of taxes paid to a particular country are as follows:

    (a) under subsection 126(1), the lesser of

        (i) non-business-income tax (see 11 below) paid for the year to the particular country excluding tax paid by a corporate taxpayer in respect of income from a share of the capital stock of a foreign affiliate, and

        (ii) Canadian tax otherwise payable (CTOP) for the year on non-business income from sources in the particular country (see 22 and 23 below), and

    (b) under subsection 126(2), subject to the comments in 5 below, the lesser of

        (i) business-income tax (see 10 below) paid to the particular country for the year, plus, for 1984 and subsequent taxation years, any eligible "unused foreign tax credits" (see the current version of IT-520), and

        (ii) CTOP for the year on income from businesses carried on in the particular country (see 22 and 23 below) plus, as discussed in 4 below, any amount added under subsection 120(1) to that CTOP with respect to income not earned in a province.

3. The non-business income referred to in 2(a)(ii) above does not include income of a corporate taxpayer in respect of shares of a foreign affiliate. However, an individual taxpayer computing non-business income under 2(a)(ii) above will include any income in respect of a share of the capital stock of a foreign affiliate even if such income includes a dividend deductible under subsection 91(5) in computing the taxpayer's income.

4. Subsection 120(1) provides for an additional tax on that part of an individual's income for a taxation year that is not "income earned in a year in a province" as determined under Part XXVI of the Regulations. Where such a tax is payable and part of the relevant income is attributable to businesses carried on in the particular country, a portion of that tax will be added to the applicable CTOP (see 2(b)(ii) above). Paragraph 126(2.1)(b) contains a formula which

basically provides that the amount so added will be equal to the portion of the additional tax that is attributable to the income from those businesses.

5. A taxpayer's claim for a business-income tax credit under subsection 126(2) cannot exceed the "tax for the year otherwise payable under this Part", minus any claim under subsection 126(1). This quoted term is defined under subparagraph 126(7)(d)(ii) and may be described as being the tax payable before making any of the Division E additions or deductions specifically mentioned in that subparagraph and available to the taxpayer. As a consequence of the deduction of foreign tax credits, the balance of "tax for the year otherwise payable" may not be sufficient to enable the taxpayer to fully utilize other available deductions. It may therefore be to the taxpayer's advantage not to claim part or all of the business-income tax credit in the year but to claim it in another year.

Foreign Income or Profits Tax

6. In general terms, a tax is a levy of general application for public purposes enforceable by a governmental authority. Examples of payments that do not qualify as payments of a "tax" include
   (a) resource royalties,
   (b) voluntary contributions to governmental authorities, and
   (c) payments made to acquire a specific right or privilege.

7. To qualify for foreign tax credit purposes, a payment must be
   (a) made to the government of a foreign country or to the government of a political subdivision of a foreign country, and
   (b) in respect of an "income or profits tax".

8. In determining whether or not a particular foreign tax qualifies as an "income or profits tax", the basic scheme of application is compared with that of the Canadian Income Tax Act. If the basis of taxation is substantially similar, the foreign tax is accepted as an income or profits tax. To be "substantially similar", the foreign tax must be levied on net income or profits (but not necessarily as would be computed for Canadian tax purposes) unless it is a tax similar to that imposed under Part XIII of the Act. Notwithstanding any of the foregoing guidelines, a tax that is specifically identified as being subject to the provisions of a comprehensive income tax treaty between Canada and a particular country automatically qualifies as an income or profits tax. Examples of taxes that do not qualify as "income or profits" taxes for purposes of the foreign tax credit provisions include the following:
   (a) sales, commodity, consumption or turnover taxes,

(b) succession duties or inheritance taxes,

(c) property or real estate taxes,

(d) franchise or business taxes,

(e) customs or import duties,

(f) excise taxes or duties, and

(g) gift taxes.

9. Some foreign tax levies are based on net income established under a prescribed formula. Such a tax is accepted as an income or profits tax if

(a) it can be considered that the formula produces a reasonable approximation of actual net income in typical situations, and

(b) an actual computation of net income would be significantly affected by arbitrary or estimated expense allocations.

Business-Income Tax

10. An income or profits tax paid to any foreign jurisdiction qualifies under paragraph 126(7)(a) as a business-income tax in respect of businesses carried on in a particular country, to the extent that it can be regarded as being in respect of income from any business being carried on by the payer in the particular country. Paragraph 126(7)(a), however, excludes from the definition of business-income tax any foreign tax that may reasonably be regarded as relating to an amount received or receivable by any other person or partnership from the foreign jurisdiction. The excluded tax qualifies as a non-business-income tax for the purpose of subsection 20(12)(see 11(e) below).

It should be noted that a foreign income or profits tax is recognized as a "business-income tax" for foreign tax credit purposes only if it is paid in respect of a business carried on outside Canada by the payer. Whether or not a payer is carrying on business inside or outside Canada is determined under Canadian jurisprudence with no consideration given to the extended meaning under section 253 of carrying on business in Canada. See 26 below for some guidelines the Department follows in determining where a business is carried on.

Non-Business-Income Tax

11. Under paragraph 126(7)(c), non-business-income tax includes any foreign income or profits tax that

(a) is not a business-income tax,

(b) is not deductible under subsection 20(11), and

(c) has not been deducted under subsection 20(12)

and excludes

(d) any foreign tax that would not have been payable if the taxpayer were not a citizen of the country concerned provided that such tax cannot reasonably be attributed to income from a source outside Canada,

(e) any foreign tax that may reasonably be regarded as relating to an amount received or receivable by any other person or partnership from the foreign jurisdiction (this tax does however qualify as a non-business-income tax for the purpose of subsection 20(12)),

(f) for the 1984 and 1985 taxation years, any foreign tax that may reasonably be regarded as attributable to that part of employment income that is equal to the lesser of the amounts determined under paragraphs 122.3(1)(c) and (d) for the purpose of computing the overseas employment tax credit, whether or not that credit is claimed,

(g) for taxation years after 1985, any foreign tax described in (f) above but only if the taxpayer claimed the credit under section 122.3,

(h) for taxation years after 1984, the portion of tax that may reasonably be regarded as attributable to a taxable capital gain or portion thereof in respect of which the taxpayer has claimed a capital gains deduction under section 110.6, and

(i) for taxation years commencing after December 17, 1987, any foreign tax that may reasonably be regarded as attributable to any amount received or receivable by the taxpayer in respect of a loan for the period in the year during which it was an "eligible loan", as defined in section 33.1, of an international banking centre business.

It should be noted that the exclusion in (b) above is an obligatory exclusion that applies even where no amount is actually claimed under subsection 20(11). On the other hand, assuming a taxpayer has sufficient non-business income from the foreign country, (c) above effectively provides the taxpayer with the option of claiming a qualifying amount as either a deduction from income or a deduction from tax, but not both. Subsections 20(11) and 20(12) are discussed in the current version of IT-506, Foreign Income Taxes as a Deduction From Income.

With respect to (g) above, where a taxpayer foregoes claiming the overseas employment tax credit, any foreign tax on the relevant overseas employment income is included in the calculation of non- business-income tax. This permits an individual to elect to include foreign tax on this type of income in the calculation of non- business-income tax where the overseas employment tax credit would be rendered ineffective by virtue of the application of the Minimum Tax under section 127.5 (see 41 below).

12. Because non-business-income tax is defined by exclusion, some foreign income or profits taxes that might otherwise be regarded as business-related can fall within the definition of non-business- income tax, as in the following examples:

  (a) foreign taxes withheld on dividends received from a foreign corporation by a Canadian trader in securities, because the trader did not carry on any securities business in the foreign country;

  (b) United States taxes on income from a business carried on by a U.S. "subchapter S corporation" but paid by its principal shareholder, a U.S. citizen resident in Canada, because the business was not carried on by the person who paid the tax;

  (c) foreign taxes paid in respect of a capital gain on the sale of a property used by the taxpayer in carrying on a business in the foreign country, because a capital gain is not business income;

  (d) foreign taxes paid to the extent that they are in respect of a business (or a part of a business) that is carried on in Canada (see 10 above).

Amount Paid by the Taxpayer for the Year
13. Before an amount of foreign tax can be considered in the calculation of a foreign tax credit, it must be "paid...for the year", whether paid before, during or after the year in question. Once paid, the Canadian dollar equivalent of the foreign tax, converted into Canadian currency in accordance with whichever method and rate of exchange described in 18 to 20 below may be appropriate in the circumstances, may be taken into account in computing a foreign tax credit for the taxation year to which the foreign tax relates. An amount of tax paid which will be refunded to the taxpayer is not considered to be tax paid for the year. For example, where a resident of Canada receives income from sources in another country which has been subject to withholding at a rate in excess of that specified in a treaty between Canada and that country, such excess is not considered to be "foreign tax paid" for purposes of the foreign tax credit. The maximum credit allowed will be determined on the basis of the treaty rate and the taxpayer must seek a refund of the excess withholding from the foreign revenue authorities.

14. Where the period ending three years after the mailing date of the original notice of assessment of Canadian taxes for a particular taxation year may expire before an expected foreign tax assessment for that year is received and paid, a waiver as described in subparagraph 152(4)(a)(ii) should be filed with the Department within that three year period. Once the expected foreign taxes have been assessed and paid to the foreign jurisdiction, such a waiver will permit the Department to accept a request for a Canadian tax refund based on the

appropriate foreign tax credit. In those cases where the taxpayer was, as of the end of the taxation year for which the original Canadian tax assessment was issued, either a mutual fund trust or a corporation other than a Canadian-controlled private corporation, the above-mentioned three year period is extended to four years provided that the original Canadian tax assessment was mailed after April 27, 1986.

15. Only a foreign income or profits tax that is paid **by the taxpayer** can be included in the foreign tax credit calculation. In this connection, but subject to 13 above, the recipient of foreign-source income is considered to have paid any amount withheld and remitted by the payer on account of or in settlement of the recipient's foreign tax liability. Payment is considered to have been made at the time the amount was withheld.

16. The payment of an amount of foreign tax by an agent on behalf of a Canadian resident taxpayer is equivalent to payment by the taxpayer. Whether or not a principal/agency relationship exists is a question of fact based on Canadian law and is not affected by the treatment of the relationship by foreign tax authorities. Thus, foreign tax paid by an agent of a resident of Canada qualifies for the foreign tax credit of the principal, even though the agent was assessed the foreign tax on the basis that the activities were for the agent's own account.

17. Where a married couple resident in Canada has paid a foreign income tax on a community income basis (e.g., by filing a joint return in the United States), an appropriate share of the foreign tax paid may be included in the foreign tax credit calculation of each spouse. The amount paid is apportioned based on the relationship of their respective foreign incomes that gave rise to the foreign tax, rather than the amount actually paid by each spouse.

18. For the purpose of section 126, an amount in respect of income taxes described in paragraphs 126(7)(a) or (c) which is payable to a foreign government in a foreign currency should be converted to Canadian dollars at the rate at which the income itself (other than capital gains) was converted. For business income, this could be done monthly, quarterly, semi-annually or annually, using the average rate for the period, depending on the taxpayer's normal method of reporting its income. For investment income which was subject only to a tax similar to that imposed by Part XIII of the Act, the conversion rate should be the rate applicable on the date of receipt of the income, although use of the average rate for the month or the mid-month rate would usually be acceptable. For other types of income, such as salaries and

wages, the average rate for the months in which they are earned is the most appropriate rate. For capital gains, the rate should approximate the rate applicable at the time the gain was realized.

19. Where the tax is not paid until after the income has been earned, the actual cost to the taxpayer in Canadian dollars of paying the tax may vary from the amount described in 18 above due to fluctuations in the exchange rate. Where this occurs, the difference will be a gain or loss on exchange to which the rules in subsection 39(2) apply. In this context, the actual cost of paying the tax is the Canadian dollar equivalent of the payment computed on the day of payment.

20. Where a taxpayer has overpaid the tax, the overpayment is not allowable as a foreign tax credit (see 13 above). The overpayment should be converted to Canadian dollars under the rules in 18 above, and any difference between this figure and the Canadian dollar value of a refund of the overpayment, computed on the day of its receipt, will be a gain or loss on exchange to which the rules in subsection 39(2) apply.

21. Evidence of payment of foreign tax is to accompany each return in which a foreign tax credit is claimed. Where a taxpayer's foreign tax liability is settled by an amount withheld by the payer of the related income (i.e., analogous to tax under Part XIII), a copy of the foreign tax information slip is usually satisfactory. In most other cases, a copy of the tax return filed with the foreign government is required together with copies of receipts or documents establishing payment. Any change in the amount of foreign tax paid as a result of an assessment or reassessment subsequent to the time of filing should be reported to the Department. Where the foreign assessment or reassessment results in additional foreign tax, proof of payment should be provided.

Canadian Tax Otherwise Payable (CTOP)
22. As indicated in 2(a)(ii) and 2(b)(ii) above, the amount of CTOP is a basic element in the determination of the limitations placed on the amount of foreign income or profits taxes paid that may be claimed as a foreign tax credit. The amount referred to as CTOP in this bulletin is described in the Act as "tax for the year otherwise payable under this Part" and is given three different meanings in paragraph 126(7)(d) for different purposes. The definition in subparagraph 126(7)(d)(i) is used in calculating both the amount under 2(a)(ii) above and the amount deductible under subsection 126(3) by an employee of an international organization, the definition in subparagraph 126(7)(d)(iii) is used in calculating the amount under 2(b)(ii) above and the definition in subparagraph 126(7)(d)(ii) is used in computing both the limitation of the

business-income tax deduction, as described in 5 above, and the amount deductible under subsection 126(2.2) where an election is made under subsection 48(2) with respect to a subsection 48(1) deemed disposition (see 40 below). Particulars of each definition are not described in this bulletin because virtually any legislative change in Division E provisions would affect the validity of such a description. Reference to the current provisions of the Act is therefore suggested when determining CTOP.

23. To determine the amount under 2(a)(ii) above, CTOP is multiplied by a fraction in which the numerator is the non-business income from the country involved (see 24 below) and the denominator is the taxpayer's "adjusted" net income. To determine the amount under 2(b)(ii) above, the CTOP is first multiplied by a fraction in which the numerator is the business income from the country involved (see 25 below) and the denominator is the taxpayer's "adjusted" net income, and to this result is added the applicable subsection 120(1) amount referred to in 4 above. "Adjusted" net income is the aggregate of income determined under section 3 and any forward averaging amount added under subsection 110.4(2) in computing taxable income, less
   (a) net capital losses deducted under paragraph 111(1)(b),
   (b) amounts deducted under the capital gains deduction in section 110.6 for 1985 and subsequent taxation years,
   (c) amounts deductible under paragraph 110(1)(d) in respect of an employee stock option benefit or under paragraph 110(1)(d.1) with respect to shares acquired after May 22, 1985,
   (d) amounts deductible under paragraph 110(1)(d.2) by a prospector or grubstaker in respect of shares received from a corporation (effective in respect of shares acquired after May 22, 1985),
   (e) amounts deductible under paragraph 110(1)(d.3) by a taxpayer in respect of the disposition of "employer's shares" previously received on the taxpayer's withdrawal from a deferred profit sharing plan (effective in respect of shares acquired as a result of deferred profit sharing plan terminations after May 22, 1985),
   (f) amounts deductible under paragraph 110(1)(f) that are amounts exempt from tax in Canada, workmen's compensation payments or social assistance payments,
   (g) amounts deductible under paragraph 110(1)(j) (which is applicable to the 1985 and subsequent taxation years) with respect to an employee benefit determined under section 80.4 that relates to a "home relocation loan",
   (h) amounts deductible under section 110.1 for taxation years before 1988 with respect to interest and dividend income, and

(i) amounts deductible by corporations under section 112 or 113 in respect of dividends,

plus, for 1985 and subsequent taxation years, any amount included in taxable income under section 110.5 as an addition for foreign tax deductions (see 43 below).

Foreign Non-Business Income and Business Income

24. As with the definition of non-business-income tax (see 11 above), non-business income from a foreign country is defined by exclusion in subparagraph 126(1)(b)(i). Thus, all foreign source income that is not excluded by clause 126(1)(b)(i)(C), (D) or (E) is considered to be foreign non-business income. Since foreign- source income resulting from a business carried on in Canada is not excluded, such income can be included in the numerator of the fraction described in paragraph 126(1)(b) (see 23 above). For example, the net income derived from a loan made to a non-resident by a lending institution in the course of its business carried on in Canada is included in the numerator.

25. All of a taxpayer's income from carrying on a business in a particular foreign country is included in the numerator of the fraction described in paragraph 126(2.1)(a) (see 23 above). Thus, amounts that could also be regarded as income from property are included as business income if such income arises in the course of carrying on business in the foreign country. In addition, income from a foreign source outside the particular foreign country is included so long as it is derived from the carrying on of a business in that country.

Determination of Territorial Source of Income

26. A determination of the place where a particular business (or a part thereof) is carried on necessarily depends upon consideration of all the relevant facts, but has been stated in general terms to be the place where the operations in substance take place. In determining where a particular type of business is carried on, the Department usually relies on the following guidelines:

(a) Development and sale of real property — the place where the property is situated;

(b) Merchandise trading — the place where the sales are habitually completed, but other factors such as the location of the stock, the place of payment or manufacture may be considered relevant in particular situations;

(c) Trading in intangible property (e.g., stocks and bonds) — the place where the purchase or sale decisions are normally made;

(d) Money lending — the place where the loan arrangement is in substance completed;

(e) Personal property rentals — the place where the property available for rental is normally located;

(f) Real property rentals — the place where the property is situated;

(g) Service — the place where the services are performed.

27. In the case of a single business comprising more than one of the above-mentioned activities, each segment is considered separately in determining in which country or countries the business is carried on. An exception is made in the case where one activity is clearly incidental to a predominant one; e.g., a vendor of machinery providing the services of an engineer to supervise installation of machinery sold.

28. The territorial source of income from an office or employment is considered to be the place where the related duties are normally performed. Where those duties require an individual to spend a significant part of the time in a country other than Canada, the individual may be subjected to tax in that foreign country on a portion of the remuneration. In such cases, an apportionment of the individual's regular salary or wages based on the number of working days spent in Canada, and in that other country, is considered appropriate in determining the foreign income from employment for the purpose of the foreign tax credit calculation. Director's fees are generally considered to be earned where the director's meetings are held and commission income is earned in the country in which the effort was expended for the purpose of gaining such remuneration.

29. Where interest is earned, other than in the course of carrying on a business in a foreign country (see 25 above), the residence of the debtor ordinarily determines the territorial source of the income. However, interest is not derived from a foreign source if that interest is received by a Canadian lender on a loan made to the foreign parent of a wholly-owned Canadian subsidiary whose principal business is the making of loans and the foreign parent reloaned the money to the Canadian subsidiary at the same rate of interest when the lender and the parent have filed a valid election under subsection 218(3), provided the parent corporation is required to pay interest in Canadian currency.

30. Where a resident of Canada receives a dividend on shares of a corporation which is resident in a foreign country and not resident in Canada, the dividend will normally be recognized as being from a source in that foreign country. However, where a company incorporated in a foreign jurisdiction is resident in

Canada, the payment of dividends by that corporation to non-residents of that foreign country (including Canadian residents) may require the payment of a withholding tax to the foreign jurisdiction. In these circumstances, the dividend paid to a resident of Canada is generally not considered as income from sources in that foreign jurisdiction but as income from Canada.

31. Where income is derived from rental of tangible property (other than income from a business carried on in a foreign country), the source of such income is considered to be
- (a) in the case of income from rental of real property, the country where the property is located, and
- (b) in the case of income from rental of other tangible property, the country where the property is used.

Where rental income is derived in the course of a business carried on in a foreign country, the income will have its source where that business is carried on (see 26 above).

32. Royalty payments have their geographical source in the country in which the related right is used or exploited. For example, a royalty received on the quantity of ore extracted from a mine is income from the country in which the mine is situated. A writer's copyright royalties are income from the country whose laws would otherwise have prohibited the reproduction of the writer's work by anyone else (i.e., the country from which the royalty payments are derived).

Income From Sources in a Foreign Country

33. The income amounts that are the numerators in the fractions referred to in 23 above are net income amounts determined in accordance with the provisions of the Canadian Income Tax Act. Thus, all direct costs as well as reasonable allocations of overhead expenses are deducted in calculating the amount of a numerator. Neither the tax treatment of the component items by the foreign jurisdiction nor any provision in a comprehensive tax treaty that prohibits taxation by the foreign country alters the calculations of income or net income for the purpose of section 126.

34. Income from sources in a foreign country is computed under the rules given in sections 3 and 4, subject to the additional directions contained in subparagraphs 126(1)(b)(i) and 126(2.1)(a)(i). Thus, items of net income or net loss from each source in a particular country are aggregated, together with amounts in respect of taxable capital gains and allowable capital losses in the

case of subparagraph 126(1)(b)(i) as described in the current version of IT-395, *Foreign Tax Credit — Capital Gains and Capital Losses on Foreign Property.*

35. The rules provided by section 4 apply to the calculation of the net income (or loss) from a particular territorial source for the purpose of section 126. Subject to the specific exceptions contained in subsections 4(2) and (3), each permissible deduction (including an outlay or expense) in arriving at a taxpayer's total net income (i.e., the remainder under paragraph 3(d)) is theoretically allocable in whole or in part to a territorial source of income. Ordinarily, such an allocation can be made on the basis of a factual relationship between a particular deduction and the gross income arising in a particular country. This is not always the case, however, and some types of deductions that frequently present apportionment problems are discussed in 38 to 40 below.

36. As provided in subsections 4(2) and (3), deductions in respect of alimony, maintenance payments, interest on death duties and RRSP premiums are never considered applicable to a territorial source of income. The other deductions described in sections 60 to 63 need to be allocated between territorial sources of income only when the duties of a particular office or employment are performed in more than one country or a particular business is carried on in more than one country. In such cases, each deduction claimed must be allocated on a reasonable basis to the territorial source or sources of income to which it can reasonably be said to apply. The amount allocated in this manner to income arising in a particular foreign country must be used in calculating the net income from that country.

37. An allocation of expenses to territorial sources of gross income for financial statement purposes is normally accepted for the purpose of computing the foreign tax credit, provided the basic rules of section 4 are satisfied. Once a basis for allocation has been established, future allocations are expected to be made on a consistent basis.

38. Various methods of allocating interest expense to territorial sources of income are accepted in particular situations. For example, a specific tracing method is appropriate when funds are borrowed and used for an identifiable purpose related to the earning of income in a particular country. For interest on a general purpose borrowing, an allocation based on relative net asset values in different countries may be appropriate. An allocation of interest expense based on the relationship of gross income from different countries is accepted only when a less arbitrary method is not readily evident. The location of property

assigned as security for a borrowing is not necessarily an indication that the funds obtained were for the purpose of earning income in that country.

39. The total amount of capital cost allowance claimed by a taxpayer for a taxation year must be notionally allocated among the countries to which it relates. No such allocation can exceed the allowable maximum under Part XI of the Regulations in respect of property situated in a particular country. In particular, the limitation in the case of "rental properties" must be respected on a country-by-country basis. Subject to these conditions, capital cost allowance deductions may be arbitrarily allocated to income sources in various countries.

Foreign Tax Credit Available to Non-Residents

40. A taxpayer not resident in Canada at the time of disposing of a property deemed to be taxable Canadian property by subsection 48(2) is allowed a tax credit on any non-business-income tax levied by the government of a country other than Canada in respect of any gain or profit. The credit is restricted by subsection 126(2.2) to the lesser of the foreign tax paid on the gain or profit as computed by the foreign jurisdiction, or the portion of Canadian tax otherwise payable in respect of the taxable capital gain from the disposition of that property. For further comments on subsection 48(2), see the current version of IT-451, *Deemed Dispositions and Acquisitions on Ceasing to be or Becoming Resident in Canada*.

Minimum Tax

41. Where an individual who is subject to the minimum tax under section 127.5 pays income taxes to a foreign jurisdiction during a particular taxation year, that individual may not claim a foreign tax credit under section 126 as a deduction from the federal minimum tax payable for that year. However, section 127.5 provides for the deduction of a special foreign tax credit ("SFTC") in computing the federal minimum tax payable in this situation. The SFTC can be equal to or, in certain circumstances, greater than the foreign tax credit to which the individual would normally be entitled under section 126. The SFTC, which is defined in subsection 127.54(2), is the greater of
  (a) the aggregate of amounts deductible under section 126 from the individual's tax for the year, and
  (b) the lesser of
    (i) the individual's foreign taxes for the year and
    (ii) 17% of the individual's foreign income for the year.
Foreign taxes, referred to in (b)(i) above, is defined in subsection 127.54(1) and may be described as the aggregate of the foreign business-income tax paid by the individual for the year in respect of businesses carried on in foreign

jurisdictions and two- thirds of the foreign non-business-income tax paid by that individual for the year. This definition takes into account the fact that the provinces provide a foreign tax credit in respect of foreign taxes on foreign non-business income.

Individual Surtax

42. Effective for 1986 and subsequent taxation years, subsection 180.1(1.1) permits an individual who is subject to the individual surtax to claim a foreign tax deduction against the surtax. This deduction is in addition to the foreign tax credit deductible under section 126 or the SFTC (see 41 above) determined under section 127.54. The deduction under subsection 180.1(1.1) for a taxation year is the amount, if any, by which

    (a) the aggregate of all amounts that would be

        (i) deductible for the year by the individual as a foreign tax credit under section 126, or

        (ii) the individual's SFTC for the year determined under section 127.54, if the tax otherwise payable under Part I for the year (see 22 above) included the individual surtax as determined under Part I.1 before any deduction under this subsection

exceeds

    (b) the aggregate of the individual's foreign tax credits deductible under section 126 for the year and SFTC determined under section 127.54 for the year.

Addition to Taxable Income

43. Where a corporation incurs a loss during a taxation year, the amount of foreign tax credit that it can claim may be restricted. This would occur if the loss reduced the corporation's total income to an amount less than its foreign source income and the CTOP is less than the foreign tax paid. In this situation, the amount that may be claimed as a foreign tax credit would be reduced as a result of the deduction of the loss in computing the corporation's income and the amount by which the foreign tax credit was so reduced would be lost as a potential foreign tax credit. To prevent this reduction in the foreign tax credit, section 110.5 (effective for 1985 and subsequent taxation years) permits a corporation to add an amount to its taxable income for the year to the extent that such an addition allows the corporation to increase the amount of the foreign tax credit it may claim. Any amount added to taxable income under section 110.5 is also added to the corporation's non-capital loss which may be carried over to other taxation years. Section 110.5 does not, however, permit a corporation to add amounts to taxable income in order to produce tax against which other tax credits or deductions may be claimed.

Taxation on a Deferred Basis

44. Where a resident of a foreign country disposes of property in the course of a corporate organization, reorganization, amalgamation, division or similar transaction and the profit, gain or income arising on the disposition is taxed on a deferred basis by the foreign country but on a current basis by Canada, a provision of a reciprocal tax treaty with the foreign country may provide a means whereby double taxation may be avoided by deferring recognition in Canada of the profit, gain or income (including recaptured capital cost allowance) so that it is taxed in the same year by both countries. Double taxation might otherwise occur if each country levies tax in different taxation years and the taxpayer is unable to make proper use of the relevant foreign tax credits. An example of such a provision is paragraph 8 of Article XIII of the 1980 Canada — U.S. Income Tax Convention, which is discussed in the current version of IT-173, *Capital Gains Derived in Canada by Residents of the United States.*

45. To achieve the deferral discussed in 44 above, the vendor and the person or partnership that acquires the property must petition the competent authority in Canada to defer the taxation (see 46 below). If the Canadian competent authority accedes to the request, an agreement must be entered into between that authority and the petitioners under which the deferral of taxation will be in effect for such time and under such other conditions as are stipulated in the agreement. Since the purpose of the deferral is to avoid double taxation, relief will only be granted to the extent necessary to avoid such double taxation. The "competent authority" in Canada is the Minister of National Revenue or the Minister's authorized representative. Refer to the current version of Information Circular 71-17 with respect to requests for competent authority consideration.

46. Where the Canadian competent authority has agreed, pursuant to a prescribed tax treaty provision, to defer the taxation in Canada of the gain or income in respect of a disposition referred to in 44 above and the vendor and the purchaser jointly elect in prescribed form (Form T2024) and within the prescribed time in accordance with terms and conditions satisfactory to the Canadian competent authority, Section 115.1 provides that the amount that the Canadian competent authority, vendor and purchaser have agreed on in respect of the property shall, for the purpose of the Act, be deemed to be the vendor's proceeds of disposition of the property and the purchaser's cost of the property. Where the property is depreciable property, paragraph 115.1(d) preserves its tax base in Canada. That is, where the vendor's capital cost of the depreciable property immediately before the disposition exceeds the agreed amount, that capital cost is deemed to be the purchaser's capital cost of the property and the

excess is deemed to have been allowed to the purchaser as capital cost allowance. Paragraph 115.1(e) maintains the characterization of the property in Canada. Section 7400 of the Regulations sets out the prescribed tax treaties and prescribed time limits for filing an election. The provisions of section 116 apply to the disposition and any forms required to be filed under section 116 must be filed at the time of filing the Form T2024. The section 116 requirements are discussed in the current version of Information Circular 72-17.

Interpretation Bulletin IT-393R2

Subject: *Income Tax Act*
              Election re Tax on Rents and Timber Royalties — Non-residents

Date: February 21, 1994

Reference: Section 216 (also sections 3, 115, 118 to 118.9 and 219, subsections 2(3), 104(7), 107(2), 120(1), 124(1), 126(1) and 215(3), and paragraphs 13(21)(d.1), 111(1)(a), 111(8)(c), 212(1)(d) and 212(1)(e) of the Income Tax Act and section 400 and subsection 2602(1) of the Income Tax Regulations)

Application
This bulletin replaces and cancels Interpretation Bulletin IT-393R dated August 12, 1983.

Summary
Certain rent and timber royalty payments from sources in Canada that are made to a nonresident person are subject to non-resident withholding tax at a rate of 25% (unless reduced by a reciprocal tax treaty) of the gross amount of the payments. However, the non-resident may be able to save tax by subsequently electing to file a Canadian income tax return and instead be taxed on the net income derived from these payments in a manner similar to that in which a resident of Canada would be taxed.

This bulletin discusses the types of income that qualify for the election, the required separate return, the unavailability of certain deductions and of the non-refundable tax credits, and certain provincial income tax implications. Also discussed are the provisions for the recapture of capital cost allowance and the non-deductibility of a loss reported under the election against income for the year reported on any other return or against income of other years. The Canadian resident payer or an agent must still withhold and remit the non-resident tax in the first place on the gross rents or royalties, but the tax return subsequently filed by the nonresident can result in some or all of the tax so remitted being refunded. Also, there is an election available which allows an agent receiving the rents or royalties to withhold and remit tax on the net amount available from those rents or royalties.

Discussion and Interpretation

1. Non-resident corporations and individuals (including estates and trusts) that receive rent from real property situated in Canada, or that receive a timber royalty on a timber resource property or a timber limit in Canada, are generally subject to Part XIII tax under paragraphs 212(1)(d) and (e), respectively, on the gross amount received. Subject to any relevant tax treaty, the rate of withholding tax is 25%. Alternatively, an election may be made under subsection 216(1) to file an income tax return and pay tax under Part I on that income as though the taxpayer were resident in Canada. This alternative is also available to a non-resident member of a partnership which receives such Income.

2. Where the renting of real property by a non-resident is a business carried on in Canada by the taxpayer, the provisions of Part XIII and the alternative treatment under section 216 are not applicable. Income from a business carried on in Canada is taxed pursuant to Part I of the Act and is also subject to the relevant income taxes of any province or territory in which such business is carried on. In this situation, the taxpayer is required to file a return reporting the taxable income earned in Canada as determined under section 115. For more details on this subject, see the current version of IT-420, Non Residents Income Earned in Canada, and of IT-171, Non-resident Individuals — Computation of Taxable Income Earned in Canada and Non-refundable Tax Credits.

3. A person who elects under subsection 216(1) to report Canadian source real property rent or timber royalty income as though resident in Canada must file the appropriate income tax return within two years (within six months, in the situation described in 9 below) from the end of the taxation year in which the income was received. It is not necessary for the person to have been a non-resident throughout the year. Thus, for example, an individual who immigrated to or emigrated from Canada during the year may elect under subsection 216(1) to report such income received during the part of the year in which he or she was a nonresident. A subsection 216(1) return must include all Canadian source real property rent and timber royalty income that would otherwise be taxable under Part XIII for the taxation year (or part of the year in which the person was a nonresident).

Furthermore, the subsection 216(1) return must be filed
   (a) as though the non-resident had no income other than the above-mentioned rent and timber royalty income, and

(b) without affecting the liability of the nonresident person for tax otherwise payable under Part 1.

As a result, the subsection 216(1) return is separate from any other return required for the year. For example, a non-resident would report section 115 taxable income earned in Canada from a business or employment in Canada on a Part I return separate from the return for subsection 216(1) income. If the non-resident had a loss from sources described in section 115, that loss could not be applied against income reported on the subsection 216(1) return.

4. Except as noted in 5 below, an election under subsection 216(1) permits a non-resident to claim those Part I deductions available to a resident in computing income under section 3. Thus, the non-resident can deduct those expenses (including capital cost allowance) incurred in earning the subsection 216(1) income, as well as any applicable amounts in subdivision e of Division B. For example, although the income reported on a subsection 216(1) return does not qualify as "earned income" for purposes of claiming a registered retirement savings plan premium, the nonresident might nevertheless, in limited circumstances, be able to claim such a premium on a subsection 216(1) return, such as in a situation where the non-resident was a resident in the immediately preceding year and had "earned income" for that year. A "subdivision e" deduction cannot, of course, be claimed twice (e.g., once on a section 115 return and again on a subsection 216(1) return). By virtue of paragraph 216(1)(c), no deductions are allowable in computing taxable income on a non-resident's subsection 216(l) return. Thus, Division C amounts such as noncapital losses are not deductible. Also, by virtue of paragraph 216(1)(d), the nonrefundable tax credits described in sections 118 to 118.9 (such as the basic personal credit or the medical expense credit) are not deductible in computing the tax payable on a subsection 216(1) return.

5. Subsection 216(8) provides that, for greater certainty, no deduction is allowed in computing the income or the tax payable of a person who elects under subsection 216(1) if that deduction is not permitted under Part 1 for a non-resident. For example, a nonresident would be denied a foreign tax credit under subsection 126(1) and a non-resident trust would be denied a deduction by virtue of subsection 104(7) for distributions to a nonresident beneficiary, since those provisions are specifically dependent upon actual or deemed residency in Canada.

6. A non-resident's rent from real property in Canada can be reported under section 216 only if it is not income from carrying on a business in Canada (see

2 above). As a result, rent that can be reported under section 216 does not represent "income earned in the year in a province" by a non-resident individual or "taxable income earned in the year in a province" by a corporation, since these terms as defined in subsection 2602(1) and section 400 of the Income Tax Regulations, respectively, include only the income from a business. Rent reported under section 216 by an individual is therefore subject to the additional tax under subsection 120(1) and is not subject to tax by any province or territory whose individual income taxes are collected by the Government of Canada. Similarly, rent reported under section 216 by a corporation is not eligible for the deduction from tax provided by subsection 124(1) and is not subject to tax by any province or territory whose corporate income taxes are collected by the Government of Canada. Income reported under section 216 by a corporation is also not subject to "branch tax" under section 219 (the branch tax is discussed in the current version of IT-137, Additional Tax on Certain Corporations Carrying on Business in Canada).

7. Where capital cost allowance has been claimed (or deemed by subsection 107(2) to have been claimed) by a taxpayer on a particular property situated in Canada for purposes of calculating the rent or timber royalty income from that property under section 216, any recapture of that capital cost allowance arising on the disposition of the property (or an interest in the property) in a subsequent taxation year will be taxable under subsection 216(5). Similar to a subsection 216(1) return, a subsection 216(5) return is separate from any other return filed for the year such as a return to report section 115 taxable income earned in Canada. In addition to the capital cost allowance recapture (or the non-resident's share of the recapture), the subsection 216(5) return must also include all Canadian source real property rent and timber royalty income that occurs in the year of the recapture (or in such part of the year in which the taxpayer is a nonresident) and that would otherwise be taxable under Part XIII. The other rules that apply for purposes of filing a return under subsection 216(1), as described above, generally also apply for purposes of filing a return under subsection 216(5). However, a subsection 216(5) return is filed because it is required when that provision applies, rather than because the non-resident elects to do so. Also, the two year filing period mentioned in 3 above does not apply, i.e., a subsection 216(5) return must be filed by the deadline that would apply if the non-resident were a resident.

8. In certain cases, it may be that what is reported on a section 216 return is a loss from rents or from timber.royalties. In such a case,the taxpayer may not set off such a loss against income for the same taxation year reported on any other return required under Part I, since to do so would conflict with the rule in 3(b)

above. Of course, if a taxpayer has a loss for the year from one section 216 property and income for the same year from another section 216 property, the loss would be set off against the income. For example, if the loss from the one property was $5,000 and the income from the other property $2,000, the net income reported on the section 216 return would be nil. However, a section 216 loss may not be deducted in other years under paragraph Il l(l)(a) because, by virtue of paragraph 11 1(8)(c), such a loss does not qualify as a non-capital loss.

9. Even though the non-resident payee may elect to file a section 216 return (which, as indicated in 3 above, can be done within two years from the end of the year in which the income is received), the Canadian resident payer or an agent, as the case may be, is nevertheless required by section 215 to withhold at the appropriate rate (see 1 above) and remit an amount to the Receiver General in payment of Part XIII tax on the gross amount of the non-resident's real property rents or timber royalties. In most cases, the difference between the Part XIII tax so remitted and the Part I tax liability resulting from the section 216 return will result in a subsequent refund to the non-resident. Where certain conditions are met, an election under subsection 216(4) may be made by an agent or other person acting on behalf of the non-resident who would otherwise be required by subsection 215(3) to remit the Part XIII tax on the gross rents or royalties. This election is available where the nonresident (or each non-resident who is a member of a partnership) has filed with the Minister an undertaking in prescribed form (Form NR6) to file a return of income under Part I for a taxation year as permitted by subsection 216(1), but within six months (rather than the two years described in 3 above) from the end of the relevant taxation year. The subsection 216(4) election allows the agent or other person to withhold and remit at the applicable rate on "any amount available" out of the rents or royalties received for remittance to the non-resident. The expression "any amount available" describes the excess of rents or royalties collected over any disbursements deductible in computing income by virtue of the election under subsection 216(1). Such disbursements would include non-capital outlays relating to repairs and maintenance, property taxes, property management fees and interest and service charges relating to the financing of the property in question. Noncash items, such as capital cost allowance, are not deductible for this purpose. Further particulars on the subsection 216(4) election may be found in the current version of Information Circular 77-16, Non-Resident Income Tax.

If you have any comments regarding the matters discussed in this bulletin, please send them to:

Director, Technical Publications Division
Legislative and Intergovernmental Affairs Branch
Revenue Canada — Customs, Excise and Taxation
875 Heron Road
Ottawa, Ontario
K1A 018

Explanation of Changes for Interpretation Bulletin IT-393R2 Election re Tax on Rents and Timber Royalties — Non-Residents

Introduction

The purpose of the Explanation of Changes is to give the reasons for the revisions to an interpretation bulletin. It outlines revisions that we have made as a result of changes to the law, as well as changes reflecting new or revised departmental interpretations.

Overview

This bulletin discusses the section 216 election that is available to a non-resident to pay Part I tax on Canadian source rents from real property and timber royalties. We have revised the bulletin primarily as a result of changes to the law under Bill C-139 and to expand the bulletin to include a discussion on the subsection 216(4) election available to an agent receiving section 216 rents or royalties.

The comments in the bulletin are not affected by proposed amendments to the Income Tax Act contained in Bill C-9, which received first reading in the House of Commons on February 4, 1994, or in the draft legislation released on August 30, 1993 (a Bill for this legislation will likely be introduced in the House in the current session of Parliament).

Legislative and Other Changes

Clarification changes: Throughout the new bulletin, there are some additions and changes to the text which we have made solely to clarify or elaborate on the information given, without changing the substance of what was said in the old bulletin. Also, the order of some paragraphs has been changed.

Old ¶ 4: This has been discontinued for the reason stated below under "New ¶ 5".

New ¶ 4 (replaces old ¶ 5): The words in parentheses in the first sentence of old ¶ 5 are discontinued in new ¶ 4 for the reason stated below under "New ¶ 5". The example regarding a deduction for an RRSP premium has been modified to reflect the amendments to the RRSP rules which became law in 1988 by the enactment of Bill C-52. The last sentence of new ¶ 4 indicates that the non-refundable tax credits cannot be claimed by the non-resident (on a return filed under subsection 216(1)). This restriction is contained in paragraph 216(1)(d), which was added to the law under Bill C-139 (as a result of the introduction of the non-refundable tax credits under the same Bill C-139).

New ¶ 5: This paragraph describes the "for greater certainty" provision, subsection 216(8), which was added under Bill C-139, preventing a non-resident who files a return under section 216 from claiming any deduction that is not permitted to a non-resident under Part I of the Act. Because of this "for greater certainty" provision, old ¶ 4 and the words in parentheses in the first sentence of old ¶ 5 are no longer necessary and have been discontinued in the new bulletin.

Old ¶ 7: This paragraph is not continued in the new bulletin. As the paragraph indicates, the general averaging provisions were repealed for years subsequent to 1981. Forward averaging is being phased out and cannot be used for income reported after 1987 by virtue of amendments to sections 110.4 and 120.1 under Bill C-139.

New ¶ 7 (replaces old ¶ 8): New ¶ 7 is similar to old ¶ 8, but has been modified to restrict the discussion on CCA recapture to that reported on a subsection 216(5) return in respect of CCA originally claimed on a section 216 return. (The discussion on recapturing CCA claimed on a section 150 return is outside the scope of this bulletin.) The last sentence of old ¶ 8 is discontinued in new ¶ 7 because the current tax treaty between Canada and the United States does not contain a relieving provision like Article XIIIA(2) of the old treaty.

New ¶ 8 (replaces old ¶ 9): The last sentence in old ¶ 9 indicates that a loss reported by a nonresident under section 216 cannot be deducted under paragraph 111(1)(a) in the previous or a subsequent year in which the taxpayer was a resident. In *Pandju Merali v. The Queen*, 88 DTC 6173, [1988] 1 C.T.C. 320, the Federal Court of Appeal found that there was nothing in the Act to prevent such a loss application in the 1981 taxation year. However, the law was then amended to nullify the application of this decision after the 1982 year: the last sentence of new ¶ 8 discusses paragraph 11 1(8)(c) the effect of which, as amended under Bill C-2, is that a loss reported under section 216 cannot qualify as a non-capital loss for the 1983 and subsequent taxation years.

New ¶ 9: We have added this paragraph to the bulletin to provide additional information to non-residents filing under section 216, regarding:
- the requirement that the Canadian resident payer or agent withhold and remit Part XIII tax on the gross rents or timber royalties; and
- the subsection 216(4) election that permits the agent or other person acting on behalf of the nonresident to withhold and remit on the net amount available out of the rents or royalties.

Interpretation Bulletin IT-497R*

Subject: *Income Tax Act*
            Overseas Employment Tax Credit

Date: February 12, 1996

Reference: Section 122.3 (also sections 114 and 126 and section 3400 of the
            Regulations)

Application
This bulletin cancels and replaces Interpretation Bulletin IT-497R2, dated June
29, 1990. IT-497R, dated August 30, 1985, and the related Special Release,
dated March 20, 1987, which applied to the 1984 to 1987 taxation years, are
also cancelled.

Summary
This bulletin deals with the overseas employment tax credit (OETC). An
individual who is resident in Canada may be entitled to claim this credit for
qualifying income from overseas employment. The OETC provides a tax
reduction for up to $100,000 of income earned in a full year of employment
outside Canada. To qualify for the OETC, the employment must be:
   (a) with a specified employer (generally, a resident of Canada);
   (b) in connection with a contract under which the specified employer
        carried on business outside Canada on a resource, construction,
        installation, agricultural or engineering project (or for the purpose of
        obtaining such a contract); and
   (c) performed outside Canada for a period of at least 6 consecutive
        months.
The bulletin explains various terms and conditions relating to the OETC. It
also provides details of the calculation required to determine the OETC and
gives an example of this calculation.

Discussion and Interpretation
General
1. The overseas employment tax credit (OETC) is available to individuals who
are resident or deemed resident in Canada for any part of a taxation year. The
current version of IT-221, *Determination of an Individual's Residence Status,*
describes circumstances in which an individual is considered to continue to be

---

* As revised by Special Release dated March 20, 1987.

resident in Canada after having physically departed from Canada. That bulletin also discusses deemed residents of Canada.

2. An individual described in 1 above who has earned qualifying income in a taxation year throughout a qualifying period while employed outside Canada by a specified employer with respect to a qualifying activity may, under section 122.3, deduct an OETC from the tax otherwise payable for the year. The terms "qualifying income," "qualifying activity," "qualifying period" and "specified employer," as well as the OETC calculation, are explained below.

Qualifying Income
3. Qualifying income of an individual for OETC purposes is the employment income earned in a qualifying period while the individual was employed by a "specified employer" (other than for the performance of services under a prescribed international development assistance program of the Government of Canada as discussed in 16 to 18 below), provided all or substantially all of the individual's employment duties were performed outside Canada:

   (a) in connection with a contract under which the employer carried on business outside Canada with respect to a qualifying activity as discussed in 6 below, or
   (b) for the purpose of obtaining a contract for the specified employer to undertake a qualifying activity.

The fact that the employment is performed in connection with two or more separate contracts of the specified employer does not, in itself, affect eligibility to claim the OETC.

The "all or substantially all" test referred to above is considered to be met if 90% of the employment duties are performed outside Canada.

4. For the purpose of section 122.3, qualifying income earned by an individual employee during a qualifying period includes salary, wages and other remuneration, including gratuities, received from that employment for the qualifying period. It also includes all or a reasonable proportion of any taxable benefit or other amount required under section 6 to be included in income that can be considered to be received or enjoyed by the individual for that same period from, or as a consequence of, that same employment. Benefits under section 7 are similarly included. This type of income is reduced by all or a reasonable proportion of any applicable amount described in subsections 8(1) to (13) inclusive that can reasonably be considered to be deductible in calculating income during that same period from that same employment.

5. Individuals are not eligible for a deduction from tax under section 122.3 in respect of self-employed income.

Qualifying Activity

6. For OETC purposes, a qualifying activity includes:
   (a) the exploration for or the exploitation of petroleum, natural gas, minerals or similar resources;
   (b) a construction, installation, agricultural or engineering activity; or
   (c) any prescribed activity.

A qualifying activity refers to a qualifying activity of the specified employer and not that of the employee.

7. As long as all or substantially all of the duties performed by the employee are in connection with a contract under which the specified employer carries on a business with respect to a qualifying activity, the employee would qualify for the OETC provided that the other conditions referred to in subsection 122.3(1) are met. For example, if all of these conditions are met, the following employees of a specified employer carrying on a qualifying activity would qualify for the OETC:
   (a) instructors or administrative staff providing supporting services to fellow employees;
   (b) staff who train the personnel of the foreign customer; and
   (c) computer hardware and software specialists fulfilling terms of their employer's qualifying activity contract.

Sub-Contractors

8. Ordinarily, the specified employer will itself directly carry on the qualified activities described in 6 (a) to (c) above, that entitle employees to claim the OETC. However, assuming all of the other requirements of subsection 122.3(1) are met, the OETC is also available to employees of a specified employer that carries on business outside Canada in other than a qualifying activity. Often referred to as a sub-contractor, such a specified employer would be one who has a contract or subcontract to provide its services through its employees to another person in respect of a qualifying activity carried on by that person outside Canada, or in respect of such a qualifying activity which that person has subcontracted to a third party. For example, assume that a specified employer (A Ltd.) has contracted to carry on business outside Canada by providing data processing services to a non-resident company (B Ltd.) whose only business is the exploration for natural gas. Assuming the other requirements of subsection 122.3(1) are met, the employees of A Ltd. providing the data processing services would qualify for the OETC, since their

employment is in connection with a contract under which the specified employer carried on business outside Canada with respect to qualifying activities.

Qualifying Period

9. A qualifying period, for OETC purposes, means a period of more than six consecutive months that commenced in the year or a previous year. The qualifying period must include part of the taxation year for which the OETC claim is made. In this context, a month means either an entire month named on a calendar or a period starting from a given day in one month to the day before the corresponding day of the next month. For example, if the starting date for the six consecutive months was December 14, 1992, the minimum qualifying period of more than six consecutive months, would run from December 14, 1992 into June 14, 1993.

10. A qualifying period may be composed of consecutive periods of time spent by an individual in one or more locations anywhere outside Canada, including the land and territorial waters of a foreign country, in international waters or Antarctica.

11. An individual's entitlement to the OETC will not be denied simply because the person was not a resident or deemed resident of Canada throughout the qualifying period. Similarly, an individual's entitlement will not necessarily be denied because the individual was not actually outside Canada or at the work location(s) for the entire qualifying period. Periods of vacation or consultation with the employer will not be considered to interrupt the qualifying period, provided they are reasonable. This will depend on the facts of each case, including the relevant industrial practice, the nature of the work performed and the remoteness from any established community. During a period of absence from the work location, an employee may perform duties of employment in Canada and still remain eligible for the OETC, provided that substantially all of the employment duties, as referred to in 3 above, are performed throughout the qualifying period outside Canada.

12. However, if an individual, such as a drill rig worker, is employed on an "on demand" basis for various periods in the year and is paid only for those periods, with no commitment for indeterminate employment or for a minimum number of days of employment in the year, that individual would usually be considered to commence and cease employment at the beginning and end of each such period. Accordingly, such an employee would not qualify for the OETC unless

one of the periods of employment that commenced in the year or a previous year, and ended in the particular year, exceeded six consecutive months.

Specified Employer

13. A specified employer, for OETC purposes, is described in subsection 122.3(2) as:

    (a) a person resident in Canada;

    (b) a partnership, provided that persons resident in Canada or corporations controlled by persons resident in Canada own more than 10% of the aggregate fair market value of all interests in the partnership; or

    (c) a corporation that is a foreign affiliate, defined in paragraph 95(1)(d), of a person resident in Canada.

Residency of Specified Employer

14. A specified employer that is a corporation is generally considered to be a resident of Canada if:

    (a) its central management and control are located in Canada; or

    (b) it falls within the criteria set out in subsection 250(4) which deem a corporation to be resident in Canada throughout a taxation year.

For further information on the residency of a corporation see the current version of IT-391, *Status of Corporations.*

The current version of IT-221, *Determination of an Individual's Residence Status,* explains the factors which apply in determining residency of individuals.

Specified Employer Carrying on Business Outside Canada

15. Whether or not a specified employer is carrying on business outside Canada is always a question of fact. In determining this, the major factors to be considered are:

    (a) the objects of the employer's business; and

    (b) the nature of the activities the employer is carrying on outside Canada.

Employment with the Government of Canada or a provincial or municipal government generally does not qualify for the purposes of section 122.3, because a body politic or government would not usually carry on business outside Canada under a contract.

Prescribed International Development Assistance Programs

16. For purposes of the OETC, employment for the performance of services under a prescribed international development assistance program of the

Government of Canada is not qualified employment. Such programs are prescribed in section 3400 of the Regulations to be international development assistance programs of the Canadian International Development Agency (CIDA) that are financed with funds (other than loan assistance funds) which are provided under External Affairs Vote 30a, *Appropriation Act No. 3, 1977-78*, or another act providing for such financing. Section 3400 of the Regulations applies even if CIDA provides only partial funding for the project.

17. The exclusion of services performed under a prescribed international development assistance program does not apply if the qualifying period started before 1984, or started before 1987 in connection with a specified employer's contract entered into before August 16, 1983.

18. As indicated in 16 above, a CIDA program financed by loan assistance funds may constitute qualified employment. However, CIDA funding rules were changed in 1986 so that international development assistance programs are financed only by grants rather than loan assistance funds. As a result, after March 31, 1986, any employment under a CIDA-sponsored program will not qualify for the OETC unless the funding agreement was initially signed as a loan agreement before April 1, 1986.

Option to Claim Foreign Tax Credit under Subsection 126(1)
19. The tax credits provided under section 122.3, the OETC, and subsection 126(1), the foreign tax credit for non-business income, are optional. A taxpayer may claim one or the other, or both. However, to the extent that a portion of an employee's qualifying foreign employment income is used to calculate an OETC, it may not be used to determine a foreign tax credit (see the current version of IT-270, *Foreign Tax Credit*). An employee may choose to claim a foreign tax credit, for example, where the OETC would be rendered ineffective by virtue of the application of the alternative minimum tax under section 127.5.

Authorized Form and Reduced Withholding of Tax at Source
20. Form T626, *Overseas Employment Tax Credit,* should be completed and filed with a T1 return when claiming the OETC. The employer is also required to complete a portion of this form. An application may be made for reduced withholding of income tax at source if the taxpayer will be eligible for the OETC. To apply, a completed copy of form T626 should be submitted to the Chief of Source Deductions at the Revenue Canada tax services office serving the taxpayer, together with a letter explaining the situation and supporting documentation, such as a copy of the contract for overseas employment. Where an employer has numerous employees on international assignment who clearly

will qualify for the OETC, the Department will consider granting a blanket waiver to cover the reduction in withholdings at source.

OETC Calculation

21. Expressed as a formula, the amount that can be deducted under section 122.3 as an OETC is:

$$\frac{\text{The lesser of limitation A and B}}{\text{Adjusted income for the taxation year (see 22 below)}} \quad \text{x} \quad \frac{\text{Tax otherwise payable for the taxation year (see 23 below)}}{}$$

where limitation:

$$A = \frac{\text{the number of days in that portion of the qualifying period that is in the year and on which the individual was resident in Canada}}{365} \quad \text{x} \quad \$80,000$$

B = 80% of the individual's qualifying income (see 3 above) that is reasonably attributable to duties performed during the number of days referred to in A above;

Therefore, the OETC provides an annual tax reduction for a maximum of $100,000 of overseas employment income earned in a full year of overseas employment. The $80,000 base amount in "A" above represents a ceiling for a one-year period which is prorated if the employee is overseas for less than the full year. An analysis of the formula components and an example of the OETC calculation is found in 22 to 24 below.

Adjusted income for the taxation year

22. For the purposes of the OETC calculation, as described in 21 above, the adjusted income for the taxation year for an individual who is resident in Canada throughout the year is the amount, if any, by which the individual's income for the year (including, before 1988, any forward averaged amount included in taxable income for the year) exceeds the total of
    (a) the amounts deducted in the year under:
        •   paragraph 111(1)(b) in respect of net capital losses; and
        •   section 110.6 in respect of the capital gains deduction; and

(b) the amounts deductible for the year under:
- paragraph 110(1)(d.2) equal to 1/4 of the amount included in income under paragraph 35(1)(d) in respect of a prospector's or grubstaker's shares received after May 22, 1985 unless the amount included in income is exempt from tax in Canada by reason of one of Canada's tax treaties;
- paragraph 110(1)(d.3) equal to 1/4 of the amount included in calculating income under subsection 147(10.4) with respect to employer shares received as part of a withdrawal after May 23, 1985 from a deferred profit sharing plan;
- paragraph 110(1)(f) with respect to certain amounts that are required to be included in income but are exempt from tax in Canada; and·
- paragraph 110(1)(j) in respect of the amount of a benefit included in income as a result of an individual receiving a home relocation loan because of an employment relocation occurring in 1985 and subsequent taxation years.

For the 1993 and subsequent taxation years, the adjusted income of an individual who is resident in Canada during part of a taxation year will include not only the individual's income for the period in the year during which the individual was resident in Canada but also the individual's "taxable income earned in Canada" (subject to certain adjustments) as determined under section 115 for the period in the year during which the individual was not resident in Canada. This is reduced by the total of·
- the amounts listed in (a) above that were deducted in the year, and·
- the amounts listed in (b) above that were deductible in respect of the period referred to in paragraph 114(a).

For 1992 and prior taxation years, the adjusted income of an individual who is resident in Canada during part of a taxation year is the amount, if any, by which the individual's income computed in accordance with paragraph 114(a) for the period or periods in the year throughout which the individual was resident in Canada, was employed in Canada or was carrying on business in Canada, exceeds the total of·
- the amounts listed in (a) above that were deducted in the year, and·
- the amounts listed in (b) above that were deductible in respect of the period referred to in paragraph 114(a).

Tax Otherwise Payable for the Year

23. As defined in paragraph 122.3(2)(b), tax otherwise payable for the year is the amount that would be the tax payable under Part I of the Act for the year before

    (a) adding any amount for:·

- the amount of tax that is, under section 120, required to be added for income not earned in a province; or·
- forward-averaged income under subsection 120.1(2); or

    (b) deducting any amount for:·

- an OETC under subsection 122.3(1);·
- forward-averaged income under subsection 120.1(1);·
- minimum tax carryover under subsection 120.2(1);·
- a dividend tax credit under section 121;·
- a foreign tax credit under section 126;·
- a logging tax deduction, a political contribution tax credit or an investment tax credit under section 127;·
- a share-purchase tax credit under section 127.2;·
- a scientific research and experimental development tax credit under section 127.3; or·
- a labour-sponsored funds tax credit under section 127.4.

Example

24. Assume an individual resident in Canada during 1994:

    (a) is employed in the year for 73 days, commencing on October 20, 1994, outside Canada by a specified employer for the performance of any one or more of the duties described in 6(a)-(c) above;

    (b) continues to be so employed until April 30, 1995;

    (c) earns income of $22,000 in 1994 that is reasonably attributable to the 73 days referred to in (a);

    (d) calculates adjusted income for 1994 to be $64,000 under 22 above; and

    (e) calculates tax otherwise payable for 1994 to be $14,000 under 23 above.

To calculate the individual's overseas employment tax credit:

(1) Determine the lesser of Limitation A and B

$$A = \frac{(a)}{365} \times \$80,000 \quad = \frac{73}{365} \times \$80,000 = \$16,000$$

$$B = 80\% \text{ of } \frac{(c)}{100} \quad = \ 80 \times \$22,000 = \$17,600$$

(2) The OETC is:

$$\frac{\$16,000}{\$64,000} \times \$14,000 = \$3,500$$

In this example, because the individual's qualifying period exceeded six months at the time the 1994 tax return was required to be filed, the tax credit of $3,500 may be deducted in calculating 1994 tax payable. However, when an individual commences the performance of employment duties outside Canada after October 31 in a particular year, the necessary qualifying period of more than six months would not be satisfied before the individual's return of income for that year is required to be filed (i.e., no later than April 30 of the immediately following year). As a result, a tax credit under section 122.3 for income earned outside Canada during the period of that year after October 31 cannot be claimed at the time such return is required to be filed unless it can be established that the individual will be performing the employment duties outside Canada for a period of more than six consecutive months. The individual can establish this fact by, for example, filing with the return a letter from the employer certifying that the individual will be performing the employment duties outside Canada for a period of more than six consecutive months.

If you have any comments concerning the matters discussed in this bulletin, please send them to:

Director, Technical Publications Division
Policy and Legislation Branch
Revenue Canada
875 Heron Road
Ottawa ON K1A 0L8

Explanation of Changes for Interpretation Bulletin IT-497R3
Overseas Employment Tax Credit

Introduction
The purpose of the Explanation of Changes is to give the reasons for the revisions to an interpretation bulletin. It outlines revisions that we have made as a result of changes to the law, as well as changes reflecting new or revised departmental interpretations.

Overview
This bulletin cancels and replaces existing IT-497R2, which deals with the overseas employment tax credit (OETC) after 1987. The OETC reduces the tax

otherwise payable by Canadian residents on qualifying income from employment outside Canada. We revised the bulletin to reflect amendments to subsection 122.3(1) enacted by S.C. 1994, c.7, Schedule II (1991, c.49-formerly Bill C-18) and S.C. 1994, c.21 (formerly Bill C-27). We have made general revisions to improve the readability of the bulletin and to reflect recent departmental opinions on this subject.

The comments in this bulletin are not affected by any draft legislation released before September 28, 1995.

Legislative and Other Changes

¶ 2 reflects the Bill C-18 amendment to paragraph 122.3(1)(b) which clarifies that the OETC may be available in connection with employment on a project in international waters (see new ¶ 10).

New ¶ 6 describes what activities constitute a "qualifying activity."

New ¶ 7 gives examples of employees who would qualify for the OETC.

New ¶ 8 reflects the Department's position that employees of sub-contractors indirectly involved in qualifying activities may be entitled to claim the OETC.

New ¶ 9 replaces the comments at the beginning of former ¶ 5 on the meaning of "qualifying period" and provides an application of this term where the period includes a part of a month.

New ¶ 10 replaces the concluding comments in former ¶ 5 to reflect the Bill C-18 amendment to paragraph 122.3(1)(b). Previously, qualifying employment had to be "in a country or countries other than Canada." It is now sufficient that the employment be "outside Canada."

New ¶ 11 replaces former ¶ 8. ¶ 11 and new ¶ 12 set out more detailed interpretative positions concerning the effect of vacations and other absences from the worksite, as well as the treatment of individuals hired on an "on demand" basis.

New ¶ 14 sets out some general information on the residency of the specified employer.

New ¶ 15, former ¶ 11, includes the Department's position regarding employment with various levels of Canadian government. The comments about commercial activities in former ¶ 11 were deleted. They were considered unnecessary because, as already stated in ¶15, "Whether or not a specified employer is carrying on business outside Canada is always a question of fact."

New ¶s 16 to 18 add new interpretive details about the exclusion of services performed under a prescribed international development assistance program.

New ¶ 19 discusses the option to claim the Foreign Tax Credit.

New ¶ 20 replaces the comment on the authorized form T626 in former ¶ 13. We have added new information about applying for reduced withholding of tax at source.

New ¶ 22 replaces former ¶ 12 and reflects Bill C-27 amendments to both subparagraph 122.3(1)(c)(ii) and subparagraph 122.3(1)(e)(ii) with respect to OETC calculations when an individual is resident in Canada for part of a year.

New ¶'s 23 and 24 replace ¶ 7 with little change to the calculation and the example. The example recognizes the 1991 amendment to paragraph 122.3(1)(b) which provides that the OETC will be available where an individual is employed outside Canada, e.g. a project in international waters, rather than in a country other than Canada.

Memorandum D2-3-2

Ottawa, February 28, 1997

SUBJECT
FORMER RESIDENTS OF CANADA
TARIFF ITEM 9805.00.00

This Memorandum outlines and explains the conditions under which former residents of Canada, residents of Canada, Canadian Government employees, and Canadian Forces personnel may import goods for personal and household use after a minimum residency or absence abroad of one year.

TABLE OF CONTENTS

Legislation

Tariff Item 9805.00.00

Goods imported by a member of the Canadian Forces, an employee of the Canadian government, or by a former resident of Canada returning to Canada to resume residence in Canada after having been a resident of another country for a period of not less than one year, or by a resident returning after an absence from Canada of not less than one year, and acquired by that person for personal or household use and actually owned, possessed and used abroad by that person for at least six months prior to that person's return to Canada and accompanying that person at the time of their return from abroad.

Most-Favoured-Nation Tariff	Free
Mexico Tariff	Free
United States Tariff	Free

The provisions of this tariff item shall apply to alcoholic beverages not exceeding 1.14 litres and tobacco not exceeding fifty cigars, two hundred cigarettes, 200 grams of manufactured tobacco and 200 tobacco sticks where they are included in the baggage accompanying the importer, and no exemption is being claimed in respect of alcoholic beverages or tobacco under another heading or subheading at the time of importation.

Where goods (other than alcoholic beverages, cigars, cigarettes and manufactured tobacco) are not accompanying the person returning from abroad, they may be classified under this heading when imported at a later time if they are reported by the person at the time of return to Canada.

The Governor in council may, by order, exempt any goods or classes of goods acquired during an absence from Canada and imported by any or all classes of persons referred to in this tariff item from any or all of the requirements, or substitute less exigent requirements, relating to the period during which such goods or classes of goods must be owned, possessed or used abroad by such classes of persons. Goods entitled to be classified under this item shall be exempt from all duties notwithstanding the provisions of this or any other Act of Parliament except that

    (a) any article which was acquired after March 31, 1977, by the person claiming the exemption hereunder and which has a value for duty as determined under the *Customs Act* of more than $10,000 is subject to the duties as otherwise prescribed on the amount of the value for duty in excess of $10,000, and

(*b*) any goods imported which are sold or otherwise disposed of within twelve months after importation are subject to the duties otherwise prescribed.

Exemption Order

ORDER EXEMPTING CERTAIN GOODS FROM CERTAIN REQUIREMENTS SPECIFIED IN TARIFF ITEM 9805.00.00 OF THE *CUSTOMS TARIFF*

Short Title

1. This order may be cited as the *Tariff Item No. 9805.00.00 Exemption Order.*

Interpretation

2. In this Order,
"bride's trousseau" means goods acquired for use in the household of a newly married couple, but does not include vehicles, vessels or aircraft;
"wedding presents" means goods of a non-commercial nature received by a person as personal gifts in consideration of that person's recent marriage or the anticipated marriage of that person within three months of the person's return to Canada.

Exemption

3. The following goods are exempt from the six-month ownership, possession or use requirements set out in tariff item 9805.00.00 of the *Customs Tariff:*
(*a*) alcoholic beverages owned by, in the possession of and imported by a person who has attained the minimum age at which a person may lawfully purchase alcoholic beverages in the province in which the customs office where the alcoholic beverages are imported is situated;
(*b*) tobacco products owned by, in the possession of the importer;
(*c*) a bride's trousseau owned by, in the possession of and imported by a recently married person or a bride-to-be whose anticipated marriage is to take place within three months of the date of her return to Canada;
(*d*) wedding presents owned by, in the possession of and imported by the recipient thereof;
(*e*) any goods imported by a person who has resided abroad for at least five years immediately prior to returning to Canada and who, prior to

the date of return, owned, was in possession of and used the goods; and

(f) goods acquired as replacements for goods that, but for their loss or destruction as the result of fire, theft, accident or other unforeseen contingency, would have been classified under tariff item No. 9805.00.00 of the *Customs Tariff*, on condition that:

  (i) the goods acquired as replacements are of a similar class and approximately of the same value as the goods they replaced,

  (ii) the goods acquired as replacements were owned by, in the possession of, and used by a person prior to the person's return to Canada, and

  (iii) evidence is produced at the time the goods are accounted for under section 32 of the *Customs Act* that the goods they replaced were lost or destroyed as the result of fire, theft, accident or other unforeseen contingency.

GUIDELINES AND GENERAL INFORMATION

1. The provisions of tariff item 9805.00.00 apply to goods imported by Canadian Forces personnel, Canadian government employees, former residents of Canada, and residents of Canada.

2. Persons in the aforementioned categories are entitled to the benefits of tariff item 9805.00.00 when they return to Canada. Unless specifically exempted by order, all goods being imported must have been acquired by the person, for personal or household use and have been actually owned, possessed and used abroad for at least six months prior to the person's return to Canada.

Value Limitations
3. A $10,000 value limitation (in Canadian funds) applies in respect of each article, acquired after March 31, 1977, which is imported under the provisions of tariff item 9805.00.00. Goods valued in excess of $10,000 are subject to customs assessment at the rate otherwise applicable, payable on that portion of the value which exceeds $10,000. Values are determined in accordance with the provisions of the *Customs Act*. In the case of an automobile for example, duties will apply on the portion of the value in excess of $10,000. Excise taxes, payable on the excess weight of the vehicle and on air conditioning units, will apply in their entirety, if the value of the vehicle exceeds $10,000.

Retention Period

4. Goods imported under tariff item 9805.00.00 which are sold or otherwise disposed of in Canada within twelve months after importation are subject to repayment of the duties initially exempted on the first $10,000. Credit will be accorded for each full month in respect of which the item was retained. For example, a US manufactured vehicle valued at $20,000 is imported from the U.S.A. on January 1, 1996. The first $10,000 is free of duties. Duties exempted on the first $10,000 = $892.60. The vehicle is sold October 1, 1996 (retained for 9 months). The repayment of duties on the first $10,000 = $892.60. Deduct credit for number of months retained $892.60 – 12 ' 9 = $669.45. The amount payable at time of sale = $892.60 minus $669.45 = $223.15.

Note: If the value of the vehicle at time of importation was under $10,000 and it was therefore exempted from the payment of excise taxes (e.g., air-conditioned/excess weight), such excise taxes become payable in their entirety if the vehicle is sold or disposed of within 12 months after importation.

Absence Requirements

5. Persons who establish themselves as residents of another country for a period of at least one year, may make return visits to Canada (as non-resident visitors) without jeopardizing their eligibility to claim under tariff item 9805.00.00 at the time of their final return to resume residence.

6. However, persons who do **not** establish themselves as residents of another country during their absence from Canada, such as those on extended vacations, voyages or world cruises, are eligible to claim goods under tariff item 9805.00.00 **only if** the duration of absence is a period of at least one year, without any return to Canada having been made during that time.

7. One year is interpreted as meaning the anniversary date of departure, in the next calendar year (for example, leave January 1, 1996, return no earlier than January 1, 1997).

8. Persons who are studying or working abroad for a period of less than one year are not eligible for the benefits of tariff item 9805.00.00 at the time of their final return to resume residence in Canada. These persons may not aggregate the time spent abroad (e.g., an athlete who spends six months in the United States and six months in Canada each year over a period of several years may not accumulate the time spent in the United States to qualify for the benefits of tariff item 9805.00.00).

Ownership, Possession And Use

9. "Ownership" means that the former resident has acquired, by purchase or other means, the legal right to have goods as personal property and to exercise control over their use and disposition. Goods which are leased do not qualify.

10. "Possession" means that the former resident has, in person, physically accepted the goods.

11. "Use" means that the former resident has actually put the goods into an action or service for a purpose for which they were designed or intended.

12. The "six month" stipulation is waived in respect of goods imported under tariff item 9805.00.00:

    (a) by persons who have resided abroad for at least five years immediately prior to returning to Canada to resume residence, provided the goods were actually owned, possessed and used abroad by them (for any period of time) prior to the date of their return;

    (b) which have been acquired as replacements for goods that, except for their loss or destruction as the result of fire, theft, accident, or other unforeseen contingency, would have qualified for importation under tariff item 9805.00.00. In order to be eligible under this provision, the replacement goods must be of a similar class and of approximately the same value as the goods they replaced, and the importer must be able to substantiate the bona fides of the circumstances. Further, the replacement goods must have been owned, possessed and used by the importer prior to his or her return to Canada.

13. The "use" requirement and the "six month" stipulation are waived in respect of the following goods imported under tariff item 9805.00.00:

    (a) alcoholic beverages owned by, in the possession of, and imported by a person who has attained the minimum age at which a person may lawfully purchase alcoholic beverages in the province in which the customs office where the alcoholic beverages are imported is situated;

    (b) tobacco products owned by and in the possession of a person who has attained the minimum age as prescribed by the province or territory of importation;

    (c) a bride's trousseau owned by, and in the possession of a recently married person or a bride-to-be whose anticipated marriage is to take place within three months of the date of her return to Canada; and

    (d) wedding presents owned by, in the possession of, and imported by the recipient.

14. All remaining requirements of tariff item 9805.00.00 apply in the usual manner.

Goods Admissible

15. Goods which may be imported under tariff item 9805.00.00 are limited solely to goods for the importer's personal or household use.

16. Mobile trailers not exceeding 2.6 metres (9 feet) in width, which the owner is capable of moving from place to place on a personal basis; motor homes, as well as tool sheds or garages which do not attach to or form part of a dwelling, are eligible under tariff item 9805.00.00.

17. Commercial vehicles are eligible for importation under tariff item 9805.00.00 only if they have been and will continue to be used solely for personal transportation. (Equipment imported exclusively for personal or hobby use may also be included under tariff item 9805.00.00.)

18. Motor vehicles as well as other goods for personal use (either husband or wife may claim, regardless of whether these goods are registered jointly or in either name).

Goods Not Admissible

19. Goods for the accommodation of others, for sale or hire or for use in a business or manufacturing establishment or as contractors' outfits, such as office equipment and furniture, dental chairs, welding equipment, metal and woodworking machines, motor vehicles and trailers for commercial use are not admissible under tariff item 9805.00.00 but are subject to the normal customs assessment.

20. Livestock, machinery, and equipment for use on a ranch or farm are not admissible under tariff item 9805.00.00 and, as such, are to be classified under the appropriate provisions of the Customs Tariff.

21. Houses and buildings used as dwellings or residences are not considered to be goods for household or personal use and are therefore inadmissible under the tariff item 9805.00.00. Similarly, large trailers used as residences, of a type or nature which require special permit and highway escort to be moved from place to place, may not be included under tariff item 9805.00.00 but are subject to the payment of duties.

22. Company-owned and leased vehicles (as well as any other leased goods) are not considered to be owned by the traveller, and are, therefore, not admissible under the provisions of tariff item 9805.00.00.

23. Goods which are shipped to Canada while the owner continues to live or travel abroad are not eligible for importation under tariff item 9805.00.00 at the time of arrival but are subject to the duties otherwise prescribed (or alternatively, they may be placed in "bonded storage"; see paragraph 33 of this Memorandum).

24. Goods stored abroad or shipped to Canada for bonded storage before all of the ownership, possession and use requirements have been met are not eligible for importation under tariff item 9805.00.00 at the time of final clearance. The time spent in transit or in storage abroad or in Canada cannot be included when calculating the six-month period of possession or use.

Listing Of Goods To Be Imported
25. Prior to importation, importers must prepare a detailed list in duplicate of all goods to be imported, showing the make, model, serial numbers (where possible) and approximate value of each item. For household items of a general nature, a group listing and overall value is sufficient (e.g., kitchen utensils - $000). The list should be divided into two headings, showing which items are accompanying the owner at the time of return and which items are to arrive at a later date as "goods to follow." This list must be presented to the customs inspector when the former resident first arrives in Canada, even if no goods are being imported at that time (see paragraph 31). Instead of a list, Form B 4A, List of Goods Imported, may be used. Refer to paragraph 29 of this Memorandum.

26. Former residents' effects arriving by commercial carrier and going forward in bond to an inland destination for clearance will be manifested on Form A 8A, Customs Cargo Control Document. If the commercial carrier is not covered by a general authorization, the carrier must obtain a single trip authorization. (Refer to Memorandum D3-1-1, Regulations Respecting the Importation, Transportation and Exportation of Goods, for bonding regulations.)

27. Former residents' effects going forward in bond are not required to be delivered to a highway sufferance warehouse but may proceed directly to the customs office at destination.

28.   Former residents transporting their effects using a private vehicle or a rented vehicle controlled by them may proceed under a Form E 29B, Temporary Admission Permit. The Form E 29B will be issued for a period sufficient to enable the former resident to proceed directly to the customs office at or nearest to destination. A copy of the list of goods referred to in paragraph 25 of this Memorandum will be attached to the former resident's copy of the permit and both documents will be surrendered to customs at the inland office. A copy of Form E 29B will be forwarded by the issuing office to the customs office of destination to ensure the formal accounting is made within the prescribed time.

Accounting For Goods

29.   When former residents first arrive in Canada, the inspector will prepare Form B 4, Personal Effects Accounting Document, on their behalf, based on the list of goods provided. The list must show which goods are accompanying the former resident and which are to follow (refer to paragraph 25). To facilitate the process, former residents may complete Form B 4 in advance and present it to the inspector when they arrive. Forms B 4 are available in French or English along with Form B 4A (for listing the goods) from regional or local customs offices.

Goods To Follow

30.   When "goods to follow" arrive, they will be released to the importer on presentation to customs of a copy of the original Form B 4. The customs inspector will initial beside the item(s) being released and date-stamp the form.

31.   Only eligible goods which were declared and listed as "goods to follow" on the former resident's original Form B 4 are eligible for duty and tax free importation at a later time, under tariff item 9805.00.00. There is no time limit for importing "goods to follow" that were declared on arrival and listed on the former resident's Form B 4.

Shipping Goods To Canada

32.   In shipping goods to Canada, special effort should be made to ensure that the arrival of the goods coincides with or follows the owner's return. Goods arriving in advance of the owner's return will be held at customs for a period of only 40 days, after which time they are treated as unclaimed.

33.   There are cases where persons residing abroad wish to ship goods to Canada for long term storage, pending their own return to Canada at some future time. In such cases, it is the responsibility of the owner to make suitable

arrangements with the shipping agent to have the goods placed in "bonded storage" in Canada. Goods may remain in bonded storage for only four years and premium rates are usually assessed by private firms for this service. When the owner arrives in Canada to effect customs clearance of the goods, only those items which met all of the criteria of tariff item 9805.00.00 before their shipment to Canada may be claimed under that item.

Requirements Of Other Government Departments
34. Customs assists other government departments in controlling the importation of certain goods into Canada. Included are such items as firearms, ammunition, fireworks, animals and animal products, plants and plant products, fresh fruit and vegetables, as well as certain food and drug products. This list is not all-encompassing but provides some examples of goods which are controlled, restricted, or prohibited. More information may be obtained by contacting:

Commercial Services Directorate
Revenue Canada
Ottawa ON K1A 0L5
Facsimile: (613) 952-1698

Endangered Species
35. Customs officers also assist Environment Canada in administering the Convention on International Trade in Endangered Species of Wild Fauna and Flora (CITES). Under this convention, the trade and movement of a large and growing list of animals, fish, birds, reptiles, insects and plants, and of any recognizable by-products made of their fur, skin, bone, etc., are restricted. Refer to Memorandum D19-7-1, Convention on International Trade in Endangered Species.

36. Goods regulated by CITES which are being transported through Canada from the United States require a temporary import certificate issued by the CITES Administrator and possibly an export permit issued by the U.S. Fish and Wildlife Service. For further details on permit requirements, contact:

Administrator
Convention on International Trade in Endangered Species
Canadian Wildlife Service
Environment Canada
Ottawa ON K1A 0H3
Telephone: (613) 997-1840

House Plants
37. Plants, generally recognized as house plants and intended to be grown indoors, being brought into Canada from continental U.S.A. do not require import permits or certificates.

38. Import permits or phytosanitary certificates are required for house plants being brought into Canada as part of household effects from origins other than continental U.S.A. Refer to Memorandum D19-1-1, Agricultural and Food Products.

Dogs And Cats
39. Dogs and cats from the U.S.A. must be accompanied by a certificate signed and dated by a veterinarian indicating that the animal has been vaccinated against rabies within the last three years. The certificate must provide sufficient description and detail to enable adequate identification. Pups and kittens from the U.S.A. that are under the age of three months do not require a rabies certificate, but must be in good health at the time of arrival.

40. Except for guide dogs that accompany you on arrival, animals coming from other parts of the world will require inspection. Customs may also require a permit or certificate and may subject the animals to quarantine requirements. Refer to Memorandum D19-1-1.

Firearms
41. Canada has stringent regulations on firearms. Former residents planning to bring a firearm into Canada should check with the chief firearms officer of the province or territory through which they intend to enter the country. For more information, and the addresses of these officials, obtain a copy of Memorandum D19-13-2, *Importation of Offensive Weapons Regulations.*

Meat, Dairy Products, Fruits, and Vegetables
42. Canada has complex requirements, restrictions, and limits that apply to importing these and other foodstuffs. Former residents can avoid problems by not bringing such goods into Canada. For more information, they should contact one of the customs offices listed at the end of this Memorandum. Those products which do meet import requirements are subject to full customs assessment in the usual way.

Motor Vehicles

43. There are restrictive importation rules for vehicles, such as motor homes, trailers, trucks, and cars that are less than 15 years old. Under the North American Free Trade Agreement (NAFTA) you can import such a vehicle from the U.S. only if it meets Transport Canada's strict safety and emission standards, or if it can be modified to meet these standards after you import it.

44. Motor vehicles manufactured to meet United States safety standards do not automatically pass Canadian safety standards. You are responsible for determining whether your vehicle complies with Canadian standards, or whether it can be modified to meet the standards after you import it. You cannot import vehicles that cannot be modified to meet Canadian standards.

45. For information on importing a vehicle originally manufactured to meet U.S. safety and emission standards, and on the federal registration fees that apply, call the Registrar of Imported Vehicles at:-
   1-800-511-7755 (from within Canada or the U.S.)-
   (416) 598-7840 (local calls from the Toronto area)

46. Vehicles less than 15 years old that meet only European motor vehicle safety standards generally **do not meet** the Canadian standards. You may not be able to import them into Canada.

47. If you are considering importing such a vehicle, make sure it meets the Canadian standards outlined in the Canada Motor Vehicle Safety Act and Regulations. It will also have to bear the manufacturer's statement-of-compliance label.

48. You should contact the following Transport Canada office for more information:

   Road Safety and Motor Vehicle Regulation Directorate
   Transport Canada
   13th floor
   Canada Building
   344 Slater Street
   Ottawa ON K1A 0N5
   Telephone: (613) 998-2174

Note: 1.   *Your vehicle may be subject to provincial or territorial sales tax. For more information, contact the Department of motor vehicles in your province or territory.*
2.   *Also, before you export a vehicle to Canada, make sure that you first check with the customs authority of the country from which it will be exported, as some countries have requirements which must be met.*

Canadian Government Employees Recalled Early

49. Situations arise where employees of the Government of Canada are posted abroad for a minimum of one year, but due to circumstances beyond their control, the posting is terminated early. As a result, duties may be assessed on certain household goods or personal effects, either because they do not meet the minimum ownership possession and use requirements of tariff item 9805.00.00 or because the person did not meet the minimum one year absence requirement. It must be noted that there is no provision for remission of duties in such cases.

50. However, persons in this category are advised to discuss the particulars of their case with their employing department or agency. The Treasury Board of Canada Secretariat has authorized Deputy Heads to reimburse employees for duties paid on goods which would have qualified for importation under tariff item 9805.00.00, had the posting not been terminated early. Certain conditions apply. For more information, refer to Directive 15 of the Foreign Service Directives, Section 15.36.

Additional Information

51. Former residents returning to Canada are also eligible to claim a personal exemption and bring into Canada goods to the value of up to $500, free of duties. For further information on personal exemptions, refer to Memorandum D2-3-1, Returning Persons Exemption Regulations.

52. Subject to the quantity limits in each case, alcohol and tobacco may qualify for free importation under either tariff item 9805.00.00 or the personal exemption entitlements described in paragraph 51, but not both. Former residents must meet the minimum age requirements, and the alcohol and tobacco must accompany them on arrival in Canada.

53. Former residents meeting the minimum age requirements of the province or territory through which they enter Canada may bring with them, without assessment, up to 200 cigarettes, 50 cigars, 200 grams of manufactured tobacco, and 200 tobacco sticks.

54. Minimum ages for the importation of tobacco products as prescribed by provincial or territorial authority are:

Alberta	18 years
Ontario	19 years
Manitoba	18 years
Quebec	18 years
Yukon Territory	18 years
Northwest Territories	18 years
Saskatchewan	18 years
Nova Scotia	19 years
British Columbia	19 years
New Brunswick	19 years
Newfoundland	19 years
Prince Edward Island	19 years

55. Former residents meeting the minimum age requirements of the province or territory through which they enter Canada may bring with them, without assessment, up to: 1.14 litres of wine or liquor, or, as a substitute, 8.5 litres of beer or ale (i.e., 24 ' 355 ml cans or bottles). Refer to paragraph 58 of this Memorandum.

56. Excess quantities of alcohol are subject to high importation costs, as provincial fees are assessed in addition to the duties which apply. In some cases, provincial taxes also apply to excess tobacco products.

57. Persons intending to ship alcoholic beverages to Canada (e.g., the contents of a bar or wine cellar) are advised to contact the appropriate provincial or territorial liquor board authority, prior to shipment, so that provincial fees and assessments can be paid in advance. In order to obtain release of the shipment in Canada, the former resident must produce a copy of the provincial receipt, and pay all of the applicable customs assessments.

58. Minimum ages for the importation of alcoholic beverages as prescribed by provincial or territorial authority:

Alberta	18 years
Ontario	19 years
Manitoba	18 years
Quebec	18 years
Yukon Territory	19 years

Northwest Territories	19 years
Saskatchewan	19 years
Nova Scotia	19 years
British Columbia	19 years
New Brunswick	19 years
Newfoundland	19 years
Prince Edward Island	19 years

59. It should be noted that provincial sales tax might apply on goods imported. For more information, former residents should contact the provincial authority where they intend to reside (see Appendix).

Penalty Information
60. A false declaration in respect of goods imported under the provisions of tariff item 9805.00.00 may result in seizure action.

REGIONAL CUSTOMS OFFICES

Region	Address	Telephone (Public Enquiries)
Atlantic	Ralston Building 1557 Hollis Street P.O. Box 3080 Station Parklane Centre Halifax NS B3J 3G6	(902) 426-2911
Quebec	130 Dalhousie Street P.O. Box 2276 Québec QC G1K 7P6	(418) 648-4445
	400 d'Youville Square Montréal QC H2Y 2C2	(514) 283-9900
Northern Ontario	2265 St. Laurent Blvd. Ottawa ON K1G 4K3	(613) 993-0534 (613) 998-3326 (after 4:30 p.m. and weekends)

Southern Ontario	1 Front Street West 2nd floor P.O. Box 10 Station A Toronto ON M5W 1A3	(416) 973-8022 (416) 676-3643 (weekends and holidays)
	26 Arrowsmith Road P.O. Box 2989 Hamilton ON L8N 3V8	(905) 308-8715 1-800-361-5603 (Hamilton only)
	P.O. Box 2280 Station A Walkerville Post Office Windsor ON N8Y 4R8	(519) 257-6400
Prairies	Federal Building 269 Main Street Winnipeg MB R3C 1B3	(204) 983-6004
	3033-34th Avenue S.E. Bay 32 Calgary AB T1Y 6X2	(403) 292-8750 (403) 292-4660
Pacific	333 Dunsmuir Street Vancouver BC V6B 5R4	(604) 666-0545

REFERENCES

ISSUING OFFICE
Travellers Directorate

LEGISLATIVE REFERENCES
Customs Tariff, tariff item 9805.00.00
(SOR/81-701; SOR/88-84)

HEADQUARTERS FILE
H.S. 9805.00.00, H.S. 9805-0

SUPERSEDED MEMORANDA "D"
D2-3-2, July 22, 1996

OTHER REFERENCES
   D7-3-2, D19-12-1, D19-13-2

Index

Directory

Name	Address	Phone #	Fax #
Canadians Resident Abroad Inc.	305 Lakeshore Road E. Oakville, Ontario L6J 1J3 CANADA	905-842-0080 **Web Site** www.cdnresabroad.com	905-842-9814
BDO Dunwoody	Royal Bank Plaza P.O. Box 32 Toronto, Ontario M5J 2J8 CANADA	416-865-0200 **Web Site** HTTP://www.bdo.ca	416-865-0887
Canadian Investment Consultants (888) Inc.	401 Bay St. Toronto, Ont.	416-368-9888	416-361-7134
Revenue Canada International Tax Office	2204 Walkley Road Ottawa, Ontario K1A 1A8 CANADA	613-952-3741 1-800-267-5177 (collect calls are accepted)	
Canadian Consulates Info Centre Department of Foreign Affairs and International Trade	125 Sussex Drive Ottawa, Ontario K1A 0G2 CANADA	613-944-4000 1-800-267-8376	